Dottie's writings are a refreshing
she found purpose from the legacy awarded her. The greatest legacy is not one of wealth and things, but a legacy of greater value is one that promotes "living with purpose". *Alabama and Beyond* reminds me of the importance of cherishing all life-time relationships, accomplishments, truths and values from those who touch my life. This book has the feel of home and gives the security of loving family and treasured traditions that "create a lasting legacy" for generations to follow.

Missionary, C. Rose Boyd, Founder/Director, Operation Teaching Tools, Falcon, N.C.

For several years, I had the privilege of serving the Gravely family as their pastor. Allan was a member of our board of elders and also established an excellent library in our church. As you read *Alabama and Beyond,* you will understand the positive effect the Gravely family had on our church family. I am not surprised by the continual favor of the Lord upon them and their children. The legacy Dottie describes continues in the lives of their children and grandchildren. One way our church remains connected to this beautiful family is through supporting Charles and Amanda Gravely as AG missionaries in Belgium. Dottie's account of their journey of faith is truly a testimony of the faithfulness of the Lord. You will definitely enjoy reading *Alabama and Beyond.*

Charles Lenn, Pastor First Assembly of God, Tuscaloosa, Alabama

Dottie's story is warm and engaging and real. Whether the reader is a young mother needing encouragement for her decision to follow God's plan for her life and for raising her family, or a grandmother like me who finds humor, connection to memories of her own childrearing years, and a "sister" in Jesus Christ, Dottie's memoirs are a reminder that He is faithful and good in all things.

Kathy Behringer, Council Member, Town of Garner, NC

Alabama and Beyond

ALABAMA AND BEYOND

CREATING A LASTING LEGACY

Dottie Childers Gravely

Cover photo by Lauren Chase Photography
Used by permission.
A portion of proceeds from this book will be donated to the Shalom orphanage in Sucre, Bolivia.

ISBN: 1508666342
ISBN 13: 9781508666349
Library of Congress Control Number: 2015903461
CreateSpace Independent Publishing Platform
North Charleston, South Carolina

CONTENTS

DEDICATION

THIS BOOK IS DEDICATED TO my husband, Allan; our four children, Charles, Sharon, Alison, and Joel; my special friend, Diane, whom you will meet in pages ahead, and, of course, the great Author and Finisher of my faith, Jesus. Without all of them, "Dottie's Story" would have been a sad tale of vanity and futility.

"I will proclaim what the LORD has done." Psalm 118:17b NIV

"Give thanks to the LORD, call on his name; make known among the nations what he has done. Sing to him, sing praise to him; tell of all his wonderful acts." ... Remember the wonders he has done, his miracles, and the judgments he pronounced." I Chronicles 16:8-9, 12 NIV

PREFACE

BEGINNING IN 2011, I BEGAN thinking about writing my life history to date. I do not have many missionary adventure stories to tell. My life has been more like Hannah's in the Bible—just doing the mother and wife things at home and offering my children for the Lord's service. Like Hannah, my husband has been as good to me as ten sons. (I Samuel 1)

But... I do have a history with God and can testify to His goodness and His wonderful faithfulness to my own soul and those of our immediate Allan-and-Dottie family. Although we made some parenting mistakes ourselves, younger parents have sometimes turned to us for advice. If such a record will help someone down the road, I gladly "take up my pen," as the great missionary John Paton said in his own autobiography preface.[1]

As God writes the script of our stories, He makes sure we leave a legacy behind that will benefit others and perhaps serve as guideposts along their journeys. To God be the glory.

"I see more and more the benefit of leaving written testimonies behind us....They not only profit the present, but will also edify the future age." George Whitefield, 1739[2]

Dottie Childers Gravely

"Come and see what God has done, how awesome his works in man's behalf!"

"Come and listen, all you who fear God; let me tell you what he has done for me."
Psalm 66:5, 16 (NIV)

ACKNOWLEDGEMENTS

I FEEL INDEBTED TO OTHER men and women who have made public the triumphs, adventures, and disappointments along their journeys of faith, providing me a pattern to follow. Some of them include my former pastors; Freda Lindsay with *My Diary Secrets*; Edith Schaeffer and her book *L'Abri;* Wayne Crook's story, *God Calls, Adventure Follows*; and John Paton's autobiography, *John G. Paton, Missionary to the New Hebrides.*

I borrowed a genre from the great novelist, Miguel de Cervantes Saavedra, who put stories within his overarching story of *Don Quixote de La Mancha.* Therefore, I have included several stories within this Gravely-story. It is my hope that the content of this book will recount God's goodness and faithfulness to my family, bring Him glory, and uplift and inspire the readers to touch others. As we live, we are truly building a legacy for those coming behind us. It need not be a tiny, constricted one.

"Let this be written for a future generation, that a people not yet created may praise the LORD." Psalm 102:18 NIV

"Not to us, O LORD, not to us but to your name be the glory, because of your love and faithfulness." Psalm 115:1 NIV

CHAPTER 1
EARLY YEARS

EVERY LIFE HAS TO BEGIN somewhere. That place is an epicenter of the ripples which that life will send out into the sea of humanity and time. My own life's ripples began on a small farm at the very top of an Appalachian foothill in north Alabama. We locals thought it was a mountain. That vantage point provided a beautiful vista of the hazy, blue mountains in the background and parts of the valley below.

Our land included several acres of woodlands and a perennial waterfall off the "Big Bluff." The smaller bluff had a small stream that trickled into a sand bed. It was fun to jump off that little six-foot bluff into the sand below. It was therapeutic to linger on the big bluff with cliffs wrapping around it like a giant horseshoe and gaze over the gorgeous landscape of patch-work fields and distant hills stretching to our familiar horizons.

The unpainted, wooden farmhouse, where most of us were born, had three rooms arranged in an "L" formation; our home was over fifty years old. Ten of us lived there—Mother, Dad, six brothers, and finally the baby sister I wished for and asked Mother to get for me. The neighbors accused Dad of trying to start his own baseball team.

One room of our house was both Mother's kitchen and the family dining room with a wood-burning stove and the wooden table surrounded by a few straight-back chairs and a long, backless bench along one side. It held several hungry consumers of Mother's good food. The corner or right-angle room with a fireplace served as a living room by day and bedroom by night for everyone except the four older sons. They slept in the third, unheated room. Everyone slept soundly after a busy day of chores.

Our church, Mountain View Baptist Church, was about three miles away. There Dad and two brothers were charter members. They had helped construct the building from cement blocks, using some of the standing water in a swampy patch of woods next door. We attended regularly, and I watched the grownups sing, conduct revival services, and get baptized, but never remembered feeling God for myself. Sometimes we traveled to "Mt. View" in the back of Dad's farm truck and watched the moon seem to shift around in the sky as Dad maneuvered along the curvy road.

Most things in my life were routine until my third grade in school. The routine was work, especially for my parents and older siblings. Sometimes I helped carry manure from the horse and cow stable to our spring garden plot or "tote" water up the steep hill from the stream behind the house. Mother needed more water than the well could furnish on her outdoor wash days. The electric washer and tin wash tub for rinsing were always outside. I helped a little with the cotton picking and corn shucking, but mostly I entertained my new sister, Judy, so that Mother could do all her many, many chores. I remember as a child playing with my doll near the old chimney, telling myself that one day when I grew up I would help Mother with all her work. Alas! That willingness vanished with maturity, and my teenaged selfishness reigned. I often resented doing the family ironing most of the day on Saturdays.

That year in third grade things changed. Dad felt he simply had to do better as a provider for the family. That decision congealed in his mind one day when he noticed that Mother had made my underwear from the fabric cow feed sacks. Even the poor people considered us poor. We could spy on the dogs and chickens through cracks in the floor. There was no plumbing, just electricity and a well!

Our family's cotton allotment was around ten acres; that meant that we were not allowed to grow any more cotton, our money crop, than that. Someone from the county agent's office came around to check on us. If we went over, even by a few rows, those rows had to be plowed up. Dad sometimes cut trees from our wooded acreage to sell as timber, but keeping the old logging truck repaired was expensive.

So, he decided to find work in Chicago, as some of our neighbors had done, and then send for the family when the school year was finished. In May everything but the house and land was sold, and we became "displaced hillbillies" in Chicago, Illinois. The oldest child, Bobby, stayed behind in Alabama to finish his senior year and lived with our grandmother. The other seven children (now aged two-and-a-half through sixteen) got acquainted with a new apartment, neighborhood, nearby store, and schools. It was quite a different world with more material benefits.

But spiritual benefits were lacking. For three years we did not go to church except for occasional visits to a Salvation Army service, and I went to a storefront church one year. It seemed that God singled me out one day to tell me about that church. I had achieved the coveted sixth grade status of "Monitor" and got to wear a round, plastic badge with that word in ALL CAPS. My "monitor" duty was to stand during recess at the gate of the kindergarten playground by the sidewalk.

One day a woman walking along the sidewalk stopped to talk to me. Her daughters attended my elementary school in the Cicero suburb where we had moved. She invited me to her church, which happened to be just a few blocks down Cermak Road, our street. She offered for her eighth-grade daughter to come by and walk me to the service. Thus, that year of church attendance began for me. My main memories include a rousing song about the "city where the Lamb is the light," prayer for a sick person with the use of oil, a long business meeting to buy property, and the skillful negotiations with a drunk man who dropped in one day. But I do not remember feeling especially drawn to serve God in a stronger way.

I never understood why our family quit attending church in Chicago. Both parents had strong commitments to the Lord. Mother's parents were not church goers, but she had had a genuine conversion experience at a Methodist revival under the preaching of a circuit rider. She even got the Methodists to baptize her immersion style. And Dad? His testimony was very unique. It started when his mother, Mary Blevins Childers, years before had taken a bold step of faith for a woman in Lawrence County. As we shall see, that legacy-maker poised herself to be instantly available to the Lord for any service she could render to Him.

Through the years Dad and Mother maintained a Christian home. On one occasion the oldest son, their little Bobby, became ill. Dad told Mother the child was not going to recover, even if he took the doctor's medicine, until they obeyed what he had been feeling led to do.

"What's that?" she asked.

"We need to start giving thanks at our meals," he answered.

She immediately responded, "Then let's do it." They did, and their son healed speedily.

Since my parents were married in 1937, the effects of the Great Depression were still felt. One day the newlyweds found themselves wondering where their next meal would come from. As they strolled across a field together, Dad offered encouragement to his bride. He began singing an old hymn line: "It may not be my way; it may not be thy way. And yet, in His own way, the Lord will provide."[1] When they reached their house, a man was there waiting to purchase a cord of wood. Dad just happened to have one already cut and ready to sell.

We had a large family Bible with family statistics recorded inside. Mother read from it at night since she was the better reader; she offered some commentary and explanation as she did. Thus it was surprising that church was omitted from our lives in Chicago.

My parents later regretted that neglect of church attendance. Two of my brothers began smoking and would later become high school drop outs. To avoid the bad influence of the city and racial tensions in the large high school, my parents decided the family should return to Alabama. Dad would remain behind and continue working, year after lonely year. He simply could not generate the income in Alabama that he could in the North. This arrangement lasted the duration of my seventh grade to mid-eleventh grade years in school. What a sacrifice Mother and Dad paid for us!

That separation was especially painful for them since they were such lovers! Their courtship and marriage proved that love can be maintained under trying conditions and certainly "many waters cannot quench love." (Song of Solomon 8:7 NIV) I was very familiar with the details of their courtship; Mother seemed to enjoy telling us about it. And it was a common sight to see my parents still holding hands.

But back to Alabama Mother must go, my parents decided, with her little brood—now of six—and leave behind in Chicago the man she loved so dearly. The two older sons had left the nest. The oldest got married, and the second son, Ronald, joined the Navy.

Dad mailed checks or money orders to Mother and tried to get to Alabama at least every three months. He seemed like a stranger to me when he came. His hard work paid off the new 1959 Chevrolet, probably the only new car he ever owned. His earnings also provided us a new home; our old house was now unlivable. The Jim Walter Company built us a "shell" home that was completed on the outside but had only electric wiring and studs inside.

Mother, Ralph, Royce, Ruel, Roland, Judy, and I helped install the dry walls and doors. Dad helped when he was there.

But my life in Alabama got turned toward God. Would that have happened in Chicago?

Since Mother could not drive and now the three older boys had left home, she could not take us to church. Most of my social life was limited to school and cousins. There was no telephone line running past our home, so communication with friends (even my best friend, Jane) ended when I stepped off that old yellow school bus "Number Eleven."

One day when I was about fourteen, Mother said, "You need to be out more with other teenagers. Why don't you ask the neighbors if you can go to church with them?"

I asked the Thompson family, and they readily agreed to pick me up each Sunday morning to attend Gum Springs Baptist Church in the valley. They actually traveled four extra miles weekly to include me in their church attendance. There at Gum Springs for the first time (since watching a Billy Graham crusade on TV in the fifth grade) did I began to feel the convicting nudge of God on my soul. It was telling me the truth: I—"good little Dottie"—was a lost sinner, unprepared to meet a holy God or even live before Him on His earth. But I managed to divert my mind from the issue until the weekly invitation to come forward and make a public surrender was over.

After about a year of this resistance, I attended summer vacation Bible school. Unlike today, there was a large crop of teenagers there, and we had a good teacher, Miss Catherine Edwards, an elementary school teacher who did Bible schools in the summer. All week, her sessions helped the "plan of salvation" to become clearer.

But why, I wondered, were some of the other kids "saved" and I was not? I never in my life doubted that the Bible was true, that God was real, and even that Jesus died for everybody—although that part was confusing. But Mother, the Bible, and the preachers all said He did. Finally, with Miss Edwards' help, I (like John Bunyan's Pilgrim) saw that He *had* to die sacrificially for *me*—a shy country girl who needed a Savior as much as anyone else in this world. He paid my terrible sin debt, and only He qualified to do that since He had no sins of His own deserving punishment.

On July 27, 1962, the final morning of the week-long school, a minister spoke in the opening exercises. I cannot remember his sermon. All I could "hear" or rather "sense" was a gentle, nearby Presence, as though God's holy eyes were peering into a heart that felt so sinful. Yet I felt He wanted me anyway and would take care of the sinfulness. The minister first asked those in the church to come forward to pray if they were already Christians but wanted to deepen their commitments. Then—that eternal moment—he invited anyone who wanted to make a public commitment to Jesus Christ as a living, loving Lord and Savior to come to the front for prayer. I could wait no longer. As the hymn writer said, "He drew me and I followed on, charmed to confess the voice divine."[2]

Actually, I never vocalized a prayer there on the front pew; others prayed for me. But God knows that my will was saying, "Here, God, you take the reins now." I was tired of directing things. I was being born from above, something I could never have done for myself. My dear old Sunday school teacher, Mrs. Dobbs with the one glass eye, leaned toward me and said, "Dorothy, I see a great truth in you." I never forgot her words.

Unfortunately, my maternal grandmother died the following day, Saturday. Everyone's focus was on the funeral. Miss Edwards had told us that when Christians die, they simply leave their bodies behind and go on to heaven. That gave me comfort through the coming days of family grieving. Somehow, Grandmother's death interrupted my church attendance a good bit. I hardly knew what to do next as a new believer. I did not know how to ask to be baptized. Doubts filled my mind. Had I just been emotional and thought I "got saved"?

God came to my rescue later through a gospel tract I found in the back of a church I was visiting.[3] The message there in that tract directed my attention toward the Bible's promises and away from my changing feelings. John 5:24 particularly gripped me. I read these wonderful words: *"Verily, verily, I say unto you, He that heareth my word, and believeth on him that sent me, hath everlasting life, and shall not come into condemnation; but is passed from death unto life."* (KJV) Believe and have. It was so simple.

I asserted my faith and said, "I did that; therefore, I am saved!!" I have not doubted my salvation since reading that leaflet and have always tried to keep copies of it on hand to share with others.

Within a year of my new birth, my next older brother, Royce, was driving, and the whole family in Alabama started back to church at Mountain View, where I became a member and obeyed the Lord's command to be baptized. Sixteen others were baptized that day (May 19, 1962) because something wonderful was starting to happen at Mt. View Baptist Church. It was a revival, a much smaller scale version of the Billy Graham meetings. Our first Sunday back in church as a family had also been the first day a new preacher came to Mt. View—Brother Bobby Couey, a short, newly ordained, fiery preacher, with clear blue eyes that reflected such a sincere heart to please God.

Obviously God had shared with Bro. Bobby His own passion to see our generation turn to His Son. Week after week, men, women, and younger folks "walked the aisle" to shake Bro. Bobby's hand and have him direct them to a waiting altar to do business with God. Deacons and other men of the church prayed at times in the pine thicket behind the church. Women prayed in a Sunday school room. They prayed for relatives and friends to know their Savior, too. And *many* of their prayers were answered as Bro. Bobby preached a bloody cross and a red hot hell, often with tears coursing down his cheeks.

What an exciting church! Never boring! Whole families came into the church. Converts became soul winners who brought others. During one revival service a young father was listening to the visiting preacher's sermon from the front porch where the overflow crowd was standing. At the invitation, he quickly handed his young daughter from his arms to someone nearby and literally ran to the altar. The evangelist gave those praying at the altar an opportunity to plead with the audience. The newly saved man stood, turned toward the crowd, and urged others, even his gray-haired father, to come and join him there. His father did not move.

It was during these exciting days at Mt. View that an early desire to be a missionary grew within me. Perhaps it resulted from the interesting stories of missionaries in our teen Sunday night Training Union quarterlies. But one time the quarterly was brutally honest and forced me to be truthful with myself. It said frankly, "Crossing an ocean never made a missionary out of anyone." Well, I had to admit I was not much of a missionary on home soil; I had entertained the idea that somehow I would become a super-Christian if I could just go to some exotic place.

Another deterrent for me in pursuing a missionary career was the quarterly's list of requirements for credentialing in the Baptist denomination—four years of college followed by three years of graduate school. That sounded like an eternity to a teenager!

But in time the crest of revival waned, and Bro. Bobby felt his work there was finished. He had laid a wonderful evangelistic foundation in my life. I read my Bible and made a few feeble attempts to witness to others. I never dreamed or thought of being anything but totally loyal to God. I did not know that I would *almost* sell my priceless pearl so cheaply (Matthew 13:45-46).

Psalms 71:17 – Since my youth, O God, you have taught me, and to this day I declare your marvelous deeds.

POINTS TO PONDER

1. Can we trace times in our lives in which God sent someone into our lives at crucial points?
2. Do children always appreciate their parents' sacrifices?
3. What is the "pearl of great price" in Matthew 13?

CHAPTER 2

TRYING OUT MY WINGS

As COMPLETION OF HIGH SCHOOL drew near, all the clubs I had enjoyed so much began to seem pointless. I was restless and ready to experience life out there somewhere. Mother cautioned me that life could be tough and dangerous. She told me the story of the baby bird who abandoned its nest before it could fly. The cat ate it. I told her another version. The mother would not teach Little Bird to fly. One day the cat climbed the tree and ate Little Bird. It couldn't fly away because it had never tried its wings. The goal that I chose to be published next to my senior yearbook photo read: "To try out my wings!"

But after high school graduation in May, 1965, I could not find a job that I needed so badly to save for college. A new junior college would be opening that fall in Decatur with bussing provided, one of the positive contributions of Governor George Wallace to our state.

In July, my oldest and married brother, Bobby, came from Chicago for vacation. He felt sure I could find work there and offered to let me stay with him. He was right. I found a job the second day out. So, at age eighteen, I had my first secretarial job, which paid $1.25 per hour, minimum wage. I was taking dictation, transcribing from a Dictaphone, and typing at Turner Mfg. Company—a factory and wholesaler for wall decorations of all types. I spent ten cents a day for a Coke to go with my lunch sandwich, and I paid my bus fare. Almost all my other earnings went to savings.

I was in the adult world all right! Everyone was older than I was. I felt compelled to act mature overnight. Not only was I surrounded by adults, but also by sinners. An older black secretary named Ethel seemed to be the only one there with a personal faith. It was harder to keep my flame glowing. Slowly my thought patterns were more filled with contriving cute remarks to make at work than thinking about God. Prayer lessened. Eventually the New Testament in my purse was left at home. I was not a good Christian example to my colleagues although they knew that I was a "nice" girl.

It had always bothered me that I was not popular with boys in Alabama, but it was against my standards to date non-Christian guys. Really consecrated Christian boys were "as scarce as hens' teeth." But during those days of shallow commitment in Chicago, I lowered my standard. I had my first-ever date with a young man at work who was a nice person but did not have a testimony of being born again. We dated casually for a while.

The reason guys didn't notice me, I decided, was because I didn't give off the vibrations of being "loose." All right then, it would be hard, but I would try to be looser. I would have to work at it since it was not my personality.

But one day a letter arrived from my mother. She had heard that I was dating and offered this advice: "Keep your purity." She never wrote me that before or since. Deep down, I loved and respected my parents so much that I never wanted to hurt them in any way. I discarded all my resolutions to be a naughty girl. On her watch, Mother was not going to stand by and see her investment into my life ruined. I'm part of her on-going legacy, preserved through her watchfulness. My siblings can also testify of her timely advice and counsels that were like apples of gold in their lives. (Proverbs 25:11)

During my five-month stay with my brother, he took me once to a "hillbilly" church in Justice, Illinois. It was great to hear the familiar hymns again.

Once I went with the two ladies downstairs to their nearby Dutch Reformed church. I had never seen so many blue-eyed, blonde people together in my entire life! Although the church had a formal air about it, I could not resist venting some tears as they sang a hymn about a deer about to falter, panting for the brooks of water, based on Psalm 42. I was that deer, thirsty and faltering, not really doing anything immoral but lost in a strange forest.

Just before Christmas, 1965, I decided to return to Alabama. Thanks to Bobby, who cared about his younger sister's education and offered his home and guidance to me in a big city, I had a bundle of savings for college. I should have been excited and expectant, but somehow I just felt "blah." Something vague was missing, and I couldn't quite put my finger on it.

POINTS TO PONDER

1. How can parents prepare their children for adult independence?
2. Are there ways we can help others around us to achieve their educational or other life goals?
3. How can we keep spiritually fit if outnumbered by unbelievers?

CHAPTER 3

COLLEGE DAYS

I HEADED HOME TO BEGIN college the winter quarter at the newly opened John C. Calhoun State Technical Junior College ("Cal Tech") in Decatur. The tuition charge was $67.50 per quarter. My student number was 640. I had missed the grand opening fall quarter and would never be a "pioneer" alumni as several of my friends were. One of them, a bouncy, friendly red head named Barbara Smith, coached me into getting a job in the library through the Work Study program. I had met her previously during high school on a state club trip with students from other high schools.

My Alabama life was resuming but would never be the same again. Although I went through the motions of church attendance, inside was a nagging conscience that condemned me for not having stood straight and tall for God in a tough place, even though I had not succumbed to immorality. My dedication had evaporated when away from my familiar church friends. I felt so hypocritical back at the piano bench. I could not bring myself to tell anyone else of my deep-seated sadness—anyone but God, that is.

One day, probably in April, 1966, alone in the peaceful woods of my parents' property, I knelt on the soft brown leaves of the forest floor and poured out the aches of my heart to Him. My face actually lowered to the leaves below me as I sobbed out my apology. Why, I wondered, wasn't God as real to me now as He had been that day I got saved? Why couldn't I feel Him all the time like that day so that I'd be a strong Christian like preachers and missionaries, who seemed to have more of God than other people did?

I remember another time of tearful repentance that was equally as agonizing while reading a novel for English literature class. Of all the books on the professor's list, I selected *Adam Bede* by George Elliott. It was a semi-true story that portrayed two beautiful women who were representative of two opposite types of women, either of which I could become as I stood at the threshold of womanhood. One, Heddy, was extremely vain and selfish and eventually ruined her life. The other, Dinah, was an early Methodist preacher woman who was modeled after George Elliott's own aunt, Elizabeth Evans. Dinah had strength of character and courage; she thought of others. One pitiful scene depicted Dinah trying to console Heddy and lead her to repentance on the eve of Heddy's scheduled execution. The words coming from Dinah's mouth, written so long ago by George Elliott, hit their target in my own heart. Tears flowed again for at least thirty minutes in the privacy of my bedroom. Still no peace came to me. Yes, I believed in God's forgiveness but could not forgive myself.

But one day. . . it was June, 1966. While waiting on the library steps for the librarian to arrive to open the library, I noticed a very peaceful fellow student reading a leaflet in her hand. It was a Christian leaflet, and I just knew intuitively that she was a successful Christian. Perhaps she could give me some pointers.

"Is that a gospel tract you're reading," I ventured.

"Yes, it is," she answered. She was immediately friendly and told me that her own father, a former Baptist minister, had written it about his life. (See Appendix I) I asked if I might see it.

From the beginning that testimony had my attention. Diane's dad told of his lack of power as a Christian minister. (Wow! A preacher struggling like me! I thought they were super-Christians.) This was good stuff, too good to quit reading when the librarian finally arrived with his key to let us all in. I was a Work Study employee, and he was my boss, and I was scheduled to begin work at that time. But I took my seat a few feet away from his desk and read that gospel tract in its entirety.

My new friend, Diane Steverson, walked past me, patted my shoulder, and said I could keep the tract since "it was a long one." Later I pumped her with questions which she patiently answered. I was especially curious about the new prayer language her dad had gotten. Was that something like hysteria? (I had seen a few country Pentecostals speak in tongues but that seemed strange and weird to me.)

"No," she almost chuckled, "I used to think that, too."

Later she shared with me *The Cross and the Switchblade* by David Wilkerson and several issues of *Voice* magazine, published by a Christian businessmen's group.[1] These magazines had excellent articles by laymen and college students from very diverse back-grounds who recounted, quite intelligently, a new-found faith and power in their lives as they had an encounter with the Holy Spirit. They all called this encounter the Baptism of the Holy Spirit, just like early Christians experienced in Acts 2, 8, 9, 10-11, and 19.

Yep, it was there in the Bible all right. I had, along with millions of others, relegated such happenings to a long ago era, completely out of reach for us moderns. Why can today's evangelicals accept the spiritual rebirth of Acts 16 but struggle with the spiritual baptisms of the other chapters in the same book? (See Appendix II for a full explanation of the Baptism of the Holy Spirit.)

Actually, I had drawn the conclusion in my young college brain that God was not dead as the "GOD IS DEAD" movement was broadcasting, but rather His interest and patience with His erring creation had been depleted. Surely He must have written us all off as hopeless incorrigibles. I was not sure why He had not ended the world yet!

But *The Cross and the Switchblade* changed my mind. It told of a God still reaching to the "scum of society" with tenacious love through David Wilkerson, a naïve country preacher on the streets of New York. He was God's Sgt. York in Satan's war zone. And did he ever take some prisoners for Christ! The book was so thrilling that I read it hungrily instead of studying for an exam. I thought it would be so neat to have God direct my life as He did Rev. Wilkerson's, to have the spiritual energy to pray an hour as he did, and to feel God loving people through me like that. Of course, when I got to chapter twenty-one, I was a little leery as I read of exuberant chapel services and Pentecostal manifestations and hoped that a good Baptist would come along and straighten them out a bit.

I guess my predicament at this juncture of my life was somewhat similar to that of Adoniram and Ann Judson, America's first foreign missionaries. They left our shores as Congregational paedobaptists but soon wrestled with and accepted the Baptist mode of water baptism by total immersion of a believer, not an infant. Ann wrote of the quandary in her soul over the question:

> But I must acknowledge that the face of Scripture does favour the Baptist sentiments. I intend to persevere in examining the subject, and *hope that I shall be disposed to embrace the truth, whatever it may be.* It is painfully mortifying to my natural feelings to think seriously of renouncing a system which I have been taught from infancy to believe and respect, and embrace one which I have been taught to despise. O that the Spirit of God may enlighten and direct my mind—may prevent my retaining an old error, or embracing a new one![2] (Emphasis mine)

Ann had never examined her embedded church tradition under such intense scrutiny. She assumed she would always be a Congregationalist but could not deny the Biblical evidence or the peer testimony of amazing Baptist missionaries she met in India, men such as William Carey. I assumed I would always be a Baptist. Ann struggled with water baptism; I was looking at a different issue, the issue of Baptism in the Holy Spirit and wondering exactly what did my church teach about it.

People at church prayed that God would fill the preacher with the Spirit so that he would preach well. They asked the Holy Spirit to convict the sinners. Since there was mostly silence about this topic, I decided to lean toward what I saw for myself in the Bible, current testimonies, and the amazing Steverson and Wilkerson families.

It is clear now in retrospect that before I could live a similar lifestyle to the Rev. Wilkerson's, I would need his total dedication to God's way and his hatred for evil. One incident really crystallized for me the necessity to *resolve* in my mind exactly which type of path I wanted my life to follow—the shameful, "stainful" way of the world or God's pure way. It could not be both ways.

I was in the back seat of Bobby's car on a trip to Florida with his family. His little daughter (approximately six years old) was beside me. I was trying to read *A Patch of Blue,* a current novel and movie about the blind daughter of a prostitute. The more I read, the dirtier I felt and the more annoying the child beside me became.

Later, I put the book aside and listened to a Catholic radio program that Bobby had tuned in at random. The speaker was encouraging American women to be pure like Mary—chosen by God to bring Jesus into the world and rear Him to manhood. I felt clean again, and my niece seemed so sweet that I spent extra time with her at our next stop and made artificial fingernails for her from rose petals (an old childhood game). The complete difference inside me was an object lesson in sowing the right seeds and choosing the right input. I was the gatekeeper to my mind, and I had the awesome responsibility of choosing purity or impurity. God would not decide for me. How badly did I want His way?

My new friend, Diane, invited me to spend the night with her one Tuesday, which just happened to be the night her church met. It was an interesting service with a Texan leading music with his guitar and Diane on piano. After a few songs, the people broke into a beautiful harmony of singing random tunes and crescendos that blended together so beautifully and harmoniously! I was impressed. This man had done well with these simple country folks to teach them harmony like that! I thought, "I'd like to see him do that with my church, where a few always seemed to be off key."

Later I learned that the music leader was not conducting this singing at all, but rather each one was singing in the Spirit as in I Corinthians 14:15. This lovely singing stopped softly without a cue from anyone. Then Diane's dad shared a simple lesson from the book of Acts, outlining the same accounts that David Wilkerson had pointed out. Later that evening in Diane's home, she and her dad prayed for me to receive the Holy Spirit. In the back of my mind, I was thinking, "I won't mention a word of this to my family." I had no false illusions about how all this would "go over" with my siblings and Baptist parents. (Although my dad's mother was a godly Pentecostal woman, our family had remained distant from her beliefs.) That night I was disappointed that nothing happened to me.

Christmas holidays, 1966, arrived. I am sure gifts were exchanged, but none of the gift giving remains in my memory. My memories are of a trip I took with Diane and a few others to a college student and young professional seminar in Waco, Texas, just after Christmas. She explained it would be free, interdenominational, and really "good" for me to attend. I readily agreed since I liked to travel and could get a Texas banner to add to my wall collection.

The eight or nine hour trip to Waco was a spiritual cultural shock for me. Everyone in the car except me had experienced the Baptism. They chattered about God all the time. One person "felt led" to stop and give money to some poor people on the roadside in Mississippi. They sang together and shared experiences (up-to-date, exciting experiences) from their lives in which they were used of God or had prayers answered. My mostly unanswered prayer list seemed so cold and stale in comparison to their "revolving" requests. It was on that trip to Texas that a quiet resolve came to me that I *must* and I *would* have this Baptism of the Holy Spirit, regardless of what family, friends, or foes thought about it. After all, it was my soul that had been miserable for the past year.

The seminar was held on a rustic campground on the outskirts of Waco. It had originally been built by the well-loved Methodist/Nazarene preacher, Uncle Bud Robinson (1860-1942), who had also built a similar one in my home county near Hartselle, Alabama. Uncle Bud's legacy did not end when the "shouting Methodists" passed from the scene. A small Waco church, named Grace Gospel Church, had purchased the Texas property some years earlier and held semi-annual homecoming meetings there. This was its first post-Christmas student conference.

As we mixed and mingled, we learned that there were attendees at the meeting from northern states, the South, New England, California, Mexico, and other countries outside the United States. Some were Baptists, Catholics, Methodists, a Russian church group, Evangelical Covenant, Presbyterian, and on and on—yet no one cared about church background. They were all excited about God and what He was doing in the earth. I found out that this wonderful experience with God's Spirit was crossing denominational and economic barriers. People were coming together around the world in a love that the ecumenical movement had not been able to produce. This was God.

I felt so fortunate to have heard about this outpouring predicted in Joel 2 and now to witness it before my very eyes. Perhaps six hundred people filled the old tabernacle building and raised beautiful praise toward heaven. Hearing that many voices singing in that beautiful harmony that I had heard in the small Hartselle church was breathtaking. Was this what heaven's music would be like?

Between teaching, sharing, and worship sessions in the tabernacle, these young people were getting acquainted and "comparing notes" on the routes they had taken in their spiritual journeys or telling about a Bible verse that had suddenly "opened up" for them. (In my own church setting in Alabama, conversation after church usually centered around the latest high school ball game.) In the dorm or around tables in the large dining hall, everyone seemed so alive with a freshness and expectancy in his/her faith. I wanted what these people had!! I made up my mind it would be mine somehow! I remembered meeting a tall seminary student from California named Allan who asked if I had received yet. I answered, "No, but I'm going to."

On the evening of December 29, 1966, a young English evangelist spoke with total confidence and exuberance. He invited those who wanted to receive laying-on-of-hands to receive the Holy Spirit to come forward. Somehow, his lively personality was overwhelming for me, and I was afraid to respond. God showed me mercy. As the service had just concluded and I bent to gather up my purse, I suddenly noticed that I felt a joy coming from nowhere. I smiled and laughed and wanted to hug everyone in sight, but I didn't. It seemed that I was engulfed in a giant puddle of God's love which just saturated me.

Diane stood next to me and noticed the visible change in me. "Dot," she asked, "are you sure you're not receiving?"

My answer was, "I don't know. I just feel like saying *encantada de la vida*."

Diane and I had learned that phrase in Spanish class. It means "enchanted with life" or maybe better in English "great to be alive." Days earlier I had thought that life was a drag. Now, I wanted to live and not miss a thing in this great awakening of my generation.

Diane and I went to the altar and talked to the gentle wife of the evangelist. I liked her, and she encouraged me. Another lady, Betty Wilson, prayed with me to receive the prayer language or tongues. I was willing, but nothing came but waves of joy, smiles, and chuckles. (The blessing of speaking in tongues, a precious gift from Jesus to me, finally came three months later.)

Later in the dorm Diane showed me Psalm 126 where God put laughter in people's mouths. I finally fell asleep around 2:00 A. M. I had received a baptismal flood of power that flushed away all my guilt and loneliness. I was truly "in love" with Jesus and stood ready to do anything or say anything for Him. I would have that opportunity very soon.

At Waco, I had asked Allan, the tall seminary student from California, how he had broken the news of his changed life to his parents. His answer was not much help since his parents were not born again Christians and would not have understood deeper spiritual matters. He assured me that God would lead me. I hoped so.

...pray to thy Father which is in secret; and thy Father which seeth in secret shall reward thee openly. Matthew 6:6c KJV

POINTS TO PONDER

1. What can we do to reach out to college students during those pivotal years when many either turn toward or away from God?

2. When should family loyalty yield to loyalty to Christ?

3. Relate how God arranged for you or others to be "filled" when there was hunger and thirst for righteousness. (Matthew 5:6)

4. Note that Jesus, the disciples, and Paul all needed the empowerment of the Holy Spirit before commencing public ministry.

CHAPTER 4
A DIFFERENT DOTTIE

MY GOOD NEWS TO MY family was met with zero enthusiasm, just as I had expected. They shared a common concern that their sister and daughter had been brain washed into a cult. I knew differently. My drooping heart had had a thorough washing. I was clean. And at last I had the power to make Jesus Lord of my life all week, not just on Sundays! The Bible came alive for me. My prayer life was energized. Even the old hymns I had sung for years took on new meaning as never before. I was no longer ashamed or afraid to speak about Jesus to anyone. Even my nervous habit of biting the inside of my cheek disappeared without any effort although I had tried to stop before. This renewal movement I had been led into was global and scriptural, not a local cult. No cult or human manipulation could have put the joy in my inner being. Doubts, fears, guilt, boredom, sadness, and loneliness were gone.

And I got a SMILE. That smile would become known as my "Jesus smile," the one He gave and has maintained throughout the years.

When classes resumed early January, 1967, I couldn't wait to tell some of my friends at Calhoun about my Christmas break. God began making them hungry, too. Some were saved and filled, and the prayer group Diane had started grew quickly. We met every day at lunch in an empty classroom in the science building, room S103.

Diane's dad, Brother Steverson, offered to bring his old reel-to-reel tape player to campus and share with students a taped account of how God was working in Russia to include those dear people in the twentieth century outpouring. We invited friends to come. One girl I had met that week came. After the Russian report, Brother Steverson had an opportunity to ask my new friend about her relationship with God. Unexpected tears came into her eyes.

She surprised herself and responded, "I'm sinking fast."

"How would you like to get on a solid rock?" he asked.

Within a few moments, she experienced the new birth right there in room S103. Later I saw her sitting outside on a bench, obviously enjoying the wind in her hair and her new encounter with a real God. She later became a roommate of mine.

Our Bible study group was dubbed "the prayer for lunch bunch," a take-off on a "Sego for lunch bunch," diet drink commercial. At times students came from the student center to debate with us. Some of them were touched by God; some scoffed and wrote us off as "nuts." College was getting fun!

Somehow we all managed to keep our grades up in spite of devoting most of our free time to witnessing or spending time in prayer and Bible study. A few of us had already been voted by the faculty into Who's Who Among American Junior College Students. We were recognized at a luncheon. In our youthful zeal, we even witnessed to faculty members. The administration could not very easily clamp down on our fervor and honor us simultaneously.

One student who joined our group was Jan. She was the first person I knew of who had come to Christ partially through my witness. Our friends-circles would not have overlapped on a Venn diagram except in the college classroom. She "hung" with cheerleaders and the party crowd, always looking for a good time. Our lives crossed in an English literature class. That is how I discovered one day that she was looking for something else besides a good time. Her soul was searching for meaning.

Our professor told us to write an Italian (or was it a Shakespearean??) sonnet with all the length, meter, and end rhyme requirements. When Jan's poem was read aloud in class, none of us could believe this frivolous, seemingly unthinking girl had penned the lines, telling of a yearning for love and happiness. To her own surprise, the poem became a prayer to God to send her happiness, and she entitled it "Prayer in Iambic Pentameter."

That was during the fall semester before I had traveled to Waco at Christmastime and received the power to be a witness. Even in that unhappy time for both of us that fall, I had wanted to offer Jan some hope. One day when we were alone together on campus, I had ventured a witnessing attempt. I first explained to her that I was not where I wanted to be with God myself, but I knew "deep down" that He was the answer. At the time, I had little more to offer her.

After Waco, I could not wait to tell Jan about what had happened. I now had something to share. The opportunity came one morning in the library. There was Jan at a table, studying.

"She must have a test," I thought.

Jan did not study unless she had a test. I debated whether or not to disturb her and hurt her test grade or share what would help her soul. I decided she could tell me if she really needed to study.

I approached that library table about to pop with excitement. In the past I had been fearful of launching into a witnessing encounter, afraid words would fail me to explain salvation. Now I simply wanted to tell a friend what I had discovered. Without fanfare or introduction, I began my narrative.

"Jan," I said, "do you remember how I was last semester?" She responded in the affirmative.

"Well, I've found my answer!!" I told her.

For the next few minutes, I described the joy and love for God I had witnessed at the meeting in Waco in the people from all over the place from different church backgrounds. I shared the tremendous change in my heart and life. There was so much more to tell her, but I had to go report for work on the Work Study program. As I glanced up, I noticed that Diane was entering the library at that time. I motioned with my hand for her to join us. She sat down, met Jan, and literally took up where I left off.

Diane had been witnessing to one of Jan's close friends, so she suggested that they both visit Diane's church on a Tuesday evening. They both came, and both surrendered their hearts and lives to the Lord. This teamwork with Diane and her family has worked well over the years. It reminds me of the analogy of two coyotes chasing the same jack rabbit. They tire out the rabbit, which is faster, by their joint efforts.

It was wonderful to see the change in Jan's life; soon it was obvious to all on campus. She later received the baptism of the Holy Spirit in her bedroom after reading *Aglow with the Spirit* by Dr. Robert Frost, a professor at Oral Roberts University.

Jan and I later took part two of the English literature class under the same professor who had assigned the sonnet. He didn't seem particularly interested in what we had found, but he was impressed that we were much better students. He even offered to recommend me to the college he had attended.

Our prayer group knew that our time at Calhoun would soon come to a close and that we would move on to get jobs or finish college elsewhere. We wanted to see what God had begun to continue after us. Some people plant a tree to leave behind. We planted a prayer. Before disbanding, one day we all prayed that God would always have His Spirit-filled witness on that campus. I never dreamed at the time that I would remain there almost three years to work as a secretary and be a part on the continuing legacy of the Prayer for Lunch Bunch.

...he rewards those who earnestly seek him. Hebrews 11:6 NIV

"Give thanks to the LORD, call on his name; make known among the nations what he has done. Sing to him, sing praise to him; tell of all his wonderful acts." ... Remember the wonders he has done, his miracles, and the judgments he pronounced." I Chronicles 16:8-9, 12 NIV

POINTS TO PONDER

1. How can we develop sensitivity to spiritual hunger in others around us?

2. Are we ready to be ostracized by our society for the cause of Christ?

3. When we are "reassigned in God's vineyard," we leave behind our spiritual toil. What mindset should we adopt in transition times? (Hint: See "Be Still, My Soul," hymn by Katharina Von Schlegel.)

CHAPTER 5

LIFE AFTER CALHOUN STUDENT DAYS

MY SPANISH TEACHER

WHEN I TOOK SPANISH AT Calhoun Community College (1966-67), I had a wonderful professor named Dr. Ramón Arias, a recent refugee from Cuba. He had no friendly sentiments for Fidel Castro and actually was involved in a failed attempt to stop him.

Dr. Arias gave me a love for his native language; students loved him and thought of him as a father figure. He had a jolly Santa Claus tummy that his wife deliberately caused, he said, in the early days of marriage so that other women would not look at him!

Spanish was so interesting that I would have changed my major from business to Spanish if I could have seen into the future when high school advanced diplomas would require foreign language. In my day, music, art and foreign language teachers were the first-to-go in budget squeezes, so I didn't want to invest a college education in so risky a direction.

After my life was radically changed at Waco, Texas, I began my second quarter of Spanish at Calhoun. Dr. Arias agreed to proofread the pen-pal letters Diane and I wrote to our new friends from Mexico that we had met in Texas. We often "witnessed" to him about the joys of the Spirit-filled life. He let us bring my guitar to class and teach the others some Spanish choruses and even

Spanish Christmas carols. His eyes became misty when we did "Silent Night" because it was the first time since leaving Cuba that he had heard it in Spanish.

Years later I paid Dr. Arias a visit with my young family. He wanted to know, "What happened to your beautiful freckles?"

I told him I never thought they were beautiful, but they had vanished. When the word "charismatic" was mentioned in our visit that day, he quickly pulled a cross necklace out from behind his shirt collar and said, "Dot, I am a charismatic Catholic." A nun from Cullman, AL, had shared the message with his wife and him. Years later, his daughter-in-law told me that in the days shortly before he died of cancer, he often lifted his arms in bed and sang, "I Have Decided to Follow Jesus." I think that was one of the songs we did in Spanish in his class, *"He Decidido Seguir a Cristo."*

A JOB FOR ME

After completing two years of business studies at Calhoun in August of 1967, I needed a job to support myself and help my parents out. I lived with them till age twenty. God graciously provided me the position of secretary to the Director of Student Personnel Services at Calhoun. My small office was just outside the director's. With my Work Study earnings I had purchased my first car, a yellow 1957 Chevy.

After two years of college and finally a real job at Calhoun, I tried out my wings again and moved into an apartment in Decatur with Jan and another friend. One day my roommates and I were enjoying a light hearted moment when the phone rang. It was my dad. The telephone company had finally installed a line along their road.

Dad usually never called me, but he wanted to tell me personally that his heroic mother had just passed away. Grandmother Childers had been a widow about a year. During that time she had made short visits to spend the night with her various children. When she came to our house on the mountain, she slept with me. I remember feeling that I was sleeping with a saint. Now Dad was telling me about her funeral arrangements. I definitely wanted to attend.

At Grandmother's funeral, her preacher nephew related some of the stories that made Grandmother a faith legend in her community. For example, once shortly before the terrible tornado in the fifties, Grandmother had felt led of God to pray all night. Although in her seventies, she took her flashlight and little dog and traveled into the woods to obey that prompting.

A few days later when she saw the funnel cloud, she understood what the prayer meeting was all about. She and Granddaddy could not close the doors of their home because of the tremendous suction of the wind. They knelt in the floor and lifted up their prayers, reminding God that they had walked with Him in the sunshine and now needed Him in the storm.

Homes within a five-mile radius of theirs were flattened. The man and woman next door were killed by flying branches. The only damage Grandmother found on her property was that the eggs had been sucked out of the nest beneath her setting hen. I recalled visiting her community after the storm and seeing sheets of tin twisted on the landscape like discarded gum wrappers.

Hearing other stories about Grandmother's faith in trusting God for physical healing, her loyalty to God, and her commitment to Him made me glad that I was her granddaughter. I was also glad that I had chatted with her in my bedroom the previous year about her Baptism in the Holy Spirit. She remembered it well, even the date: April 10, 1910. A man had come to her home with the message and prayed for her and another girlfriend.

Grandmother said, "I prayed through. The other girl didn't."

She knew that what I had experienced was real. I felt a special bond with her, a kindred spirit.

Another special time I had alone with Grandmother Childers was by the hospital bed of Granddaddy Childers about a year before when I still lived on the mountain. He had slipped on his front porch steps and broken his hip. Surgery was the only option to repair it. However, he slipped into a coma during or after the surgery. When I went by to visit him, Grandmother and I stood beside his bed and prayed for him. She began praying in tongues softly. I marveled that her prayer language was identical to mine although we had acquired this wonderful enablement miles and decades apart. Neither of us had been taught "how to do it" by men but by the same Holy Spirit. Both of us clung to hope that Granddaddy would recover.

Just a few days later I was praying in Dad's woods. I felt that I should "release" Granddaddy. If God wanted him to come on home, that was God's business. When I went to the house, I learned that someone had just called with the news. Granddaddy was safely home, his eternal home. He had never regained consciousness on this earth.

Shortly before her own death, Grandmother had told an old preacher friend, "I don't have a pain in my body." She simply got tired and went home in her late eighties. Jan attended her funeral with me and thought the silent, still face reflected a victorious champion. She left behind a brighter path for others to follow.

A faith test lay just ahead for me. My fledging faith seemed small compared to Grandmother's. I needed another car. The 1957 Chevy was just beginning to be a popular model in the late sixties, but mine was not popular with me. It was leaking gas, water, oil, and brake fluid. I constantly had to refill all the above. I sold it for $150 to two brothers, who had big plans for it, and took their old Rambler as a trade-in. Later on I found a 1963 Chevrolet Econoline van to use to carry more people to church. That car payment stretched my faith and my meager secretary paycheck, but each month God met my needs in unexpected ways. Sometimes I got an unexpected telephone refund. Someone returned money that I had loaned earlier. Someone needed a ride and offered to put gas in my van.

My Decatur apartment became a revolving door for various roommates in transition. One of them was my Calhoun buddy, Barbara Smith. She had now finished college and was ready to become a teacher, but she needed a few things to get started. The first thing was a teaching job for the fall. Then she would need a good car, some teacher clothes, and some cash to get started. I had a front row seat and saw her faith level rise higher and higher that summer of 1969. She fed her faith the rich Bible promises and soaked in the principles of "The Kingdom Way" described in Brother Andrew's book, *God's Smuggler.* It's an excellent mentoring tool.

Barbara even quit asking God about her needs and just began saying, "I just accept a job, a car, clothes and some money." Before fall, she had a teaching contract in another town. It opened the door for a bank loan for a car, professional clothes, and extra cash to get started in her dream job in an elementary school classroom. Her new 1969 automatic-shift Volkswagen later came in handy in another adventure we shared.

In April, 1970, my third year as secretary at Calhoun, I had a visitor at work that rocked my world. It was one of my older brothers, Ralph. I was alone in the office when he broke the sad news to me that my "just-older" brother, Royce, had been killed that day in a motorcycle accident. His words seemed surreal.

"Are they sure? Has a doctor pronounced him dead?" I queried.

He affirmed it was true. With tears mounting in his eyes, he reached for my hand across the desk. Just then my boss entered the room and took a second look at the scene, a man holding his secretary's hand. Ralph's tears told him this was some special, private moment, so he passed silently through the room into his own office.

The following days were a blur. The wake was held in Royce's home. His widow, Brenda, was heartbroken and hardly wanted to eat. She was left with two small children, a boy about four and a girl about three. At the funeral, Royce's casket stood in our beloved Mountain View Baptist Church near the spot where he had knelt to receive His Lord and Savior, Jesus, just a few short years before as a teenage boy under Brother Bobby Couey's ministry. Royce was now twenty-four; I was almost twenty-three.

What I remember more vividly than anything else during those sad days was looking up into the clear, sunny April sky in 1970 as I stood near that open grave that was ready to receive my brother's coffin. I just knew there had to be more to life than this ending of death. I promised the Lord that I would live thereafter with that glorious resurrection in view, that moment when I would hear the divine trumpet sound that would summon my brother to come forth and live eternally in his glorified body. (John 5:25) Many times along my journey here on earth I have been called to attention and reminded of that commitment when I heard the sound of a motorcycle engine. Often a parked cycle without its rider has reminded me of my fallen brother, just as the horse carrying empty boots in the stirrups of an empty saddle in John Kennedy's funeral procession spoke volumes to our grieving nation.

Royce, my dear chum from childhood, was absent and would be absent the duration of my lifespan, but his memory spurred me on daily. Often I arose in the morning to think, "He's not here to make a difference for the kingdom of God, but I am!!"

His widow told me something about Royce that I had not known before. This shy guy felt inept at witnessing, so he left gospel tracts in the bathroom at work. How I wished that my light could burn twice as brightly, with enough brightness for Royce and for me. I longed for God to give Royce major credit for anything I would ever accomplish here.[1]

With his passing, heaven and eternity became realities for me. Heaven was not just a word in a hymn or Bible verse. Royce was there. I knew it!! It would be my business to help as many as possible find their way to heaven's door.

POINTS TO PONDER[2]

1. What scriptures teach us it is our responsibility to build up our faith?
2. How can we keep our faith strong while waiting for answers to prayer?
3. How has the memory of a godly person influenced your life? (Proverbs 10:7)

CHAPTER 6

AH, MEXICO!

In June, 1970, because I knew some Spanish and felt some nudging from the Lord, I decided to go along with a group from church on a mission trip to Iguala, Mexico, in the same state as Acapulco. Some of the details of that trip seem to be a lesson in how *not* to do a mission trip, but God did honor our naïve attempt to please him.

A frequent speaker at Waco from Mexico, missionary Earl Kellum, often invited us to come down, stay with him, and help out with mission work. He always quoted the friendly Mexican expression "*Mi casa es tu casa.*" Then he gave the translation in its entirety, "My house is your house. All's that's lacking is for you to occupy it" [the house]. So our group decided to take him up on his offer.

Our group of seven girls and one guy pooled our money and headed south in my van and Barbara Smith's new Volkswagen bug. Gas cost about twenty-five cents per gallon then, so we figured that $20 each would cover gasoline expense. We packed sandwiches, drinks, water, and lots of cookies.

I got my van serviced the day before we left, so it should have been in top shape. But during the first leg of the trip to Waco, Texas, the team members following behind in the Volkswagen noticed that oil droplets were trailing behind the van. We just bought extra oil and pushed on. At Waco, the old van went to a mechanic, and we were delayed a good part of the day. Finally, we moved on and crossed the border at Laredo, Texas. We were in Mexico!

Unfortunately, the thin air of the Mexican mountains was a strain on the carburetor in my 1963 Chevy van. About thirty miles beyond San Luis Potosí, I heard a clang under the hood, and the engine died. It never moved again. We all quickly held a council meeting to decide what to do with a sick van on the roadside in a foreign county.

"Let's go to a nearby village and find a mechanic," someone suggested.

I waited in the van so that both groups would have a Spanish speaker on hand. Diane, the other Spanish speaker, and all those that could fit into Barbara's Volkswagen found a friendly, charming little village called Oyo Caliente. It had a natural hot springs that the villagers used for washing clothes or bathing. They had erected a building over the springs. But no mechanic was to be found.

With Diane's broken Spanish, she learned that it was siesta hour. No help would be available right away. There was one telephone in the village. Another girl, Carolyn, in our group had an idea. She had a boyfriend who worked with missionaries Roger and Linda West about one hundred miles away in Celaya, Mexico. Why not call him since he would know the ropes on car repairs and was fluent in Spanish?

But Carolyn did not have the Wests' phone number. The council met again. This time it decided to send Carolyn, Diane, and the one male in our group, Fred, to Celaya. Again I waited on the roadside with the remainder of the group. We still had cookies and water. We managed to put makeshift curtains over the van windows for privacy and locked the doors.

After dark, a few local people surrounded our van and began to rock it gently. Probably they were just having a little fun with us, but it was not fun to us. Then, suddenly one of the girls inside spoke out a bold declaration of God's certainty to protect us. I wish I had recorded her words because they instantly gave all of us an unlikely, unexplainable peace that everything was going to be all right. We all felt that we had just heard a New Testament type prophecy, one that "speaks to people for their up building and encouragement and consolation." (I Cor. 14:3 ESV) Worries disappeared. The curious folks outside retired for the night, and we did too.

About twenty-four hours after seeing the little blue Volkswagen drive away, it came back with help. The missionary boyfriend, Paul, knew how to get a wrecker and get us all checked into La Panorama Hotel in San Luis Potosí, a large city. The only problem was that it was around 10 P. M., and all the restaurants were closed. Finally we found some young boys selling corn-on-the-cob from a tin wash tub filled with warm water. We became their satisfied customers; corn never tasted so good. We all slept well that night and said that we went from rags to riches.

The next day, Paul helped us deal with the van problem. We found that the engine would be very expensive to repair. None of us could afford that. One government official told me that I had three choices: repair the van, ship it to the border, or give it to the Mexican government. Their law said that if I entered the country with a vehicle, I must exit with it or donate it to the government. The latter seemed to me the easiest option. I became "car-less."

Now we needed another council meeting to find a Plan B to get to Iguala. Some overly friendly taxi drivers offered to take us the whole distance. We opted for a bus ride. Carolyn called missionary Wayne Myers in Mexico City to see if second class buses were safe. He said it would be fine, but we might have to travel with a few chickens. The bus rolled into Iguala safely with no feathers on board. We had reached our destination.

Brother Kellum was a gracious host. We attended and helped in his Iguala church and others he had established over the years. We helped him stamp addresses on gospel tracts, sang Spanish songs, and typed up song sheets and invitations for meetings. His cook made delicious oatmeal with sweetened condensed milk.

We traveled to outlying villages in the back of Brother Kellum's pickup truck with its camper cover. Several of us crowded into that small space and held on as we bounced and jostled over roads that resembled my dad's logging roads through his woods.

In one village, Coacoyula, we met a church elder, Brother Plácido, who was once about to be hanged by other villagers for embracing the new religion that Brother Kellum brought. Suddenly a man on a horse had appeared and ordered the people to "cut him down or answer to me." They obeyed and never seriously bothered the grateful elder again. Brother Plácido treated us to some wonderful *pan dulce,* a slightly sweet bread, after the evening services.

Our team went throughout the streets in Brother Plácido's village and invited people to come to the services. A few pigs wandered around on the cobblestone streets. An annoying type of stinging flies bit our legs. Diane and I had the privilege of praying for salvation with one woman who had gotten our invitation and come to visit one night. All the discomfort was worth it for her.

Brother Kellum announced one day that all of us were going to the state of Vera Cruz on the Atlantic side of Mexico. A special conference for people from various churches was going to be held there on Mexico's highest mountain, Pico de Orizaba. It proved to be a very interesting trip. It was an honor to be included.

Into the camper compartment we went and rolled along the highways and toll road all day until we reached the base of the mountain at Sumidera about nightfall. We could see the towering snow-capped mountain reaching about 18,000 feet in elevation. We slept that first night on our inflated air mattresses, placed on wooden pews of a humble church in Brother Kellum's network. We needed our rest for the next day's exertions.

As soon as possible after sunrise the next day, we drove a little farther up the mountain. Then we left the truck behind in Tetla because the last five miles to our destination could only be covered by horseback or on foot. We walked along clearly defined trails with picturesque mountain slopes and vegetation all around us as we wound upward into thinner, cooler air. We noticed an old Franciscan church with huge stones and wondered how they had been placed together in such a remote place. Fields were cultivated up the sides of mountains; they would have impressed any Tennessee farmer.

At one point Brother Kellum hastened past us; he was excited about the meeting and wanted to get to the indigenous village church that was hosting the event. One of his "preachers-in-training," Juan from Peru, carried a fifty-pound generator on his hip. The village of Xocotla had no electricity, so the generator was needed for lights at night. The village lay at an 11,000 foot elevation.

A goatherd family in the church moved out of their home those few days of the conference to provide us with lodging; they stayed with in-laws. We slept on the floor on air mattresses and ignored the horse kicking the outside wall sometimes. The men shaved near the well before a fragment of a mirror. The cornfield served as a restroom.

We ate our breakfasts and suppers of beans and rice just outside the smoke filled kitchen house. The "most-delicious-coffee-ever" was brewed over an open fire in a former motor oil container; the coffee beans came from trees grown on the mountainside.

I had the privilege of sharing a Bible story during one afternoon session of the conference. I absorbed all that I could from the teaching sessions and admired the faith of my Mexican family of faith. Attendees had come from many places in Mexico.

In Mexico I really developed a love for the Mexican people. They seemed so humble and genuinely "hungry" for God. One poor family in the church at Iguala made a special meal with red *mole* for us, sacrificing their meager resources to buy Cokes and killing their chicken. Their home had a dirt floor and no plumbing or electricity. The mother's eyes filled with tears as she told me that her little girl was learning to read. Oh, I would have stayed in Mexico for years just to teach that mama how to read!

I believe having a willingness to extend ourselves for others is a key to leaving a lasting legacy. How can "love ripples" go out from our lives if we keep what we have to ourselves? That family certainly extended themselves for strangers from afar.

When time came for most of our team members to return to the U. S., they traveled again in Brother Kellums's truck. A young Texan named Ronnie Fowler, who assisted Brother Kellum, drove them to the border. He developed a friendship with Diane. Her parents met the team at Brownsville, Texas, and took them home.

Three of us were able to stay a little longer in Iguala and help out with some of Brother Kellum's office work. We finally headed home in Barbara's VW. We made a brief stop in Celaya to thank Paul for his help. We stayed in the home of Roger and Linda West, but they were out of town during the evening church service.

Another giant of faith spoke at that meeting. He was Daniel Ost, an American missionary who loved Mexicans so much that he took on Mexican citizenship. Over the years he had flown his airplane over villages and dropped tracts, started a Bible correspondence ministry, fathered several churches, and mentored many pastors. All of his eight children served the Lord. He invited us to pay a visit to this home in El Carmen, near Monterrey; there we met his wife and shared a meal with his family.

During one stop on our return trip, we visited a large market in Monterrey. I asked a little boy if he knew what he needed to do to go to heaven.

He shrugged his shoulders and guessed, "Go to First Communion?"

With my limited Spanish, I told him the good news that heaven is a free gift provided by God through the sacrifice of Jesus; we cannot earn it or deserve it.

In that market I saw the poverty of spiritual truth all around me. In my Morgan County, Alabama, almost anyone in the public market at least knew what was meant by "being saved" and had heard about the gospel. In Mexico's masses, such familiarity was unknown. Again, I would have given the rest of my life to be able to share this good news with them.

No doubt this notion of sharing came from the Lord, my pastors and church teachers, and also from my mother. I recall one day as a child at the old house, Mother sent me on an errand. My job was to carry a bucket of sweet potatoes up to the top of a hill where Dad would one day plant our second home, then go further up the road a little, and finally up a steep driveway to a neighbor's house. Oh, I dreaded that uphill journey with that load for my skinny little arms to lift and bear such a great distance!

I asked, "Why can't the neighbors grow their own sweet potatoes?"

Mother seized a teachable moment and answered, "When you come into something good, you should share it with others."

I never forgot her words or how much heavier those potatoes became with each step. Mother was an incurable giver.

But I realized in 1970 that any sharing in Mexico would have to wait. I had to return to my homeland and watch for the opportunity to return to Mexico. I worked on my Spanish. Two more trips came along in 1971 and 1972. Finally, I began corresponding with Linda West, wife of veteran missionary Roger West, in Celaya, Mexico.

Although I had never met her, upon Paul's recommendation, Linda offered me a position in their home, helping with their children, and said that she would believe with me for the finances. I transferred my utilities to my roommate's name and began paying off my last outstanding debt, about $150 to the Goodyear Tire Store. I would not leave the U. S. owing money. But before the last payment was made, a detour had been set up just ahead.

POINTS TO PONDER

1. Pastor Steverson once remarked that "occasionally we may find ourselves in situations that we would never have had the faith to enter into, but we must use our faith to get out of them!"

   Can you think of an example of this in your life?

2. Simple assistance or hospitality can be remembered for years by the recipients. Reflect on someone's kindness to you at home or abroad.

3. Can you see yourself going on a mission trip?

CHAPTER 7
MY DASHING YOUNG HUSBAND

BY MY MID-TWENTIES I HAD made those three mission trips to Mexico and thought it might be good to put off marriage until maybe age twenty-eight, as Mother did. After all, a husband would slow me down, and I wanted to travel and get some things done before settling down. Sure, I had felt lonely in 1970, living alone for about five months in an apartment, and had prayed one day on U. S. Hwy. 31 near a Flint Creek bridge, "Lord, provide me a husband."

But later several of us church girls rented a large house, and I forgot about that prayer. Well, once I did feel very "unloved" among that group and did tell the Lord I that just wished someone would pick me up and love me, maybe like a stray puppy?! I had not felt "special" to anyone since I was Dad's little girl.

Shortly after this time of feeling unloved, Diane returned from the spring Waco convention, and this little conversation followed.

"Remember Brother Allan?"

"Yeah."

"He asked me for your address."

"Oh, really?"

Allan was the tall seminary student I had met at Waco. But no letter arrived.

In the spring of 1972, Allan stopped off at Diane's Hartselle church (where I had begun attending) en route to his home state, North Carolina. I was at work and missed his visit. He told my pastor that he was considering relocating to Hartselle, wanting to get back closer to the east coast.

Our church had launched intensive prayer for one hour before every service in the spacious "upper room" on the second level over the empty apartment in the back. Since this prayer had begun, prophecies from church members had been given saying that God was going to begin bringing people there from the north, south, east, and west.

Apparently Allan would be one of those brought from the Southwest. He arrived from Texas late October or early November, 1972, in his little cream Volkswagen, packed with his books. He was allowed to move into the church apartment provided for those in transition who were moving from a distance to join the church.

I was the main church pianist (since I could play the worship choruses that had become popular in the Charismatic movement) and usually sat on the front row after the song service in order to step back to the piano for the closing song. Allan began sitting next to me. I could feel every eye watching that little scene. Sometimes my handy guitar ended up between us to make some distance. I knew, like it or not, that after the closing prayer, he would be there. I made only cordial conversation. Not my type, I thought. He had no interest in being a missionary to Mexico as I did. Besides, he was still a stranger.

ALLAN'S STORY

I learned that Allan's life was very unlike mine. He had only one sibling, a younger brother, Ben. His dad was always the branch manager of Swift & Company meat distributors in various North Carolina cities–Greenville, Raleigh, Wilmington, Charlotte, and

Asheville, respectively. Their lives were comfortable. During Allan's adolescent years, he lived in a two-story brick home near the upscale Myers Park area of Charlotte. He attended Myers Park Methodist Church, a Gothic-like structure. He did not work in cotton fields but landed a job at an A & P store near the boyhood farm of Billy Graham.

After high school, then college at all-male Davidson, and then some graduate work in philosophy at the University of North Carolina (UNC), Allan decided to take a break from graduate work to fulfill his mandatory military obligation, which was universal in his day. In 1962 the young, ROTC 2nd Lieutenant left for a tour of duty to Korea, taking with him some philosophy books.

There in the bachelor officers' quarters, a Quonset hut, another young officer inspired him to read the Bible every day. As he read through the gospel of John, he was able to push aside the liberal criticisms of the Bible he had been taught. He was so moved by words from Jesus in John 7:37-39, words about living water inside, that he could only conclude that (1) if this was fiction, then this fisherman, John, was a greater literally genius than Jesus and other classic writers or (2) this was true. He asserted his will against his doubts and said, "I'm going to believe this." Things begin to change in his life. The Holy Spirit convicted him of the reality of his sin before God, and he confessed Him as Lord in the fall of 1963.

When he got out of the military in the summer of 1964, he resumed graduate work, sought water baptism, and found a Church of Christ group on the UNC campus that baptized him. Then he got involved with the Intervarsity Christian Fellowship there. One day one of its members invited him to a meeting that changed his life forever. There he heard about God's outpouring of the Holy Spirit today. In one of the buildings there on campus in Chapel Hill, Allan experienced the same baptism of joy that I did in Waco, Texas.

Now, what should he do with seven years of studies in philosophy? He no longer dreamed of teaching "that stuff." It had not led him to the truth and peace he had sought. They were not found in Plato but in Jesus.

Without taking a degree in philosophy at UNC/Chapel Hill, he headed for Fuller Seminary in Pasadena, California. There a friend of his told Allan about a great meeting in Waco, Texas, just after Christmas, 1966, before the spring semester started. That is where our paths had crossed and where he eventually met my pastor and considered moving to our church, Spiritual Life Church in Hartselle, AL.

Allan later transferred (1968) to Southwestern Baptist Seminary in Ft. Worth, TX, for his final year and earned his Masters of Divinity degree. Here he even had a short term serious relationship with another seminary student. After seminary, he lived in Texas for a time, working for the state employment service until he injured his upper back through playing too much golf, carrying his clubs. He was forced to work part time for a friend.

During this trying time, he began to sense two growing desires in his heart, the need to migrate closer to his home state and the need to seek a wife. The latter need compelled him one night in October, 1972, at a weekly Bible study to request special prayer. The meeting was hosted by a group of single ladies in their apartment. Allan explained that he was tired of not having a wife. The group placed him in a chair and gathered around him, praying fervently for a real, tangible wife to be given him.

Allan had two wife candidates in mind, both lived in Alabama. I was his number one prospect. He made plans to relocate to Hartselle, AL. Not only was prospect No. 1 there, but also a good, thriving church with a free apartment. He was now living on savings and his withdrawal of funds from the Texas retirement system. He packed his car, said goodbye to his friends, and headed east.

The Courtship Begins

Eventually Allan asked me out for dinner at the "one-and-only-one" Hartselle restaurant, The Corral. I sent up a quick prayer before accepting his invitation and felt it would be all right. He used some of the last of his savings to buy those steaks on our first date. He had not yet found work.

Then one night he offered to accompany me as I took a single mom and her five children home after church. After helping her get her little charges inside, I returned to the car where Allan had waited. Immediately he turned to me and said, "Dot, I'm in love with you." Umm, that had a nice ring to it. Wish it could be true, I thought, but this guy has been here only a few weeks, and he's "in love"? Here we go again. Two other guys had recently had crushes on me; this was getting annoying.

But I had to be careful. I did not want to encourage Allan, nor did I want to be cruel and possibly drive him away from church or maybe even from following the Lord. I weighed my words carefully as I responded, "I had thought you did, but wasn't sure." Nothing more.

That was not the answer he had hoped for. He didn't know how to respond to that, so the conversation was dropped.

Life went on as usual, usual except Allan kept creeping into my thoughts constantly. Even one of the preschoolers where I had begun working as four-year-old teacher kept calling to his friend, "Allan" and reminding me of that other Allan at church.

I began thinking that if I told Allan to stop pursuing me, he might move away, and I would **never, ever** see him again for the rest of my life. Somehow that thought carried a pain with it. What! Was I falling in love with him?

But what about Mexico? I was working down that debt to the Goodyear Tire Store so that I could join the Wests in Celaya, Mexico. I began trying to get some answers from God. One day after work I fell asleep while praying about it; I had to open that learning center where I worked *early* each morning.

Allan was unrelenting. After one evening church service, he asked if he could talk to me. I told my roommates I would be home later. The only private place I could think of after 9 P.M. was the well-lit parking lot of a local hospital. All hamburger joints had closed. Allan assured me that his feelings for me had not diminished at all. He waited for my response. Truthfully, I had to admit that, yes, I loved him too.

When I got back to the girls' house, a roommate queried, "Well?"

I answered, "Oh, he just wanted to know how he stood with me."

"Well," she prodded, "how does he stand with you?"

"Pretty tall," I said and ended the interview.

One of my other roommates (or rather, housemates) happened to be a new friend who had recently started attending our church. I first met her when I was a secretary at Calhoun and often spent most of my lunch hour "witnessing" in the student center. At the time, she thought I was "nuts" because I knew the definite time and place that I became a Christian. She later transferred to a four-year school and roomed with a Campus Crusade girl who prayed for her daily to understand being born again. When that finally happened to her, I was the first person she thought about, and she wanted to see me again to tell me. Unknowingly, Allan and I met her future husband one night.

We were becoming more and more serious about each other, but church people or housemates were always around. One evening at the "girls' house" in Decatur where about five of us were living, he turned to me and said, "The walls have ears. Let's go for a ride."

I had been wanting to show Allan my old college, Calhoun, so we headed over the Tennessee River to tour the campus where

God had worked so wondrously previously. As we were entering the library where I once did my Work Study duties, a young fellow said, "Hi, Dot."

It was Tommy. He had been one of those who used to invade our daily prayer groups at Calhoun, just to debate with us, never agreeing. As we chatted outside the library this night, however, it became obvious that Tommy had also changed after leaving Calhoun for higher education. Now he was open to visiting my church. Soon he was a regular attender and began wooing the hand of my housemate.

On December 5, Allan officially asked the question, "Will you marry me?"

By faith, my reply came, "I sure will."

And that has made all the difference. I still did not have an answer about Mexico; I only knew that I had a wonderful peace when I felt God was leading toward Allan and an agony when I thought of going the other direction. The "Mexico question" was finally resolved in my mind several years later.

At Christmas, 1972, six years after meeting him, we took a trip together so that I could meet his family in North Carolina and tell them our good news in person. We had hardly entered the Asheville home of his father and stepmother when they informed us that the husband of one of his father's sisters had died suddenly of a heart attack. All the Gravely clan would be gathering in Charlotte for the funeral.

We traveled through the gorgeous Carolina mountains to the city where Allan had spent his high school years, and I met his extended family. The recent widow told Allan, "She's the one."

I had Aunt Virginia's blessing! All the relatives were gracious to me, a typical Carolina quality I have observed repeatedly.

We set our wedding date for March 24, 1973, again by faith since he still had some back problems and had not secured a job. But soon God provided a desk job at a local plant; he was officially

"Assistant Materials Manager" at Baker Industries. We began looking for our first home nearby.

Out searching for a rental home one day, we saw a vacant house with no rental signs out front. We went to a nearby home around the corner to inquire about it. After stating our business and mentioning Allan's job and our future plans, the homeowner there told us that he had a rental property on the block behind the one we were checking on. That gentleman became our landlord and gave us the key to a charming little cottage on Sherrill Street near the public library. It was semi-furnished with organza curtains, a Persian rug, piano, large dining table with golden, velvet cushioned chairs, a Victorian sofa, French doors, and hardwood floors. Wow! God was so good to us.

The week before the wedding, I wanted to go out to "the mountain" and spend one more night in the home of my parents. I asked Mother if she had any last minute advice for me. She thought a moment and then said, "Well, my mother always told me: (1) 'Remember your husband is your sweetheart, and (2) if you're going to live with him, don't talk about him.'"

I wonder how many generations of my past grandmothers passed that advice down to their daughters. It is true for any generation.

By March 24 all the wedding plans had been made. Diane, her Texas husband, Ronnie Fowler, and their new baby daughter were able to come from Waco, Texas. She and Jan were my bridesmaids. My sister, Judy, was my maid of honor. It was a joy to have my family a part of our wedding plans, rehearsal dinner, and wedding. They were so happy for me. Dad teased me, "I thought you were never going to make it."

I was almost twenty-six. Big brother Bobby and younger brother Roland stood on either side of me and posed for a photo, each kissing me on one cheek. Bobby even offered his car for our honeymoon trip to Bradenton, FL.

That day in March was the launch date for many "Allan & Dottie" adventures ahead. Most (or rather *all*) of them took faith and prayer to get through. One of the first was just ahead. I was about to face something I had hardly considered before, pregnancy. It was definitely a doorway or first installment into one of the most wonderful legacies any woman could invest in.

POINTS TO PONDER

1. Think of times when the principle of inner peace has been a deciding factor in major decisions. Colossians 3:15-17
2. Can we act in faith before we have all the answers?
3. Someone's "no" to the gospel today can change to "yes" later. Relate examples

CHAPTER 8

OUR NEW ADVENTURE – PARENTING!!!

OUR WHIRLWIND ROMANCE AND MARRIAGE quickly led to whirlwind parenthood. Little Charles was conceived the second month of our marriage and was due on our tenth month anniversary. Decisions had to be made during the nine months of pregnancy—a doctor, names for Baby X, and childbirth method.

Someone recommended a Decatur doctor. Allan had wanted a son to name "Charles Isaiah." Charles W____ was a high school classmate he admired; Isaiah was a Bible prophet he admired. I suppose we had a female name picked out, but I do not remember what it was. We simply thought of our unseen baby as "Little Charlie." Ultra-sound photos were uncommon or maybe non-existent in those days. We just assumed it was a boy.

The childbirth method was a little more complex. Allan was inspired to have a natural delivery, having heard stories of success in rural Mexico. An older missionary-turned-midwife named Harold Davenport had shared with Allan and his Dallas friends some interesting accounts of Mexican women giving birth on an improvised birthing chair, a toilet seat with legs. Necessity was the mother of invention in remote villages with no doctor. Mr. Davenport based his method on the lively Hebrew women using (literally) two stones for a birthing chair in Exodus 1:19. Both appliances were effective.

My friend Diane spent some time with me relating in detail her experience with natural childbirth during her recent delivery and also suggested some books to read. My doctor was agreeable, although Decatur General Hospital had no type of birthing chair, primitive or otherwise. We decided to use the hospital rather than do a home delivery since I was "new" at all this and no experienced person was available to be with me at home for the birth. My mother probably could have been on hand to coach me but did not feel comfortable with that role. She had had nine babies at home successfully. Midwives were illegal in Alabama.

The delivery went well on January 17, 1974, although I was lying on my back and wished for that birthing chair. The pushing made Charles's head a little pointed at first, and I thought he looked purple in color.

Little Charles Isaiah entered the delivery room just fine late afternoon, but his dad was not allowed to be there. Nor was Allan permitted to touch the baby until we left the hospital in our own car two days later!! Nurse's orders. (The hospital wanted to avoid being blamed for any germs from the outside world.) After leaving the hospital, we stopped in the parking lot of the first shopping center. Allan parked the car and said, "Let me see my son."

We loved our new roles as Mama and Daddy. Charles was a hit at church and with relatives. He was always smiling.

My daily routine was getting Allan off to work and caring for Charles. My Bible reading became a little *routine* also, and I felt it needed some refreshing. I just told the Lord so and asked for His help in revitalizing my time with him.

One day I held Allan's old Scoffield study Bible and thought, "Where should I read?" I was very, very familiar with all of it; the last thing I wanted was a bland, trite time in the Bible. "Well, it is always good to read about Jesus," I thought. I began turning in the direction of Matthew, the first New Testament book. But at the end of the Old Testament I saw an interesting chart about the names of God in scripture. Dr. C. I. Scoffield had prepared a little treasure hunt for me.

Starting with the first time a particular name of God was used, he provided background information, then told me to go to the next place of use. There I found additional information and the reference for the next location. On and on I went from *El Shaddai* to *Adonai* to the Lord of Hosts to the compound names. Then one day as I reached for something on the floor, I noticed on the bottom shelf of Allan's growing, copious library a book entitled, *The Names of God in Scripture* by Andrew Jukes. I read it hungrily.

This whole experience of seeking-and-finding spoke to me of the goodness, the faithfulness, the shepherding expertise, and the wonderful watch-care of God for a lowly housewife and mom in small-town Hartselle, AL. Yes, He knew my address, and He knew my longing to know more about Him. He did not turn away my prayer. But our address was soon to change.

POINTS TO PONDER

1. Think of times when the principle of inner peace has been a deciding factor in major decisions. Colossians 3:15-17
2. Can we act in faith before we have all the answers?
3. Someone's "no" to the gospel today can change to "yes" later. Relate examples

CHAPTER 9

GOODBYE TO HARTSELLE, NEW THINGS AHEAD

ALLAN BEGAN TO FEEL THAT he was not adequately prepared vocationally to support his little growing family. Baby Number Two was due in June, 1975. Allan had left the desk job because of severe back pain from the continual sitting position and had taken up paint contracting. His business was sometimes profitable and sometimes not, after paying his team of men from our church. He looked into going back to school on a few remaining GI bill benefits. After comparing programs at the University of Alabama in Huntsville and the main campus in Tuscaloosa, he decided to enroll in the latter. He would major in history for a Master's degree, hoping to teach someday. We sold his painting equipment, packed up our U-Haul truck, and headed south toward Tuscaloosa via Birmingham. I followed behind the truck in our little Dodge car with Charles in his baby seat beside me and Sharon Annette "in the oven."

Our new home was an apartment in married student housing of the University of Alabama, the old Northington campus with an interesting history and future. The old red brick buildings had served as WWII Army barracks or hospital rooms before becoming the city hospital. Then the University had converted them into student apartments. We moved into Apt. D6A in January; it was in row D, building 6, and apartment A at the end of the structure. All the floors had black tiles. There was no air conditioning.

But we had community and dignity!! Yes, indeed. There was no ghetto spirit there. One neighbor had put layers and layers of liquid floor shine on her black tiles so that they resembled polished marble. One couple put a brass door knocker on their door.

The orderly rows of buildings made me think of a field and harvesting. Yes! That was what I had been missing in my routine household-and-wife-and-mommy duties. I wanted to get back into the harvesting for the kingdom of God. Opportunities for sharing the gospel were limited while living in our private homes in Hartselle.

The Northington campus had a community playground area with swings and a sandbox. My new German friend, Godula, and I often waddled to the playground together with our little boys. She was also expecting her second child, due in April. There near the sandbox I had the privilege of sharing with her the wonderful story of Jesus.

Godula's husband was a brilliant man from West Virginia, of German descent, majoring in math. He respected God as the Great-Physicist-in-the-Sky but was not sure about "this Jesus business." As Allan and I did Bible studies with this couple and showed them how the life of Jesus was predicted in minute detail centuries before by Hebrew prophets, faith came into their hearts, and their lives were changed. They also were intrigued with accounts of finding remnants of Noah's ark in Turkey and attended with us a current movie on the topic. They also went with us to hear the young author Josh McDowell when he spoke in the infamous Foster's Auditorium on campus (where Gov. Wallace once defied integration). Josh's book, *Evidence That Demands a Verdict*, and the Thompson Bible were useful when showing Anton and Godula the fulfillment of the Messiah verses.

Another new friend I met was from Colombia, South America, Rosa Maria F___, also pregnant with her baby Number Two. Her first child had been still born. I give Rosa credit for my fluency in Spanish. She learned that my Spanish was dormant and began challenging me in her beautiful accent to "speak Spanish, Dorothy."

Rosa and I decided to eat lunch together and speak Spanish-only one day, then English-only another day. Rosa's English was as bad as my Spanish, so we felt comfortable with each other and corrected each other's mistakes. For example, when I used the archaic word for "pregnant" from my sixteenth century Spanish Bible, she quickly said, "Oh, no, we only use that for animals." I decided I needed a modern Spanish Bible. Rosa had faith, but it seemed that the concept of the new birth never registered with her. We lost touch.

In June our little Sharon Annette arrived. The home delivery went well. We had gained more confidence in home deliveries after reading Dr. Robert Bradley's book, *Husband Coached Childbirth*. We lived only three blocks from Druid City Hospital (DCH) and would have gone there if a problem had arisen, but that trip was not necessary. We chose a home delivery because we wanted Allan to be present with me this time. DCH did not allow fathers in the delivery room. Some women tried to reach the Catholic hospital in Birmingham to deliver so that their husbands could attend, but I feared one of those roadside deliveries en route and preferred a home delivery.

I knelt on the floor by my bed, and gravity was my best friend as I easily pushed our little lady out into our world into her daddy's arms. He had a tender side to him that had not surfaced until he put his delicate little girl on his shoulder. It just seemed right to call her a princess. We felt royal. Our Prince Charles liked "baby" and learned we could go outside *after* the baby finished nursing. One of his first sentences was "Me bye-bye *after*."

In August our dear old Northington campus was condemned, deemed no longer fit for housing. We relocated to another red-brick

University married-student housing site, Belmont Apartments (now Harbrooke Downs) on the corner of 10th Avenue and Hargrove Rd.

The old Northington campus was soon used to film a Burt Reynolds movie, *Hooper*. From Belmont, we could see smoke rising on some days as the script called for burning buildings. The old smoke-stack tower came tumbling down in one of the movie scenes. After the filming, the site was later completely cleared and became home to University Mall, the toast of the town. Only the ship's mast display from Northington years was left standing as a point of reference. (Years later Sharon worked in that mall in the McRae's store, approximately on her actual birthplace.)

All the new friends, new surroundings, and new opportunities for Allan and me in Tuscaloosa did not seem to be intimidating challenges to us but rather exciting adventures. We had joined up to do life together, believing that "two are better than one." (Ecclesiastes 4:9a) That had proven true so far and made us hopeful for traveling on down other new paths. I adopted the philosophy of hymn writer C. Austin Miles, "If Jesus goes with me, I'll go anywhere."[1] In that new Belmont apartment we met new friends and two very special new Gravelys.

POINTS TO PONDER

1. Reflect on Bible heroes who left familiar surroundings to follow God's call. (Rebecca, David, the disciples, others)
2. If we pray for witnessing opportunities, we seem to be more aware of them when they occur. Thoughts?

CHAPTER 10
GROWING IN
MANY WAYS

THE BELMONT APARTMENTS COMPLEX WAS not arranged in military rows but snaked around slopes in various horseshoe formations. Inside some of the horseshoe or *U* shapes, the developers had placed mini-playground areas with an assortment of fun equipment for the children. With delight, Charles and Sharon got acquainted with swings, teeter-totters, monkey bars, *and* little friends who shared their enthusiasm for such fun things. There was also a clubhouse available for parties or social events. Later some of us poor, innovative college-student-wives formed our own moms-morning-out day in the old club house by serving on a revolving shift as babysitters.

In 1977 and 1979, apartment 9B became the birthplace for our last two children, Alison and Joel respectively. Only Allan attended me, and he caught them just fine. The births went well. Allan registered the home births at the local health department through their department of vital statistics. The local hospital finally began permitting fathers in the delivery room about two months after Joel's birth after some lobbying by young couples. It was too late for us. By then, Allan was already an accomplished "baby-catcher."

Alison arrived just before Christmas, so Charles and Sharon opened their gifts early. We were house bound together. Charles and I played with his new safari set on the "mountainous terrain" of the bed covers. I rang the doorbell of Sharon's Fisher Price doll house and paid her several imaginary visits there. Alison was a jewel, a low-maintenance baby. Charles was almost four, and Sharon was two and a half. Life became a little busier.

Then, life got even busier fourteen months later when a "surprise package" we named Joel joined us and fulfilled our wish for two boys and two girls, just what we wanted. I had wished for a little "Joel" since our newlywed days.

Our first house guests as a couple back in Hartselle had been out-of-town guests attending our church's conference. They were a young mom and her three young children; her husband could not attend. She introduced her children one by one, beginning with the oldest, "This is Bobby. This is Ruthie...."

"I'm Joel," interrupted the blonde three-year-old with a smile. What a sweetie! I decided to remember that name for future reference.

Now with the birth of our Joel, the family grew to include four preschoolers; I began to feel some stress and did not get to enjoy the last baby as much as the earlier ones. Two were in diapers and needed constant care; two were old enough to go outside to play with some watch care. Of course, meals and laundry had to be done. Time for "me" was really rare; I trimmed my fingernails at red lights.

During these busy times, we attended a church conference and heard Rev. John D. Reese of Dothan, Alabama, speak about "Keeping Perspective" during life's stressful times. He used Biblical Esau as an example of someone who could not see past the urgent moment directly in front of him. That is why he traded a bowl of beans during a hunger attack for something vastly more important.

Later I told the speaker how his message had helped me and described my current circumstances. He and his lovely Italian wife, Gemma, had raised four children. All or most of them were current students at the University of Alabama in Tuscaloosa. He wisely told me, "Believe me, sister, they will grow up faster than you think."

I believe the Holy Spirit helped me apply this godly advice about perspective. Here is an example. Once a week I volunteered as an English teacher for international students, mostly wives of students. That was an outlet for me, and my children enjoyed the free nursery with friends from all over the world. Classes were held in the campus Baptist Student Union building. One day while walking through the student lounge area, I noticed a tall, slender, blonde co-ed with a nose shaped somewhat like my husband's, the aquiline or Roman nose. It occurred to me that our lively Sharon might someday look like this elegant young lady, who sat there so poised and composed. That scene became my "faith image" for the future so that my focus was not always on the immediate need of those four little blue-eyed blondes around me but on what they would someday become.

Another technique I had for coping in those days was to sing this little poem by an anonymous author. I improvised a tune.

Lord, give me patience when little hands
Tug at me with their small demands.
Give me patient and smiling eyes;
Keep my lips from hasty replies.
Let not confusion, weariness, or noise
Obscure my vision of life's fleeting joys.
So when, in years to come, my house is still,
No bitter memories its rooms may fill.

I also sang hymns, especially one that said "It will be worth it all when we see Jesus. Life's trials will seem so small when we see Him." **Yes, perspective mattered.**

While Allan pursued his graduate work, he worked part-time as a paint contractor, shoe store salesman, and jewelry store salesman. Then he tried real estate.

NEW EVANGELISTIC TOOLS

While living at Northington, a friend showed me how to do flannel graph Bible story lessons with children and told me about Child Evangelism Fellowship (CEF) materials, 5-Day Clubs, and Good News Clubs in neighborhoods. After moving to our second University of Alabama married student housing, Belmont Apartments, I began holding Bible clubs for children in our small apartment. I remember having twenty-eight people there one time. They were from around the world since the University of Alabama had many international students. There were Nigerians, Taiwanese, South African, German, Korean, and Haitians. Our own children grew up feeling comfortable with people from around the globe since they played together with them on the lawns of Belmont, our common back yards.

One little American girl, whom we will call Julie, was especially precious. Since I had a nursing baby, I arranged for the local Child Evangelism director to teach for the one-week outreach. When I invited Julie, she wrinkled up one side of her nose, curled up her lip, and explained why she could not attend.

"I have to watch *The Little Rascals* then," she said.

Somehow that sounded so trivial a thing to do when God's eternal agenda was going on in our midst. I heard myself saying, "You know, Julie, you have the rest of your life to watch *The Little Rascals*. We are doing the Bible club this week only."

The first day Julie did not attend but came by later in the day to see if she too could have a piece of candy as the children who had attended got to have. I gave her one and encouraged her again to attend. She did come, got involved with memory verses, and wanted a Bible of her own like her friend had. The CEF director gave her one.

Julie loved it. Her mom told me later that this little scholar sat in bed at night reading her Bible. She insisted on beginning at Genesis and plodding onward from there. Her enthusiasm was still high about six weeks later when she and her mother moved to other apartments in our school zone.

One day one of Charles's friends told us the sad news that Julie had been hit by a car as she crossed a street en route to school and was in the hospital in a coma. I did not have a chance to visit her before she left us for her forever home, but I did visit with her mother soon afterwards and took her a *Living Bible.* She told me that she believed if Jesus had come to that hospital room during the coma and offered Julie the choice of staying on earth or going with Him to heaven, she would have chosen heaven. That was how evident her passion for the Lord was.

During another Bible club meeting, a neighbor knocked at my back door to tell me of tornado alerts. The children became concerned.

I assured them, "Don't worry, kids. In Tuscaloosa, if they really see a tornado, they turn on the sirens all over town."

Within minutes, the sirens went off. Little eyes glanced around, needing more assurance.

Then I asked my co-worker, Joanna Jennings, to pray that the tornado would not even touch down but just go on away up into the sky!!! Joanna was the daughter of long-time missionaries to India, Ray and Dorothy Jennings. She had seen miraculous healings in her dad's crusades and knew about prayer. She prayed as I suggested. We continued with our lesson; we were already in a center part, ground level of the building and sheltered by God.

Later the local news confirmed that her prayer was answered. That funnel cloud spun off into the wild blue yonder.

On another occasion, Joanna helped me most by offering to stay in my apartment to babysit little Joel during his nap time so that I could take the older children and help conduct a five-day Bible club on the campus of the University of Alabama in the old Presidential Apartments. Just like Belmont Apartments, they were largely rented to student families.

When I returned home the last of the five days and was walking into my apartment, Joanna told me that I had a long distance phone call waiting for me. The voice on the other end of the phone was that of a Decatur, Alabama, man whom I had met on two occasions back in my single days. He was calling to thank me for witnessing to him on those two occasions. Yes, I did remember him and recalled vividly how he had been coolly polite but showed absolutely no interest in what I was saying. Now he was a Christian attending a church where some of our friends were pastors. He just wanted me to know how much those two times in his life meant to him because of my boldness to approach him for Christ.

"You just walked right up to me," he said.

That was on the Shoney's parking lot.

Shoney's parking lot! I also remembered why I was there witnessing on Shoney's parking lot. My Hartselle church hosted a weekend retreat at some nearby facilities. During one afternoon between sessions of the meetings, some of us in the "twenty-something" age group got a little bored. Someone in the group suggested, "Let's go witnessing."

Soon we were in cars heading for Shoney's in Decatur. At the time, the restaurant had several drive-up stalls with microphones for placing orders, which the smiling "car hop" delivered to the car. It was also a place for boy-meets-girl situations, or maybe better said, girls-flirt-with-boys opportunities. Usually there were extra "customers" hanging around or cruising around checking out prospects, not menus.

The Shoney's manager actually gave us permission to stay on one side of his lot and approach people with the gospel! That was when I decided to talk to the man now calling me to say "thank you." I had also witnessed to him briefly one day in my Calhoun office. He had learned from our friends that I had married, moved to Tuscaloosa, and now had a growing family. He simply felt compelled to let me know about his changed life. (Allan was not jealous of that phone call.) The call came at the end of a grueling week of teaching Bible lessons during those precious hours of my usual nap-time. My sacrifice for the Lord that week was rewarded in the best possible way. He sent me assurance that my work for Him was not in vain, regardless of my assessment of it. (I Corinthians 15:58)

During these Bible clubs, my children heard and saw not only the flannel graph Bible stories but also missionary stories. Thus the lives of great heroes such as William Carey, Hudson Taylor, and Mary Slessor were portrayed in large drawings in continued segments right before their young eyes. Be assured, children will have heroes. Good stewarding of young lives should dictate that we put good heroes before them. Their hearts will envy those life styles.

In some of the CEF literature, I found an old, anonymous poem that never failed to give me a lump in my throat and often extra moisture in my eyes. It stressed the awesome importance of leading children to know the Lord and confirmed to me that I was on the right track with my Bible clubs.

Dear Lord, I do not ask that Thou
Shouldst give me some high work of Thine,
Some noble calling or some wondrous task;
Give me little hands to hold in mine;
Give me some children to point the way
Over the strange sweet path that leads to Thee;

Give me some voices to teach to pray;
Give me shining eyes Thy face to see.
The only crown I ask, Dear Lord, to wear
Is this…that I may teach the children.
I do not ask that I should ever stand
Among the wise, the worthy, or the great;
I only ask that softly, hand in hand,
The children and I may enter at Thy gate.

When Charles was about six and found his first "true love," Kirsty, from South Africa, we had been learning in Bible club about nineteenth century missionaries, Hudson and Maria Taylor, in China. They lived in an upstairs apartment, using the lower floor for a medical clinic throughout the week and a church gathering place on Sundays. One day I overheard Charles checking with five-year-old Kirsty on an important matter.

"Kirsty, are you still going to marry me when we grow up?"

"Yeeess" was her reply in her lovely South African accent.

"Then we'll have to live upstairs so we can have church downstairs," he said.

Missionary hardships were no big deal for him; he just had to be sure his mate was in agreement with that. Today, Charles and his wife (not Kirsty) spent their first years as missionaries on the fourth and fifth floors of an apartment building in Brussels, Belgium, and the third floor was reserved for church meetings or college student ministry gatherings.

I was not the only one who did Bible clubs in Belmont Apartments. Forest Lake Baptist Church sent a team of young people over on Saturday mornings to host their "Big A Club" in our Belmont clubhouse. During our tenure as resident managers there, I opened the clubhouse weekly for Miss Judy Fondren, the local Child Evangelism Fellowship director, to hold her Good News Club after school.

One day after Miss Judy's class, she wanted to talk to me. She told me some good news. Our five-year-old, Alison, had prayed to receive the Lord into her heart.

Miss Judy told me, "Dottie, I told her about Revelation 3:20, if we ask Him, he will come in. When I asked Alison where Jesus is now, she pointed to her heart."

Alison has always stated that she became a Christian that day in her early life. She has always had a simple, childlike faith in Him.

That faith grew in Alison's childhood, along with that of our other children, when Allan stumbled upon some special material at a garage sale. The literature from David C. Cook Publishers was in comic book format, illustrating Bible stories. Neat! Then we learned that the series came in a one-volume book called *The Picture Bible*.

That book began a family tradition and end-of-day routine. After all the kids had gone through their bath times and were in their pajamas, we lined up on the sofa for "bedtime Bible stories" from *The Picture Bible*. It really laid a foundation for their future Bible learning, and I heartily recommend it for families. Before they could read, I pointed to the characters as I read their words. Early into elementary school, they could read it for themselves, and they did. A campus ministry pastor once told me that college students with a Bible story foundation have a better grasp of Bible concepts than others who do not.

When Joel was a toddler, Sharon had some issues with hearing loss. The doctor said that there was a hole in her eardrum and he would need to insert tubes. Also, her adenoids should be removed. We had church leaders to pray for her, but no improvement came.

One day I noticed Joel was headed toward a volume of a child's picture encyclopedia left lying on the floor. He had a reputation for damaging books by tearing the pages with his "not so gentle" touch while turning them. I rushed to get there first, but he reached the book and flipped it open. As I rescued that "A" volume from his grip, I noticed the article he randomly "found" was on "adenoids." It said that hearing often improves when they are removed. I sensed that this was one of those mini-miracles, one in which God chooses to remain anonymous, a "coincidence." The prayer for healing was not answered as we had wished, but we got an answer nonetheless through the means of little fingers and an encyclopedia page. The surgery went well; I spent the night in the hospital with Sharon and got to witness to another mom. Joel looked around the house for me that night, Allan said. Sharon's hearing improved.

When Joel was just a little older, one evening at twilight I let him play outside near our front porch with the other children in our apartment complex who had gathered there for end of the day time together. I thought it would free me up to get a few things done quickly since he would be entertained watching the older kids. Wrong! A few minutes later a man came up carrying Joel. He had found him in the middle of the busy four-lane 10th Avenue. We were so stunned that we failed to shake the man's hand, and he was gone. I clasped Joel in my arms and kissed his innocent little face over and over again. The whole episode showed me a wrong priority: a desire to get house work done to the neglect of my children and even resentment toward constant watchfulness over my children. That little boy in my arms could never be re-placed. Housework was recurring.

I was not the only one in the family who was doing some teach-ing during those Belmont Apartment days. Our local church pas-tor, Joe Fowler, asked Allan to tag-team with Jack, another church history lover in the church, to do a series on church history. The meetings were held in various homes. Allan and Jack alternated teaching sessions. For variety, occasionally Pastor Fowler showed us some rented, full-length films on lives of some of the key figures of the past, men such as Martin Luther, John Huss, and Hudson Taylor.

Allan's main textbook was *The Pilgrim Church* by E. H. Broadbent. Thus, this farmer's daughter from the cotton patch learned about many unsung Christians throughout the years. Allan told about Roman persecutions and faithful old Polycarp, a disciple of John the apostle. He outlined the struggles of the courageous Waldensians of Italy who retreated to the mountains as the Roman Catholic Church restricted their beliefs. Allan's years in seminary were not wasted.

As our children grew, they were active in school and sports teams. I was a stay-at-home mom, doing some typing and tutoring to help the budget. I was able to sell Tupperware for three years (1980-1983) and did not have to leave the children except for Tupperware parties. They went with me to the warehouse to pick up merchandise and supplies and also to deliver items to my hostesses.

When Charles was about nine years old, we attended an evangelistic meeting held in the auditorium of Shelton State Community College when it was housed in an old Gaylord's Department Store building, newly renovated. The guest evangelist was Clark Whitten from Roswell, New Mexico. His church had recently led the Southern Baptist Convention in baptisms. (Allan was not present when Whitten gave the invitation because his chronic back pain forced him to go to a side room to lie on the floor.)

The evangelist pleaded, "If you are not sure you would go to heaven if you died, come forward."

I was standing next to Charles. He looked up at me and said, "Mama, I need to go down there."

I asked, "Do you want to go alone or have me go with you?"

He wanted me to accompany him. There in that setting, Charles entered the kingdom of God. He was always a "good" child, but that day he was reborn from above and has served His Lord faithfully since.

There was another memorable event in Charles's life when he was about nine. It affected our entire family.

POINTS TO PONDER

1. Promises for our children to live for God: Isaiah 44:3; Psalm 102:28. Think of others.

CHAPTER 11
MY DAD

In January of 1983, Tuscaloosa, Alabama, said "goodbye" to its well-loved football coach, Paul "Bear" Bryant. His admirers lined the street to see his funeral procession. Just three months later, I had to say "see you later" to my beloved father, Robert Lee "Bob" Childers. God's amazing grace both prepared me and carried me through those days in early April.

I remember sometime beforehand hearing an announcement on a friend's TV that there would be a homecoming episode with the original cast of the old *Leave It to Beaver* sitcom. I really had a desire to see it since that show was a weekly favorite of mine back when the series was *current*; Wally was my contemporary. But we did not own a TV set at the time that I heard the announcement. However, I happened to be spending the night at my parents' home the night that the special show aired. There was a touching scene showing the grown-up Beaver and Wally with their TV mom, June Cleaver, and others in the rain at the cemetery for the interment of Ward Cleaver. I thought, "I'm so glad I still have my dad."

About two weeks later, I got a phone call that Dad had become ill on a Thursday evening with his old problem, a gall bladder attack. He had just bought a new garden tiller and enjoyed using it for spring plowing. Three years earlier he almost died from the poison his defective gall bladder had pumped into his system. He still refused to get it removed, perhaps from fear of bleeding to death or of never waking up from surgery, as his own father had done. After that phone call announcing the second attack, I began praying for Dad earnestly, just as I did during that first attack.

Three years earlier I had seen a mental vision of the sunrise on the horizon of our farm and felt God was saying that Dad would return there. He did. This time as I prayed, I saw a cemetery, as unwelcoming as the one in *Leave It to Beaver*. So, Allan and I were not surprised when the phone rang very early Sunday morning, Easter Sunday morning, 1983, and heard my sister's voice say that Dad had left us, just three days after the onset of the illness.

Our family hurriedly prepared for our trip back to that mountain that Dad loved. As we ascended the final steep mile up the road, we were silent in the car. I looked upward through the windshield and noticed the wooden electric power line poles as never before. Each one was a perfect cross shape. One after another loomed in front of me as we moved onward, reminding me that because of the cross that Jesus accepted on Calvary and his three-day ordeal with death, that shy country boy now had an eternal home with Him "just over in the glory-land," as Dad often sang.

Mother filled in more details of my champion's passing. She said just before the doctors asked her to step out of the room, Dad had sung to her the words of one of his more recent favorite songs, "I'll Live On." It declared that when the body is lifeless, "I'll live on, through eternity, I'll live." Yes!! Jesus had said so. John 11: 25-26 (ESV) "...I am the resurrection and the life. Whoever believes in me, though he die, yet shall he live, and everyone who lives and believes in me shall never die...."

Dad's funeral was held in Mt. View Baptist Church where he had still served as a deacon and song leader. His burial took place at Andrews Chapel cemetery near Danville where his parents, his second (still born, full-term) son, and other relatives were laid to rest. The rain was falling so steadily that all attendees simply waited in their cars. We all watched the men who had been employed for the task of depositing and burying the casket carry out their duties. Dad was home forever, finally home. Mother, at age seventy-two, continued to raise the last two of some twenty foster children entrusted to her home. These last two were siblings; the younger was just a few days older than Charles, a nine-year-old. He and his sister remained with Mother through their high school days. Our family was glad to have them there so that she would not be alone as she grieved for her lost love.

I was so thankful that I had had a conversation with Dad one day sitting together in the shade of his cedar tree. I tearfully thanked him for being willing to work all those years in Chicago away from Mother and his family. He just said, "Oh, we were glad to do it."

It wasn't until I was married and discovered the incredible bond between man and wife that I could understand the hurt in that separation. But Dad saw fatherhood as his responsibility, whatever it cost him.

Another adult conversation with Dad that I will always cherish was about his decision to follow the Lord. He never volunteered the information but did not seem to mind at all telling me about it when I asked him. I recently shared his testimony, in story form, by incorporating it into a Mother's Day speech and focusing more on his mother, who was a key player. Here is how the story went.

GRANDMOTHER CHILDERS' STORY

This story is about a young housewife named Mary. She lived in the remote area of Alabama in Lawrence County, where much of the land is now in the Bankhead National Forest. In 1910 she had two little girls and a fourteen-month-old son whom we will call little Bobby. In that year—just four years after the 1906 Azusa Street Revival that spawned most of our Pentecostal churches —somehow the Pentecostal message reached Mary in that remote area of Alabama (like a dandelion seed that found its way to a distant crevice). Mary heard that God was moving again today. People were asking God to fill them with His Holy Spirit, and it was happening. A messenger told of Christians' lives being empowered, their prayer lives energized, and the Bible becoming more real. This sounded good to Mary, so she prayed for this baptism of the Spirit and received.

<u>Fast forward twenty years</u>. Now it is about 1930. During the previous twenty years, Mary has become known as a woman whose prayers reach God. Sometimes people make their way to her door to request prayer for physical healing. She has affectionately become known in the community as "Aunt Mary." Little Bobby is now twenty-one years old, known by his more mature name, "Bob."

One night Mary told the family that she would be staying up that night because it was time for her chicken eggs in her incubator to hatch, out in the shed for chickens. (We once incubated some eggs. We put a big *X* on the eggs and had to rotate them each day—*X's* up, *X's* down, *X's* up, *X's* down.) Mary had nurtured these eggs the twenty-one days required for hatching them. She had to be there to move the chicks from the incubator to their pen.

Unknown to her, back in her house, the son she had nurtured for twenty-one years was struggling. Bob went to bed as usual that night, but suddenly his heart began doing something extremely unusual. He feared he was going to die. This should not be happening, he thought. He was only twenty-one years old, but it appeared he was being called upon to die with hardly a moment's notice. Eternity loomed before him, a frightening thought because he had not "bought into" his mother's holy-roller religion or yielded his life to Jesus. He had some rowdy friends. But now, at that time of night with no preacher around to counsel him, his only hope was to make it out to the chicken shed to find his godly mother.

Together Mary and her son prayed, and Bob settled his account with the Lord that night. He said that such a peace filled his mind that it would not have mattered if he had died. Things changed after that prayer. Bob gave up his tobacco use in all three forms, along with alcohol and rowdy friends. Instead, he began playing his guitar and singing with a friend in area churches.

I did not call Bob's mother "Aunt Mary." I called her Grandmother Childers. She was my grandmother, and Bob was my dad. Largely because of Grandmother's faith, one of her nephews was a Church of God preacher till his death. Three of her great-grandsons are senior pastors; one is a part-time preacher; one is a foreign missionary; and another has completed seminary to prepare for Christian ministry. One great-granddaughter is licensed in her denomination and was once a nationally appointed home missionary; another great-granddaughter was a worship leader in a church. Timothy can thank his Grandmother Lois for embracing Paul's teachings and being "different" in her day; perhaps she was one of those who "sided with the apostles" on Paul's first stop in the Lystra area and set an example for grandson Timothy. (Acts 14; 16:1-5; II Tim. 1:5; 3:10-12) Likewise, all of Mary Childers' descendants can say, "Thank you, Grandmother Childers." She was willing to check out the message of a fuller spiritual life in the scriptures and be "different" in Lawrence County. Both of these grandmothers (mine and Timothy's) spearheaded a new spiritual lineage in their respective families.

What a legacy Dad and his mother left us. Dad was the one who first showed me some guitar chords. Although he was not perfect and had his weaknesses, as we all do, I was very thankful for my godly father. After his passing, I knew he had joined the ranks of "just men made perfect." (Hebrews 12:23) He is perfect now! I was sorry that our little Gravelys would not remember much about their Granddaddy Childers; they were all too young. (Allan's dad died in 1975; only toddler Charles met him.)

POINT TO PONDER

1. The anonymous wise woman of II Samuel 14:14 says that God "devises ways so that a banished person may not remain estranged from him." (NIV) Think of examples of God's engineering ways (some as unusual as the chicken shed story) to bring someone back to Him.

CHAPTER 12
GOD LIFTING THE POOR

ALLAN HAD FINALLY COMPLETED HIS Master's in history on Alison's fourth birthday, December 21, 1981. But no job was to be found. He had launched a new career as a real estate agent the week of Alison's birth in 1977, but the market was difficult in subsequent years, and sales were low. His recurring migraine headaches limited his ability to do jobs with paperwork. He felt he could not work an eight-hour-a-day job with his migraines and chronic back pain. So, he got out his paint brush again. He needed a "help meet" to step up to the plate at this time and help meet the expenses in a more substantial way than Tupperware sales had done.

One night in early 1983 at a Tupperware party, my hostess re-marked that anyone walking into her office seeking work would be hired on the spot to be her secretary. She was desperate. My ears perked up. I told Allan about the position with hours compatible for our schedules, 8:30 A.M.-2:30 P.M. I could still car pool the three school children; only Joel would have to be put in daycare. That Tupperware hostess became my boss for two years as I func-tioned as secretary, bookkeeper, volunteer coordinator, and fund-raiser for United Cerebral Palsy of West Alabama. That monthly check was very helpful. But I regretted not getting to spend that year alone with Joel, just the two of us, since he had been short changed on the "Mama attention" the others had had.

Our tenth wedding anniversary was approaching in March of 1983 when I began to pray that we could do something special to celebrate. We did not have many extra funds for a big celebration, so the day came and went without too much fanfare. But it seemed that my prayers did get answered after all, just three months over-due, in June instead of March! We had a second honeymoon. This one was almost free!

Several events coincided to make that second honeymoon possi-ble. First, a couple of old friends told us that God put it on their hearts to give us $300. Then Allan won a scholarship to pursue his doctor-ate. As Allan's graduate program had wound down, the University recognized him by bestowing the Albert Burton Moore Memorial Award for Outstanding Graduate Student in History. (I knew all along he was outstanding.) He also won awards at the University for his thesis work, *The English Seekers: 1643-1656.* It won the "Outstanding Graduate Student Research Writing Award for M.A. Thesis."

But it was the third award that prompted us to take that sec-ond honeymoon trip. It was the Richard M. Weaver Foundation Fellowship Award for 1983 for an essay written with the sponsor-ship of Dr. Forrest MacDonald at UA, "Education in a Free Society: Vision and the Demonic Legacy." That award, one of thirteen na-tionally, was for full tuition in the graduate program of his choice.

After investigating all his options for earning a doctorate, Allan was keenly interested in doing church history research at the University of Wisconsin. Ironically, a friendly guest lecturer from that school spoke to the history department at the University of Alabama and told Allan that he would be glad to host us if we decided to make an exploratory trip to Madison, WI.

When our friends put that $300 in our hands, we decided to make that trip to Madison in June. First, we treated our children to a rare surprise, a trip to the movies to see the current film, *Return of the Jedi.* They enjoyed it, but Joel fell asleep during the second half. Our wonderful church friends agreed to watch all four of our kids during our time away on our trip. So, we drove off in our little gray Datsun.

Allan and I enjoyed our time together. We stopped the first night in Paducah, KY. We arrived in Madison the next day. To us, it was chilly that June in Wisconsin, and we were glad we had light jackets. But the locals thought they were having a heat wave, and some of them even put on tank tops and shorts.

Our friendly hosts there told us that the couple living in the downstairs apartment had left on an out-of-town trip and offered us their apartment while they were away. Their apartment had a luxurious, king-sized water bed. We were up and away daily checking out the graduate program, a local church, elementary schools, married student housing, the Tupperware possibilities, and even jobs for me.

We knew that I would have to work full time for our family to survive financially. Allan's scholarship paid only tuition; he would have to spend the majority of his time doing research and writing. Then, two haunting questions filled our minds: (1) Would Allan be able to do all that reading necessary to earn a doctorate when eye-strain constantly brought on migraines that forced him into a dark room for days? (2) If he was studying at the library all the time and I was working full time, who would be raising our children?

As we pondered those two uncertainties, we had a growing conviction that moving to Wisconsin would not be the most favorable move for our little family of four tender plants. We were the stewards of their souls. I never wanted another woman raising my children; I knew that someday I would give an account of how I (not the village) performed that responsibility. As tempting as it was, Allan turned down the Richard Weaver scholarship.

We had moved to Belmont Apartments when Sharon was two months old. Nine years later, we were still there since Allan had been a part-time student. But things had changed. The University of Alabama had not upgraded these married student units; couples could find more modern apartments for comparable rates. To increase occupancy, the University opened the apartments for rental to any staff member. Crime increased; playmates were more aggressive.

Alas, we felt trapped there because we did not own a stove, dining table set, or refrigerator; they were all provided. Also, the rentals listed in the newspaper required deposit money—which we did not have. The University had already refunded our initial deposit earlier when we had served there as resident managers for a time. Our utilities were provided at Belmont, so we did not have utilities deposit money either. My mother, now a widow, came to visit with brother Ruel and family. She detected the hostile environment and began praying for something to happen to enable us to move out. God listens to widows; check it out in the scriptures!

One night I read Psalm 10 very slowly and noticed that God was really on the side of the poor. He cared. The next day we got a phone call from a friend in our church. He wanted to know if we would be interested in assuming his lease on a small house since he felt his family should move into a half-way home as house parents. No deposits would be necessary since we were subleasing. Also, they would be leaving their stove and refrigerator for our use. We accepted his offer.

Church friends came in a caravan of trucks and moved us across town to a small yellow cottage in the Cedar Crest neighborhood situated between the hospital and the new mall where Northington apartments had once stood, near Krispy Kreme Doughnuts!!! Someone in the church had a dining set he did not need. When our friend's lease expired, the landlord allowed us to paint his cottage in lieu of a deposit. Some of our church friends lived in Cedar Crest, and our children had good friends to play with. They could even walk underneath the six-lane McFarland Blvd. to swim in a community pool. They all became good swimmers. That was something I always wanted for my children since I cannot swim at all. Ain't God good?

(Note: On the April 27, 2011, a terrible tornado "wiped out" this Tuscaloosa neighborhood between the hospital and the mall, along with Krispy Kreme Donuts. Even *Southern Living* magazine covered the story.)

While living at Cedar Crest, one day in May, 1985, Allan and I set aside a day to fast and pray about our finances. At that time he was self-employed as a paint contractor, but could only work part-time because of back pain. Friends agreed to keep our children that day. As I prayed and read my Bible, a verse in Haggai 2:19 seemed to be a direct promise to us: "from this day I will bless you." Soon afterwards, we attended a home Bible study through Riverwood Presbyterian Church. A young man there mentioned to Allan that local Stillman College was in desperate need of a religion professor since a full-time professor had suddenly had a stroke. Allan applied and was hired for the fall term.

That summer of 1985 I became so grieved with leaving my children daily to go to work during their summer vacation that I thought, "Where can I work so that I won't have to leave them when school is out?" The only answer I could think of was this: at a school that closes for the summer. A school!! Yes. I would be willing to be a "janitoress," a library aide, teacher aide, lunchroom worker, or secretary. I was qualified for any of those support personnel positions.

I applied to Tuscaloosa City Schools and interviewed for both of the current secretarial openings. With some sixteen other applicants competing, God gave me favor with Mr. Jack White, principal of a vocational high school. During his interview, I showed him a recent family photo and commented, "These are my four reasons for wanting to work here. I'm not interested in climbing a social ladder.

If I were, I'd stay downtown. I want my kids to turn out right." He hired me to be the school secretary to work the front desk.

I served in the same corner, same desk at that vocational, technical high school for fifteen and a half years during the tenure of several principals and one name change. The school at first was Tuscaloosa Area Vocational School (TAVS), then Tuscaloosa Center for Technology (TCT). The low-stress position was ideal for child rearing. I was off summers, Christmas and other school holidays, and spring breaks. Also, I had no preparation for work, and I left my work at school so that I could focus on my family after 3:30 P. M. The Auto Body and Auto Mechanics shops at the school repaired our old cars often at minimal costs.

A HOME OF OUR OWN

But these two jobs (mine and Allan's) were only the beginning of God's blessings to our family. One day when I was not at home, the children prayed with their dad for a larger house, one with stairs like on TV, one with a separate bedroom for each one of them, a fireplace, and a dishwasher. They wanted that dishwashing chore eliminated for good!

When I heard about their request, I kept quiet so as not to destroy their faith but had serious doubts about a family with our income getting a five-bedroom home! I was impressed with their prayer for their dream house. Within months we got that house. Here's how it happened.

Allan had done a painting job for Don & Betty Brandon. They mentioned to him that they had an older, family home in Northport they would love to sell. It was a rambling frame house with a basement. Allan told them that if it did not sell, he would be interested in renting it. That we did and moved into 2706 20th Avenue, Northport, AL, during Labor Day weekend, 1985, where we remained for sixteen years.

Like my job, the house was ideal in many ways. It was near good schools, within walking distance for the middle school and high school, Northport Jr. High and Tuscaloosa County High. The children had a bedroom apiece in the basement; a fireplace was on the new den addition to the house. There was roooommm, sssppppaaaaccee. After so many years in a small apartment or a small cottage, we had room to move around at last. The modernized kitchen had plenty of counter and cabinet space and a dishwasher. The beautiful colored glass front door panels and pine hardwood floors in the front room had come from materials of an old, dismantled hotel in Tuscaloosa. The only negative feature was a leaky basement that required a sump pump. The next year we were able to buy the home!

Our house was built in 1927 by Mr. Levi Brandon, Don's grandfather. Levi's brother, Henry Brandon, was in his late eighties and lived next door. He had once been a World War I era flying ace who could fly a plane in and out of a hangar. He said that his grandfather had stood as a lad on the roadside there on our street, 20th Avenue, and watched Union soldiers file by on their way to cross the Black Warrior River to reach the University of Alabama to burn it to the ground. It had been a Confederate cadet training center. The Union soldiers had met little resistance there. They did leave the president's mansion and a guard house standing. We learned that our street and Main Avenue were the two oldest streets in Northport, a town just across the river from Tuscaloosa. As far as I know, the house is still standing today. It deserves a historical marker.

We knew that Allan's job at Stillman College would be a temporary assignment since the school's grants required faculty with doctoral degrees. A replacement for him was eventually found, and we were again looking for gainful employment. Allan tried selling encyclopedias and working part-time on a church staff. Through a friend, he heard about a program at the University that offered free tuition and a stipend for earning a Master's degree in vocational rehabilitation counseling. He was accepted and was able to complete this program in his fifties while working at his latest job, repairing dings in windshields, thanks to his gracious employer, Robert Hart.

The windshield job required Allan to be outside in the heat and in the cold. I remember looking outside the window of my cozy office one bleak, cold winter day and thinking, "Allan is out there working in that cold." I wanted something better for him.

One day, the children and I gathered around Allan, laid our hands on his shoulders, and prayed for his job situation. I felt no extra faith, just a need to express our needs to God. We asked for a new job for him, one with (1) retirement, (2) adequate income, and (3) inside work. We had been hopeful that his newly earned Master's degree would lead to a better job, but we were told that he had to be "reachable" on a state list in order to be hired for a state job in vocational rehabilitation counseling. His name was too far down the list of potential candidates. But we were not forgotten by our heavenly Father.

The Lord impressed me that He was "in our corner" one summer day while returning from a trip to spend time with my mother who lived two hours away from us. Along Interstate 65 was a slender man walking slowly uphill. My, my! His walk was identical to Allan's. If I had not known that Allan was home with the kids, I would have thought surely it was Allan. As I drew closer, I noticed that this man carried a simple plastic shopping bag in one hand. It appeared he had few earthly possessions in that bag. With a lump in my throat, I saw what God saw in our financial struggles: the effort was like an uphill walk with little accumulation of goods. But I also felt an assurance, a "knowing," that things were going to improve somehow, hopefully soon. That fall, Allan was unexpectedly hired as a counselor at State Vocational Rehabilitation Services. He would work there eight years and purchase two years of military time in order to become vested and retire with a pension. His income was adequate for us, and he was indoors!!!!

Another source of income for us for about ten years came through renting a room in our 20th Avenue home to international students. A carpenter friend was able to divide off one end of the large living room to make an additional bedroom and wanted no compensation for his work. His son and Joel were buddies. That half of the large front room already had electrical outlets, an air conditioning vent, and a closet. All it needed was two walls and a door.

We secured boarders by putting up a sign on the bulletin board at the University of Alabama's English Language Institute, which prepared students from around the world to take the TOEFL exam to prove English proficiency for college entrance requirements. Some of the students wanted additional conversation practice and were eager to move in with an American family. Their rent money paid our mortgage, and our children got to know young people from Spain, Venezuela, Korea, Kuwait, Jordan, Saudi Arabia, China, and Japan. Today our children seem comfortable with meeting individuals from other countries.

Our children have actually told us when mature that they are glad we were once so "poor." They noticed some of their friends with all the material comforts had become selfish and demanding, never learning to take honest needs to God. Another benefit of experiencing low income is to have a genuine empathy for others in similar circumstances and to have an assurance that God cares about their plight as well. Although I would never preach a "prosperity gospel," it is true that God does care about the afflicted. He is good to His obedient children.

POINT TO PONDER

1. Psalm 113:7 "He raises the poor from the dust and lifts the needy from the ash heap." (NIV) Would God also not lift the poor before he reaches such dire straits if he calls out in faith?

CHAPTER 13

THE WONDER YEARS

THE SIXTEEN YEARS SPENT ON 20th Avenue were like Part II in our parenting adventures. Infancy and preschool were behind. Now elementary and junior high days were upon us. They reminded me of the TV show, *The Wonder Years*, with its nostalgic recounting of these years of transition. I was enjoying this stage of the wonderment of parenthood as well.

During Allan's hectic real estate career, he discovered that clients were not very interested in properties on Friday evenings. Therefore, he set aside those times for "Family Night." We knew that we would have Daddy's full attention on Friday night and we could do something fun. Allan has always served as our "social director" who sought diverse resources of fun for us. (When the children outgrew our family nights and sought their own amusements, Friday night became our date night! Still is!!!!) The children also knew that Mama and Daddy loved each other. Someone has said that kids can endure a lot if they just know that their parents love each other.

Our oldest, Charles, entered seventh grade at the prestigious Tuscaloosa Academy via a scholarship. The other three all attended a local elementary school nearby. My old north Alabama friend, Diane Steverson Fowler, moved to our community, and our children became friends.

During the "Wonder Years," Allan was able to impart things into our children's lives that I could not. He once paid Charles to read Herodotus's *Persian Wars*. One year he bought all four of them children's tennis rackets and taught them to play and keep score correctly; I still have not mastered either skill. (In high school, Charles, Sharon, and Alison all played on the TCHS tennis teams.) Allan taught them chess and golf; he got Joel involved in a Junior Golf Tour in Tuscaloosa. Allan was on his school's junior varsity basketball team and has quick reflexes. I did contribute a little to the basketball practice since I had played on the eighth grade intramurals team. Sometimes those youngsters said, "Come on. Let's play an old-timers game." That meant they wanted Dad and Mom to play basketball with them. Off we went to our amateur indoor basketball court in the two-level garage. Mom and Dad had to have "breathing" timeouts. Allan also got our family a ping pong table. Some summers we took advantage of traveling to South Carolina to Uncle Ed Gravely's cabin on beautiful Lake Waterlee near Camden, a little south of Charlotte, North Carolina, and did some boating and fishing.

Our family tried one camping endeavor in the none-rustic section of Mt. Cheaha, Alabama's tallest mountain. It turns out that Allan and I are softies, just Holiday Inn-type campers. On this one-and-only camping trip, we had an electric outlet on a post near our tent so that I could use my electric griddle, and the brick shower and bath house was nearby. The ground felt hard through the air mattress. I got lots of chigger bites, but the others did not because they got into a swimming pool after lying on some grass and washed their "critters" away. The children loved camping; Allan and I did not.

Allan did impart his love for the beach to us by getting us there even if we sometimes had to borrow some funds to be able to go. He had lived in Wilmington on the North Carolina coast from age five through ten and had learned to swim in the sound between Wrightsville Beach and Wilmington. He cherished those happy boyhood memories at Wrightsville Beach. He wanted good memories for his inland offspring, even if he had to settle for the Gulf of Mexico instead of the Atlantic coast. I learned to like the beach, too. Gulf Shores and Dauphin Island on the Alabama coast "grew" on all of us, and I did not mind going there whenever possible so that the family could get their "beach fix." After all, I was able to get my "mountain fix" every time I went back to see my relatives in north Alabama.

Our historic home had another feature for developing athleticism in our growing-up tribe. There was a large area of concrete surface under the large carport and side porch. I found four used roller skates at a garage sale. Soon the children were skating back and forth between the two areas, spinning around a support post for the carport roof. I had never learned to skate and felt so awkward at a club skating party in high school. I was confident those old skates would eliminate such future embarrassment for my children. I do not remember their ever falling down or getting hurt while skating.

How about that? We had our own skating rink and indoor basketball court. The yard had ample space for a badminton net and outdoor basketball goal. The nearby TCHS walking track and tennis courts were available after school hours. We saw that we didn't have to have great resources to be resourceful.

Since we discouraged a lot of TV viewing, we always looked for alternative outlets for our children's youthful energy, or they came up with their own ideas. The next door neighbors shared their huge front lawn with all the neighborhood kids, and many a game of softball took place there. One day a newspaper reporter stopped by our house to photograph our three youngest making their own tree swing with a rope and an old bicycle tire. That photo was on the front page of the paper. Many good things in life are free.

One humorous vignette of these years is of note. As I was driving Joel and Alison to church one day, they began disagreeing in the back seat. I told them, "We are not taking this into church." I pulled over into a parking lot, turned toward them, and started singing a little tune by an unknown writer to them:

Oh, how sweet it is to see
All my children in unity.
Makes my feet jump up with glee,
All my children in unity.
Praise the Lord, I'm beginning to see
All the blessings that are coming to me
When in Christ we all agree.
All my children in unity.

Within moments, those two belligerents were laughing and forgot what they were quarreling about. Allan and I always cherished the harmony in our home and guarded it. Peace, unity, and harmony in a family are rewarded perpetually in life.

Allan and I sought churches that were best for our children, not us. Our preferences could wait until they were grown. We saw that church camps were excellent for boosting a child's own commitment to the Lord. Sharon and Joel were both saved at camp, and all four later received the baptism of the Holy Spirit at a church camp site, at either youth camp or college events held there.

My mother sometimes recounted a "church" regret of my Pentecostal Grandmother Childers. During her children's growing up years, Grandmother had thought that her obligation was to be often at church, even if her children were roaming the creek banks. She confided in Mother that if she could redo those years, she would have been with her children more. Her rural church had little to offer its youth, and only one of her children became involved in her church.

I remember very clearly when Alison returned home one summer from the state camp of the Assemblies of God. (She had probably finished the eighth grade in school by then.) I took one look at her and knew that something was different. I was right. She had something special to tell. At camp she had prayed for the Baptism of the Holy Spirit at the end of a sermon by evangelist Sam Rijfkogel. He admonished her to just focus on Jesus. She did, and He gloriously filled her. During high school, Alison got up almost as early as I did before the rest of the family stirred. Through a crack in my upstairs cabinet wall, I could see that the downstairs bathroom light was on. She was having her quiet time there with her 365-day Bible before washing that beautiful long, blonde hair before her school day began.

Sharon was about fourteen when she traveled to the North Carolina mountains near Asheville to attend Ridge Haven Camp, sponsored by the Presbyterian Church of America. During her eighth grade year at West End Christian School, pleasing God had seemed lower on her list of priorities than in the past. Being popular had occupied her mind. But a dear youth leader, Kathy Andreason, had challenged her to give all to Jesus.

One day before Sharon left for camp, I was upstairs in my kitchen and began to feel an urgency to go downstairs to give Sharon some advice. I found her alone in her room. I urged her to be sensitive to the Lord at camp, especially the closing evening. I remembered how the final chapel service of my week at vacation Bible school had culminated in my decision to surrender to the Lord for salvation. Sharon seemed open to my counsel. When she returned from North Carolina, she said she had publicly committed herself to the Lord the final evening of the camp. That commitment has been in place since that summer day. We would have to wait longer for Joel's surrender.

During this Part II of our parenting, we were involved in our children's dreams and activities and also our efforts to manage the income and household. The old desire to be a missionary to Mexico rarely crossed my mind until one day I happened to mention it in passing to a friend. Later, thoughts about why I had been "turned down" for missionary service began to trouble me. Surely I had not missed God's will for my life, or had I? I decided to fast about all that and see if I could get an answer. For some reason Allan took all four kids somewhere and I had the house to myself.

There I sat at his desk praying, thinking. I noticed a well-known book on his desk top, *A Man Called Peter* by Catherine Marshall. I flipped through its pages and found my answer shortly before the famous scene of Peter Marshall's hearing his named called by a mysterious voice in the dark just seconds before he would have fallen over a cliff. He, too, had once questioned God about why he could not go to China and be a missionary as his heart desired, just as his Olympic winner friend Eric Liddell had done. (Liddell was the hero of the *Chariots of Fire* movie.) The door of opportunity to China had slammed shut in Peter's face. Then it seemed the Lord showed him that his heart was right in being willing to go, but China was not the place God wanted him to go. Peter came to America instead and later became chaplain of the U. S. Senate. My, how those words soothed me. My own heart was right in wanting to go to Mexico, but it was not the place for me. The matter has been settled since that day.

While I never became an official "missionary," representing a group, God arranged something special for Allan and me to make us His missionaries. While Allan was serving as a part-time staff member at a local church, he took advantage of a week-long training session in Evangelism Explosion (EE). That seven-day absence from Allan, our longest time apart until then, was worth every moment. The event was held at the new building of Briarwood Presbyterian Church near Birmingham, situated high on a hill there to shine for Jesus. Some sixty team members went out witnessing on those chilly February nights; one member was the founding pastor himself, Frank Barker.

Allan returned to train me and others at church. It was exciting to see our teams begin to go out to share their faith. One evening Allan and I called on a home that had responded favorably to a phone questionnaire. Before we left that home, the man there repented of his sins and committed his life to the Lord. Later he shared with us that just before we knocked on his door, he had been sitting alone plotting revenge against his ex-wife's boyfriend. That new Christian got involved at our church.

With EE, at last I had a skill that helped me to "close the deal" if I felt God leading that way when I witnessed to someone. Beforehand, I usually just shared my testimony and felt inept at telling someone else how to receive eternal life. The old Training Union quarterly was right; crossing an ocean never made a missionary out of anyone. "Wanna-Be" missionaries need to be trained. When I was single, my strategy was merely to tell those who listened all that I knew; then I would take them to Bro. Steverson, Diane's dad. That harvester knew how to lead people into salvation or the baptism of the Holy Spirit. Someone has compared the "know how" gained through EE training to pitching skills in baseball. Without EE, often Christians seem to throw the ball here and there, but EE helps them put it right over the plate.

In the Gravely household, the "Wonder Years" rolled on into high school. Before long, Charles and Sharon had been awarded scholastic scholarships to Tuscaloosa Academy and later West End Christian School. One year, the latter closed about two weeks into the school year, forcing Charles and Sharon to transfer to Tuscaloosa County High School (TCHS), very near our home. I wanted Charles to take Spanish, but we were told the same thing we had heard at Tuscaloosa Academy–all Spanish classes were full, and he would have to take French. I pouted. I wanted all my children to take my beloved Spanish. But French it was. (Today he is fluent in French, living in Belgium as a missionary and preaching in French.)

Another door was closed to Charles at TCHS, basketball. Because he had attended a private school that year (a few days), he was disqualified from joining the team. Alas! The following year, his feet were so sunburned from a beach trip that he could not put on his gym shoes for basketball tryouts. He did join the Tuscaloosa Eagles, an independent team. He was that team's successful free-throw shooter and was called upon for scoring technical foul penalty shots. In practice he once rang over forty consecutive baskets without missing from the free-throw line, but mothers should not brag. I am glad he had a higher calling than the NBA. The missionary family of Daniel and Ruby Ost of Mexico often said, "If you're called to be a missionary, why stoop to be a king?" (In the 1980s, their immediate family of eight children and their spouses had already contributed around 188 years of full-time missionary service to the Lord.)

When the defunct Christian school closed its doors, all its scholastic records were forwarded to the Tuscaloosa City Schools. I went there personally trying to locate Sharon's eighth grade records, but they could not be found. We still have no proof that she completed that year. There is no trace of evidence. That was the year she was most ashamed of because of her shallow commitment to the Lord. What an analogy of the forgiveness we receive for our hideous sins, i.e., all the evidence against us is gone forever. (Colossians 2:13-14)

Doesn't Cancer Happen to "Other" People, Not Me?

I guess wives and mothers can be so focused on their family units, that they become susceptible to surprise attacks from danger. That was my story the summer of 1991.

Everything on the "things to pack" list for the beach was taken care of, and off we went to Gulf Shores, AL, on the beautiful Gulf of Mexico. The sun was especially bright one day, so it seemed perfect for tanning my legs below the knees a little. My skin was so pale. Soon, really soon, the leg skin was pink and pinker. The sunburn healed up all right in the following days. All that discomfort was gone, but a larger-than-usual freckle remained. I gave it little thought, but some annoying little moles around my waistline were bothering me. I made an appointment with my dermatologist for their removal. I planned to have him look at that huge freckle on my left leg calf that had grown to the size of my pinky's fingernail since the beach trip.

The day of my doctor's appointment was the day that doctor became my hero. He took one look at my "big freckle" and said, "The moles bother you. This bothers me."

Dr. Johnson did a biopsy immediately. A day or two later he called with the results: melanoma cancer. His voice was serious over the phone, "Dottie, you have four kids. Let's get this taken care of."

He arranged for surgery as soon as possible at the University of Alabama in Birmingham, and I did some research on what "melanoma" meant. I don't remember ever hearing that word before, but it turned out to be as unwelcomed and as fatal as a rattlesnake. I was very willing to stretch out on that out-patient operating table to have the "freckle" removed. I requested just a local anesthesia so that I would be alert when my seventeen-year-old driver, Charles, would take me home through Birmingham traffic, which he had never experienced before. The incision required stitches, and I used crutches for a while. No skin graph was necessary.

The post-surgery lab report read, "all margins clear." Those were three special words to me. My life was spared to continue on in this world in the roles I enjoyed most, Allan's wife and my children's mama. Allan and I never discussed the danger of melanoma around the children. We reasoned, "Why disturb them if it will all be over with surgery?" Their school year and mine was about to begin. The Wonder Years had evolved into senior high for our older two, and college was on the horizon for them and for me.

POINTS TO PONDER

1. There are fewer regrets if we prioritize in this order: God, family, church.

2. We may not have to wait till the "sweet by and by" to understand perplexities. Sometimes God grants enlightenment here. Proverbs 28:5

3. Peace, unity, and harmony in a family are rewarded perpetually in life. Psalm 133:1 "How wonderful it is, how pleasant, when brothers live in harmony!" *The Living Bible*

CHAPTER 14

ALABAMA VS. AUBURN

SHARON AND CHARLES WERE THE ones who led the way for our family to discover how the system of earning college scholarships works. I say "earning" because it does require some work. They had a wonderful counselor at TCHS, Ms. Fuller, who coached them in finding and applying for scholarships. She kept their files with recommendation letters, transcripts, and other pertinent items to complete the kit for each application. They won several college scholarships.

Charles landed at the University of Alabama, right there in Tuscaloosa, fall of 1992. He declined other scholarship offers (including Auburn's), but we delivered Sharon to her Auburn University dorm room in 1993. Both of them had worked hard throughout their high school days, only doing part-time jobs in the summer. Alison worked three summers and saved enough money to pay cash for her first car. All of our children paid for their own cars; we shared the family car with them until they had enough money to buy one. We told our children that those meager school-year job earnings (just "peanuts") could never compare to big scholarship dollars ahead if they did *not* work September through May but kept up their GPAs. We were right!

Charles became active immediately in the Chi Alpha Christian Fellowship at the University of Alabama, led by his mentors, Al and Heather Baker. I knew where to find Charles every Friday night. He moved to campus his sophomore year. He majored in English and thought of being an English teacher, but during his senior year, he felt a call of God to enter campus ministry through Chi Alpha, the secular college ministry of the Assemblies of God. Since college, he has been pursuing that call full time. Many of his former disciples are now in full time ministry as well or are serving the Lord in some capacity.

Sharon was active with Chi Alpha her freshman year at Auburn. God used her to reach another girl who later did children's ministry overseas.

But Sharon's dream of attending Auburn and becoming an architect had to be tweaked somewhat because the department did not offer scholarships for sophomores. Her freshman scholarship was not renewal. In addition, she decided that she did not care for some of the aspects of that occupation, things like planning sewer lines. She wanted to decorate rooms. So she returned to Tuscaloosa, moved (reluctantly) back in with Mom and Dad for a while, entered the University of Alabama, and began earning a degree in Interior Design, just as her younger sister had predicted all along.

The wonderful Chi Alpha and high school friends were always welcomed at our home. (Today many of them are my Facebook friends.) We gave our children permission to invite over anyone they wanted to entertain for Sunday lunch. I always cooked a large meal in order to have plenty to share. Afterwards, I usually excused myself and took my standard Sunday afternoon nap. Just after one such luxurious nap, I emerged from the bedroom and noticed Erick, one of Charles's friends, enjoying a snooze of his own on the den sofa. I was thrilled that he felt that "at home" with us.

Often on Thanksgiving weekends, after we returned from our annual trip to the Morgan County mountains, we welcomed lonely Chi Alpha students who were too far from their families to make the trip back home both then and again at Christmas. I called them the "Chi Alpha orphans." Sometimes we took them to the mountains with us. My inspiration for including them came from a dear friend, Wyoma Jackson, who had led the free English class for international students and wives on the UA campus through the Baptist women's ministry.

Wyoma's story always brought a lump to my throat. In her youth, her family lived on the Virginia coast near a naval base. Every Thanksgiving her mother prepared a generous meal. When every delicious detail was complete, she sent her husband out to check the streets for lonely sailors, far from home and their mother's cooking. They got invited to Wyoma's home.

I adopted Wyoma's mother's strategy. Although I expected no "pay back," I have observed over the years that when my own children were far from home on Thanksgiving, someone extended hospitality to them. That gave me one more thing to give thanks for.

One year Sharon took off a semester from college to do a tour with Youth-With-A-Mission (YWAM) in Belarus. She struggled with that decision for a while, praying alone in our old two-story garage. That dear old garage had once had a second level apartment during World War II. Now the upper flooring had been partially removed so that the high ceiling afforded enough space for a tiny basketball court for our family after we mounted our indoor hoop. The small area of upper flooring still intact provided us an "upper room" prayer get-away to escape from family interaction and to be alone.

During this season of prayer, a former "YWAM-er" encouraged Sharon to "go for it" and believe God for the finances. That year, as usual, I gave my first day off for my three-month summer vacation to the Lord as a "first fruits" offering by praying and seeking His kingdom. I drew up a mailing list of every Christian friend I could think of to receive a support letter from Sharon. I reviewed that list and felt my eyes grow moist with tears. Those names represented some of the most wonderful people on earth. And they were *our friends*!!!! Their response was amazing. One old friend from Belmont Apartment days sent $100; we had not seen her in years.

Sharon reported to the Elm Springs, Arkansas, YWAM base for training before going to Eastern Europe. She trained with some of the dedicated family members of singer and songwriter, Twila Paris. Sharon saw some marvelous things on her mission trip, including one healing of blindness, several salvations, and even deliverance from stalkers.

Seeing God provide for Sharon and Charles in their college and ministry efforts gave me faith that He would provide for me to go to college someday. Allan and I knew college was important. How I regretted not having earned a degree. Our income would have been so much better over the years. I tried to return part-time once when the last two children were in diapers. After two semesters and losing ten pounds, I decided the time was not right.

About four years after making that decision, something happened that served as a catalyst, that "dangling carrot" before my nose, to intensify my desire to complete my education—someday, somehow. A professor in the University of Alabama Spanish department whose class I took during those two semesters there recommended me for a Spanish teacher job in an adjoining county. A school official had called him for a recommendation. When that official called me, he told me that if I had a college degree in *anything*, he could hire me with an emergency certificate since he was desperate for a teacher. I had my wonderful "Mrs." degree, the only letters associated with my name and two years of college. I lacked credentials. He hired one of my Hispanic friends who majored in physical education. My college experience would have to wait.

I waited and prayed about the right time to return to school. I waited as Allan finished his Master's in Vocational Rehabilitation counseling so that one of us could be more "on duty" as parents. Allan was also working full time during his studies. Teenagers, not just little people, need *available* parents too. Alison had her first boyfriend, always a time when Mom needs to be there. I was very busy as the family chauffeur. When Joel got his driver's license, I finally felt a peace and a "green light" to pursue a college diploma. I was forty-seven years old.

POINTS TO PONDER

1. God can make dreams come true. Nothing is impossible with Him

CHAPTER 15

MAMA IN THE COLLEGE CLASSSROOM

I REMEMBER DRIVING ALONG "THE Strip" on University Blvd. in the heart of the University of Alabama campus, thinking about college. "Do you really want to do this at age forty-seven?" I asked myself. Immediately I thought of what my mother was doing at that same age–weaning a three-year-old and raising seven other children ages five through eighteen on a poverty level budget. I thought, "I think I can take a few classes if she could do that."

One day I noticed an envelope on my desk when I returned from my lunch break at work. It was from Allan. Inside was a note reminding me that I was not too old to go to college. After all, he said, God changed the courses of many lives of older people in the Bible. What an ally and friend I had in Allan!

My decision to finish college that January, 1995, was need-driven, two needs: (1) Our family needed more income, and (2) I needed to finish something I had left undone in my life.

Financially, I had contributed as best I could in a job that allowed me time with my maturing family. At this time, I had worked at that same school desk for almost ten years, eventually "maxing out" the pay scale.

The unfinished business needed addressing. Mother, the great believer in education, had often told me, "You ought to finish."

My educational pursuits reminded me of a French drain project I had begun years earlier with such ambition; I had only dug the small ditch beside the front walk's monkey grass to carry off gutter water. But I left it incomplete, intending to lay the gravel and pipe and cover dirt later. One day as Alison chased Joel across the front yard, her foot tripped into that ditch, and she fell. I resolved to complete it, and I did. Getting up early one Saturday morning before the family stirred, I told myself, "I won't stop until this is done." I put down gravel and pipe and covered the ditch.

When I decided to be a "returning" college student, I resolved, "If I start this, like the French drain project, I'm going to see it to the end. I'll finish what I start."

My study time was Saturday mornings, on the living room sofa so that the children knew I was accessible to any of them who needed me. One time Sharon sat herself down next to me on that sofa and began, "Mama, I have a problem, and my problems are your problems." I cannot recall what the problem was but can never forget that brilliant introduction to it.

How I transitioned from being a junior college dropout to having a Master's degree is a chronicle of God's faithfulness to me. He backed me up all along the way as I diligently plowed through scholarship applications, chapters of texts, lectures, papers, practicum sites, practice teaching, and deadlines. Before it all began, Allan called a family meeting and let our children know that Mother would be needing more help around the house. He told them, "We need to step up to the plate."

I read once that Alabama's famous Coach Paul "Bear" Bryant advised, "Have a plan, and work your plan."

Well, *my plan* was to get a bachelor's degree in Spanish without teacher certification since the BA in Spanish alone could be earned with evening and summer courses. The BA degree would then qualify me for the Master's level Alternative Certification program, also offered nights and summers. The four-year degree in Spanish education was out of the question since most of the required courses were day-time only and I simply had to work for the family budget. After the Master's, I hoped to work at least *three* years as a teacher before reaching retirement age; the state retirement pension rate was based on an employee's *highest* three years.

How I *worked that plan* took some effort. Step one was securing finances. I visited the financial aid office on campus, applied for Pell Grants, and got a large newsprint booklet listing all scholarships administered through that office. With my hi-liter in hand, I marked every scholarship for which I qualified and started working on applying, sometimes on my lunch hour. I did not have a guidance counselor to help me, but I knew what to do since I had been involved with Charles and Sharon's triumphs in scholarship hunting.

In 1995 I had little time for journaling but did record a few things indicative of that year of transitioning into course work and scholarship pursuits. For example:

- May 20 – DG to Montgomery to accept scholarship ($600) from Business & Professional Women's Club.
- June 16 – Read three plays in Spanish this week...Spanish American Drama class, plus studied for geography class.
- Dec. 7 – Turned in the last of eighteen correspondence lessons yesterday. Won $500 scholarship from University Women's Club this week. Will go Jan. 9 to [their] luncheon.

God's favor was with me, and my efforts were rewarded with good grades and additional scholarships from Capstone Women's Club, Adult Education, Anderson Family, Nancy Coleman Memorial Scholarships, as well as some Pell Grant money. Finally, in December of 1997, I completed my BA in Spanish and was ready to begin graduate school *as planned* in the College of Education's Alternative Certification program, designed for working people like me.

The College of Education was a different animal from the College of Arts & Sciences, with the latter's Department of Romance & Modern Languages. The education classes were not difficult; many were practical in preparation for a teaching career. I printed off the list of classes required for my course of study and began checking them off one by one, "jumping through all the hoops" mandated for them.

God's corrective hand had to guide me once near the end of those years. I had a particularly stressful semester doing a ninety-hour practicum in a public school Spanish classroom. My principal at TCT agreed to let me use my lunch hour plus some extra time to attend the practicum. Then, I worked after school to make up the time beyond my lunch break. I made sixty trips from my desk to that classroom and back to clock in those ninety hours. I rushed down Interstate 59 with my sandwich in one hand on the way there and had an apple on the return trip.

During this particular practicum, occasionally I had to present a lesson, and a graduate student teaching assistant from the University came to evaluate my performance. She sent me her scores (usually "Cs") via emails.

One day I thought I had done very well on my lesson and hoped for a better grade. When I opened the scoring email and again read "C," anger and a *profanity* rose up in my heart. The profanity shocked me. It was something foreign to me. I sat still a moment then said, "You, Dottie Gravely, are backslidden."

But how could that be? I attended church weekly and read my Bible daily. But there was an idol in my life, my high GPA, so necessary for scholarship competition. This grad student evaluator was damaging my idol. It was time to surrender that GPA to God. I made a B on that course. Now I am glad. My boast is in the Lord Jesus Christ and Him crucified and no accomplishment of my own. After all, whatever I have accomplished was possible only through His enablement. (Isaiah 26:12b) I keenly felt that hardness of heart had crept into my life. As I listened to a song by Small Town Poets, I let its words describing the Lord's Supper (communion) meal heal me. The song spoke of letting the tremendous price paid for our salvation heal us from all that has hardened us. Thank you, Lord.

The last hurdle to cross over was doing my practice teaching or internship. That would mean quitting my job and serving full-time under a local Spanish teacher. I prayed that I could be placed with that glowing Debra Downs at the middle school. I had done a brief practicum with her and immediately liked her, a devoted Christian. When I got my placement assignment, I was thrilled to see Debra Downs would be my supervising teacher. Although she did not have the required Master's degree for that position, the University waived that requirement because of a shortage in intern sites and willing teachers to oversee the interns. Debra had actually requested one.

Thus, at the end of the fall 2000 semester, I resigned from TCT after fifteen and a half years, along with my adult-education-friendly principal, Ms. Crawford, who had enabled me to reach my goal. The faculty honored us with a meal and farewell gifts. I still have their crystal vase.

Finally, I crossed the Master's degree finish line in May, 2001, a few days before my fifty-fourth birthday. My children said I should "walk" during the University's 2001 graduation ceremony. I did. There was a "closure" moment that day as I shook hands with President Sorenson and was handed my diploma case. I felt a HEAVY load lift from my shoulders. Graduate school was over!!!! More stress did lie ahead, but not the grad school kind.

Soon afterwards, I was interviewed for a summer school English class position. A teacher had quit unexpectedly, and I was needed. I was hired, and my teaching career began. I was about to discover the reality of being a teacher, an authority figure, in public schools. Before, I was the nice secretary who dispensed Band-Aids and checked out students. Would I be up to this new task?

POINTS TO PONDER

1. Can we get so focused on details or accomplishments that we forget God?

    Dear children, keep yourselves from idols. I John 5:21 NIV

2. Preparation for life roles takes time and work. The results are rewarding.

CHAPTER 16

MEANWHILE ON 20TH AVENUE

THOSE SIXTEEN YEARS ON 20TH Avenue had some other struggles besides Allan's health issues and college, but we also had some ministry opportunities besides just children's Bible clubs. One struggle was finding a church all of us liked. We assisted with two small church plants, but the children wanted and needed thriving youth groups. They are great for teenagers because they provide peer examples, relevant leadership, and social outlets in groups, not single dating!!!! Riverwood Presbyterian Church was good, as well as Daystar Assembly of God. Allan preferred Trinity Presbyterian Church and attended there for a time, letting the children continue at Daystar. I was torn between being with him and attending Daystar, my preference. I considered that disunity my lowest valley to date in our marriage.

In time, we were all led to First Assembly of God in Tuscaloosa in the summer of 1994 and were so thankful that God brought Pastor Charles Lenn and his wife, Brenda, to our city. There I served a while as children's church director. Allan was recommended and elected to the church board and became the church librarian and a Sunday school teacher for an adult elective class. The class came to a consensus (Allan's idea) and chose its own course of study. We did attributes of God, church creeds, and a series on biographies of earlier Pentecostal leaders. Since I was very busy with college then, I was simply his "First Lady" in Sunday school class, my spiritual role at that time.

While at Daystar, I had the wonderful opportunity to work three years alongside my buddy and co-laborer, Diane Steverson Fowler, each Sunday morning in a women's jail service. During those three years, I got up extra early on Sunday morning and prepared our lunch meal. Wives can't neglect the family's care, even in doing the Lord's work. I left our four teenagers in the charge of my loving husband. He never complained but always supported my efforts for the gospel. He had to "crack the whip" at the four sleepy-heads and get them up for church.

At the old Tuscaloosa County Jail, I was allowed to bring my old 1972 Mexican guitar (that Jan and her husband had provided for me) up to the cells on the second floor. We sang and shared God's word with the women. I often wrote to them during my lunch breaks. (We make time for what matters to us.) Sin had carried them farther than they had wanted to go, as it always does. There were often tears of regret.

One day at the jail, a young woman wept the entire time we were there. A dear sister, Delphine, who accompanied us that day, heard that soul's sad story. She had endured a painful divorce by turning to alcohol. One day while driving "under the influence," she had struck and killed—in her words—a good Christian woman. Now, she would be leaving soon to serve time for manslaughter in the state women's prison, Tutwiler.

Another inmate was a sixteen-year-old awaiting trial for murder. She was given a life sentence; before she left for Tutwiler, another Christian worker was able to lead her to Christ on her seventeenth birthday.

Pastor Rick Warren has spoken of our lives having two tracks running along in parallel fashion, one track of blessing and another with struggles or trials. These wonderful ministry years were concurrent with some trying times brought on by our youngest, Joel.

OUR JOEL

We had not foreseen a major struggle with Joel during those 20th Avenue days. As a youngster he had shown concern for the soul of a neighborhood boy and was open to the things of God. But in junior high he was influenced by some worldly friends, even one in the Daystar youth group. In high school, his life further deteriorated when he joined the TCHS soccer team. Most of the sin he dabbled with was unknown to us, but our whole family knew he was drifting far from God and all he had been taught. Charles was then living on the University of Alabama campus and used to walk across its beautiful quad praying for his brother. Pastor Lenn prayed for him in the beautiful language of intercession: "Lord, spare no means to bring him to Yourself."

All of us prayed for and loved Joel. He was spared in a single vehicle accident when he and some friends flipped over.

One evening our family watched a free outdoor movie from our quilt on the grass at an amphitheater on the University campus. The movie was *A River Runs through It*, depicting two sons of a minister. The older son lived a respectable life; the younger son (Brad Pitt) chose a wild life-style. He ended up dead in an alley at a young age. That graphic storyline reminded me of my two sons and jolted me into more intense prayer for my younger one. He would NOT end up like that movie son. I became determined to do battle in prayer for my child.

One day on my knees interceding for him, I could see him outside sitting on the top of our picnic table. He was dangling and casually swinging his feet. I remembered when those feet of his once pushed into my upper ribs when I carried him full term. (He was nine pounds, twenty-two inches at birth.) Watching him now on the picnic table, I prayed, "Lord, I gave him birth, but only You can give him new birth. O, please do it, Lord."

Sharon prayed for Joel in an unusual way. Her Sunday school teacher challenged Sharon's class one day in early 1996 to write a special prayer request on a slip of paper, make it a really "hard on God" request, put the paper in a small box, and wrap it up in Christmas paper. The teacher instructed them to open their boxes at Christmas and see if God had answered. Sharon not only prayed that Joel would turn to the Lord but also be used to reach many young people with the gospel.

Those dollars we invested in church camps paid off in the summer of 1996, between Joel's junior and senior year of high school. One day he announced that he wanted to go to summer camp. That surprised us because he seemed to hate attending church with us and slumped on a back pew. His camp experiences had been positive enough to make him—out of the blue–decide to go to camp and even take one of his rowdy friends along. Later, this decision seemed like a divine nudge to all of us, once we heard what happened there at the state Assembly of God Camp Springville. He described it in an essay for his senior English teacher:

"CHURCH TRIPPIN'"

This year I walked into Camp Springville with an attitude of heaviness and deprivation. I sat in the night service inside the chapel and saw hundreds of young people much like myself exalting and worshipping the Lord. I noticed some teens that were having such a supernatural experience that they were shouting, dancing, and even falling over on the ground as if they were unconscious.

As the young people continued, something made me want that peace and joy that seemed so real. Drug abuse and bad friendships had left my life in literal "ruins," and I wanted something that would last and that would free my soul from bondage. Well, my chance came. The speaker stated as follows: "How many young people here tonight are suffering for whatever reason, and you want to be set free? If you are one of those people, then I would like for you to come up and be delivered and set free." So I thought to myself, "I can either sit right here and go back home and never pay attention to any of this, or I can go up there and be changed into a new person with peace and lasting joy like everyone else." The choice was simple, and the results were dramatic and life changing. That night I left my old self at the altar and was reborn into a Christian. When I left that camp, I was so different from the way I was when I entered, that people who saw me said that I acted different, and the good thing is, I am different. Amen

His teacher wrote a comment, "Good for you!"

Joel's church friends told me they saw a 180° change in him at the camp. Unfortunately, his rowdy friend left the service without making a similar commitment. When Joel got home, he told us what happened and asked us to forgive him for being "such a hellion." It was easy to do so. God had given us back our son. Sharon knew long before opening her Christmas-prayer-gift-box that her prayer request had been answered.

During the fall semester back at TCHS, Joel had some struggles with his old friends and old temptations. He returned to Camp Springville just after Christmas in 1996 to attend a Chi Alpha Christian Fellowship meeting called SALT. Joel's three older siblings were all involved and encouraged him to come. There he received the wonderful empowering of the Holy Spirit that he so desperately needed in his life. That was exactly thirty years since my after-Christmas encounter with the Holy Spirit at Waco, TX, in 1966.

When Joel returned to TCHS after Christmas break, he was on the offensive for God. He returned to the Daystar youth group and was mentored by a peer named Ben Rodriguez, Daystar's Pastor Pat Schatzline's nephew. One day Joel and Ben wore dress shirts and ties to school to attract attention. When classmates asked why they were dressed up, they responded that it was in order to tell them about God's love. Joel and a friend painted our old two-story garage and began a student-led prayer group there after school. It continued at least another year at a different location after Joel graduated.

Joel's example inspired all of us to shine more for Jesus. His older sister, Alison, had graduated a year ahead of him and won a presidential scholarship to the University of South Alabama (USA) in Mobile, AL. Her Christian commitment had become slack toward the end of high school. At Mobile she renewed her determination to make her life count for God and was mentored by an excellent woman of God in the Chi Alpha ministry there, Susan Ricketts, now a missionary in Japan.

I have mentioned the various mentors in our children's lives because of their importance. It seems to me that a mentor can take someone to a higher level than the parents can. A high school teacher knows that the college professor can direct a learner to a greater depth or thoroughness in a field of knowledge. Likewise, parents should value and seek out for their children (if possible) worthy role models beyond themselves to reinforce and further develop the strong foundation laid in the home.

Mentors now were invaluable because our influence over our grown children was diminishing and our nest was becoming emptier, although sometimes "elastic" as our children left and returned. Alison's USA scholarship proved inadequate for her financial needs, and she returned home in 1998. Just before moving back home, she managed to squeeze in her first mission trip to a Latin American country, Mexico. She loved working with the children on that trip.

Back in Tuscaloosa, Alison eventually finished her undergraduate degree in Spanish Education and her Master's in English as a Second Language at the University of Alabama. So, all of us

Gravelys except Joel earned degrees from hometown "U of A," and he probably would have followed our examples if different opportunities had not come his way.

We attended Joel's high school graduation one spring evening in 1997. The next day we put him on a bus bound for Branson, Missouri, for a summer job as cook in Kamp Kanakuk's system of Christian summer camps. For two years he was a busy man, and we saw little of him. He worked summers in Branson and did two years of ministry with Master's Commission (MC) through the Alabaster, AL, Kingwood Assembly of God.

MC's directors were Mark and Peggy Sims, two champions for Christ who took young "diamonds in the rough" year after year and polished them for the Master. One year Pastor Sims reported over 2700 decisions for Christ through MC's street ministry, high school outreaches, and other efforts. The founder of MC, Tommy Barnett of Phoenix Assembly of God, felt that Pentecostal youth could give two years in ministry if the Mormons could. MC helped Joel develop as a worship leader, using his guitar and keyboard skills which surfaced when he was around seventeen.

With that two-year commitment behind, Joel was now ready for college. He did one semester at the University of Montevallo; then he completed his freshman and sophomore years at the local Shelton State Community College in Tuscaloosa. There he was awarded a music scholarship to the University of South Alabama in Mobile, and he was gone again. Tuscaloosa was too small anyway for this adventurer. In Mobile, he began a track in Music Performance but later changed his major to Physical Education. He is one of those rare individuals who can sing in operas or coach sports. But by moving away, he did miss an interesting development for our family just around the corner.

POINTS TO PONDER

1. Someone has said that parents should not live with a "guilt trip" if their children become wayward after a godly upbringing. Do you agree?

2. Books, movies, and friends are major influences that shape our lives. Do we always choose these carefully?

Rescued from "the cruel streets" of Sucre, Bolivia

Mother's parents

Mother at Livingston State Teachers College, 1928-29

Mother, top right, Templeton School, c. 1930

Dad's parents

Dad and his car

My parents, Easter, 1937

L-R: Royce, Ralph, Bobby Ray with Roland, Ronald, Dottie, Ruel (Photo courtesy of Richard Childers)

Allan with his mother

Royce Coleman Childers, 1945-1970

Mt. View Church today

Allan's father

Dottie, Edsel Steverson, Allan

The Wonder Years

Ana Colque, Sharon, & Luis in Sucre, Bolivia

Our young family on my parents' mountain farm

Luis and Sharon's wedding

Mother (age 96) with my sister, Judy

Charles and Amanda's wedding

Amanda, Charles, Aidan in Belgium

Daniel & Alison, engaged

Sharon, John Moore, Luis in Auburn, AL

Joel's infectious smile

Daniel & Alison's wedding

Gabriel Scott Gravely born Nov. 13, 2013, in
Belgium, – newest member of clan

Allan's grandfather, William Goggin Gravely, Jr.

Photos courtesy of Desmond Kendrick, Henry Co., VA

CHAPTER 17

NEW DIRECTIONS AND ROMANCE AHEAD

THERE WAS ANOTHER MAJOR CHANGE in our family in 1998-1999. One of our own was falling in love. It happened unexpectedly to Sharon, the so-called Ice Princess who could keep unwelcomed suitors at a distance with skillful precision.

In junior high, her Riverwood Presbyterian youth pastor, Mark Woods, had told his young flock that finding a mate was like taking a walk in the woods. If the walker strolls along and looks up at the sun, he will bump into a tree. Brilliant! Likewise, he explained, if an unmarried Christian walks through life with his eyes focused above on the Son of God, he will bump into his future mate. That made perfect sense to Sharon, so she adopted that strategy. It worked. Here's what happened.

The same year that Sharon reluctantly transferred back home from Auburn to live with Mom and Dad and attend the University of Alabama, a young man from the University of North Alabama in Florence decided to change his major and attend the University of Alabama in Tuscaloosa. His name was Luis Antonio Saavedra. (Years before Luis's Bolivian father had been an exchange student at the University of Alabama, where he met the lovely north Alabamian, Monica Armstrong, and they were married and raised four outstanding children.)

Luis became active in the Chi Alpha Christian Fellowship group and "noticed" Sharon. Eventually she "noticed" him too, but both were very unsure of what the other thought about the other. There were a few clues scattered around that onlookers could see. Then, during their senior years in college, they became co-leaders for a morning Chi Alpha prayer session. Sometimes they were the only two in attendance and had time to pray together and talk and get better acquainted and talk and share and talk.... Luis joined Allan's Sunday school class, which Sharon attended. She visited Luis in the hospital *twice* when he had an appendix attack; all other friends had come by only once. He asked her to be his date for Chi Alpha "swap night." Thus, the Ice Princess began to melt, and soon Sharon and Luis had a DTR. That was a Chi Alpha code name for "determine this relationship." It was settled. They were boyfriend-girlfriend.

That was how Sharon "bumped into her tree." Before long they decided to get married, but they wanted to do the engagement Bolivian style. That meant that both extended families needed to be present as the prospective groom publicly proposed to his prospective bride. The date was set for April 10, 1999.

Allan and I hosted a meal for the Gravely and Saavedra clans, a headcount of about twelve. One of Luis's sisters was married and brought her husband along. Charles was away in Washington State doing his Chi Alpha internship. Since I did not have a matching set of dishes with that many settings, I used the $40 check I earned that month from a part-time job to purchase several plates and bowls from an open-stock selection from Wal-Mart. (I taught Spanish once a week after school at Westwood Elementary School in Tuscaloosa County.)

After the meal we all gathered in our large den. Luis's sister, Ximena, sang for us with her guitar. Then Luis got down on his knees and asked for Sharon's hand in marriage. She accepted both his marriage proposal and the beautiful sapphire ring he had purchased for her. She did not want the usual diamond but one similar to Princess Diana's of Britain. God worked some financial miracles for Luis to buy that ring since he was working a part-time job. He found full-time work before the December wedding, and the love birds started their lives together as man and wife. For them, college days were over.

CHARLES FOLLOWS HIS CALLING

As Sharon and Luis navigated through the first years of marriage and Allan worked at the State Vocational Rehabilitation job, and Alison, Joel, and I persevered through college course after college course, what was Charles up to? Well, he left behind a college dream of being an English teacher and instead actively began pursuing a kingdom dream born in his heart. He set his course to better serve in college campus ministry. That preparation led him to a two-year internship at Western Washington University in Bellingham, WA, near the Canadian border, under the watchful care of veteran campus pastor, Brady Bobink. Brady had trained Charles's Alabama mentors, Al and Heather Baker.

After the internship, Charles spent a year and a half in Mobile working with the University of South Alabama Chi Alpha. It was a comfort to me to know that he was there at the same time as his freshman "little sister," Alison, although I have been told that at times she looked after him!!! Charles's ministry there may seem small in his eyes, but some of the young men he mentored are still walking faithfully with God today.

After Mobile, Charles was offered a staff position with Eric Treuil at the University of Louisiana at Lafayette, known among Chi Alphians as "ULALA." During Charles's five-year tenure there, he had the opportunity to preach, lead much of the international ministry, and head up a mission trip to Belgium. Some of his students later worked with him in future ministry. He formed a lasting friendship with one of his co-workers, Amanda Meadows, from Colorado. She was a charming girl, but Charles thought it best not to date a fellow worker in the event that the relationship should end and the two would still have to work around each other and feel awkward. Staff members shared a common kitchen and lived in "modest" studio quarters. Modest quarters did not affect this boy who had once explained to little five-year-old Kirsty that she must live upstairs over their ministry post, that is, if she still planned to marry him when they grew up.

Allan, Alison, and I had the privilege of visiting Charles in the spring of 2003 in Louisiana. Our income tax refund came just in time to book a hotel and travel down during spring break. One morning during our hotel continental breakfast, we watched the news on the TV set mounted on the wall. We saw a U. S. soldier helping the Iraqis pull down a statue of Sadam Hussein. We had invaded Iraq.

Charles was a gracious host who introduced us to his friends and showed us around the beautiful campus with its mini-swamp, complete with an alligator. Later, he joined us on a real swamp tour via boat on a bayou. Our Cajun guide welcomed about eight of us aboard his unusual craft. It had his small engine in the rear mounted to a long pole that he could use as a lever to lift the motor up and over floating logs, then lower it again and continue on with the journey and with the narration about what we were seeing around us. For example, that green coating on the water surface was not scum but duckweed. Over there on the logs were the turtles taking in the sun. Near the cypress roots were those pesky little nutrias someone had brought in from South America or somewhere. Big mistake!! They were eating away at the cypress bark and killing the trees; they were multiplying like rabbits too. At one time a bounty of $4 was paid to anyone bringing in a nutria tail. Since they were vegetarians, their meat was good, we were told.

Early on in the tour, the Cajun guide assured us that alligators do not attack humans unless first provoked. No doubt, he explained, some alligator ancestor had sampled us and spread the word that humans are not tasty. Dogs and chickens are a different story.

About mid-way through our peaceful tour, our guide directed our attention toward a bank just ahead. There was a huge alligator, fully grown. It was an old fellow about one hundred years old, apparently blind in one eye. His snout was pointed toward the water, and he was poised to come on in if provided any motivation or provocation. Allan and Charles were closer to the front of the boat and grew a little nervous when the old fellow on the bank made a sudden turning movement toward us. We were relieved when he settled down and we moved onward without incident.

We stopped near a tree so that our guide could lift up a crawfish cage/trap. We "innocents abroad" in this Louisiana world could not believe our ears when he told us that the baby crawfish eat their mother's tail. No worries, he explained. It grows back.

God's world of nature was a marvel to us, but we saw another beauty in the world of His church. Back on campus we witnessed Christianity in action. The ULALA chapter of Chi Alpha advertised a free Wednesday "Meal and a Message." Yes, a free meal at the Chi Alpha Café, along with a gospel message. A ladies ministry of a local church provided some delicious lasagna that day for the students. A speaker provided the everlasting gospel message. This was teamwork for Jesus.

Seeing the surroundings where Charles labored and meeting his friends made his newsletters more real to us. For instance, later he reported that he had addressed the "free lunch" crowd one day when a Chi Alpha student had invited a new friend. The new friend said that the whole time that skinny guy was speaking, she was feeling a drawing toward God. She accepted Christ that day. I could picture that scene in my mind and prayed harder for the

"Meal and a Message" time in the old campus Lutheran church turned "Chi Alpha Café."

Charles saw an invaluable example of godly leadership in his ULALA campus pastor, Eric Treuil. Eric just kept on keeping on year after year and earned the respect of his peers, students, and the community. Campus officials called on Chi Alpha to carry the game banner and lead in prayer at football games.

POINTS TO PONDER

1. Someone has observed that it is easier to steer a moving ship or car than one standing still. Is God sometimes steering us behind the scenes in our transitions?
2. Does God get involved with finding a mate? (Psalm 68:6)

CHAPTER 18

GOODBYE TO 20TH AVENUE

IN MAY, 2001, WITH THAT hard-earned college diploma in my hand, I was ready to leave a secretarial desk behind and begin competing in the teacher job market. Someone asked me during my Master's studies, "What will you do if you can't find a job after all this work?"

I answered, "Well, Tuscaloosa County is surrounded by six or seven other counties. If I have to drive, I will."

Fortunately, that driving was not necessary, at least not the first two years after college. My first small temporary stint as a teacher was in the summer school program of Tuscaloosa City Schools. I taught eighth graders remedial English. The class was offered at the Central West campus, where ninth and tenth grade classes were held during the school year. During that short tenure with eighth graders, I was hired as a Spanish I & II teacher on the Central West campus to replace a teacher who was retiring.

At last–after all those scholarship applications, classes, job interviews—at last I signed my first teacher contract at the age of fifty-four. Our income soared several thousand annually. All that effort was beginning to pay off.

Allan felt that it was time to move to a better home. He loves lakes, rivers, and oceans. His research found that the "closest-to-town" subdivision that links up to the beautiful Lake Tuscaloosa was one on Hwy. 69 north, Lakewood, just five miles from our dear old 20th Avenue historical home. And, yes, there was a home for sale in Lakewood.

We worked like ants to make the old home place saleable. It sold fairly quickly, and we purchased a brick, one-level home in Lakewood subdivision on a shady lot. After years of marriage and raising four children, it was our first home in a real subdivision. We had access to a boat landing on Carroll's Creek, which fed into Lake Tuscaloosa. The neighborhood seemed like a vacation get-away for us and our family. The back deck under the trees was so relaxing. The downsizing in rooms and floor space proved to be worth it. Now we had only three bedrooms and a great room instead of a living room, den, and six bedrooms.

At the time of our move, our family unit consisted of Alison, Joel, Elimar (a female university student from Venezuela), Sharon, Luis, Allan, and me. Elimar's name was a blend of Elizabeth and Maria; she was our last international student to board with us. In order to move with us, she had to give up a room of her own and share Alison's bedroom in Lakewood and live farther from campus. That fall I dropped her off at the University sometimes. She was genuinely impressed with the beauty of the fall leaves along the highway; Venezuela was always green. She soon married an American man and seemed very happy.

Sharon and Luis were temporarily staying with us as they finished up their Alabama itinerating to be nationally appointed home missionaries with the Assemblies of God. They had heard a call to campus missions but had to raise their budget. They occupied the dining-room-turned-bedroom. Joel had a room of his own. It was good to have him home again for a while in our "elastic nest."

Eventually Sharon and Luis exhausted their Alabama contacts and decided to move on to Arkansas to raise the balance of their budget needs closer to where they planned to work, at the University of Arkansas with campus pastor Ronnie Hoover. Their stay with us had really helped me in my transition into teaching. They often prepared the evening meal; others cleaned up the mess. It was a good arrangement!!! Their contact with Ronnie Hoover set the stage for some future adventure in Bolivia.

An Unforgettable Day

Just as I was getting into the groove of teaching that first year, the unexpected happened. On September 11, 2001, a student in second block Spanish I class mentioned that our country was under attack and wanted to check it out on the classroom TV set. I agreed and watched along with my students the awful scenes of that infamous day when radical extremists crashed into the New York Twin Towers. I told the students that they would always remember where they were when they saw those news releases. I knew that to be true because I could remember where I was when President Kennedy was shot; I was at school that day and was about the age of the kids before me now there in my classroom.

Later that year I took my first field trip with two busloads of students. They were excited about getting off campus and going to a Mexican restaurant for lunch. My mentor teacher on campus had walked me through all the paperwork and money handling that preceded that day. The administrators were holding their breath (along with me), hoping everything would go well with this novice teacher. I sat on a seat near the front of the bus and happened to glance up into the driver's rear view mirror. There I saw an unbelievable mini-scene before my eyes. There I was in the mirror's reflection with a full load of students seated behind me. And I was responsible for all of them and the happenings of the day!!! It was surreal and a little scary, but there were no problems at all, and we garnered some good memories that day around some delicious food and a little leftover time at a park.

ALLAN'S RETIREMENT

In the fall of 2002, Allan had to make a decision he did not want to make. It seemed he had no alternative but to retire from his job with the Alabama State Vocational Rehabilitation Services where he had served eight years. The state did not replace his secretary who had succumbed to cancer. Instead, Allan had to do all his data entry for his large caseload himself. The old migraine enemy then reared its head. Even the sound of his computer and the screen's brightness triggered constant pain that made him dread each day at work. Since he had been able to "buy back" his two years of military service to transfer them to his state retirement years, he became vested with ten years. He had wanted to work at least five more years to set us up for a more comfortable retirement, but circumstances forced him to turn in his office key. We knew God would be faithful in our future as He had been in our past.

After retiring, Allan took upon him many home chores, such as laundry and grocery shopping, to free me up for the demands of teaching. In addition, he managed our finances and maintained our cars with zero neglect, as he always had done. We were a team.

FROM HIGH SCHOOL TO JUNIOR HIGH TEACHER

Near the end of that first year, I learned that a new Spanish teacher position was to be opened in the fall at the middle school where I had done my practice teaching. I applied for a transfer to Eastwood Middle School, and it was granted. So, during 2002-2003, I repeated the courses I had taught during my internship under Debra Downs's tutelage, beginning Spanish for seventh and eighth graders and Exploratory Foreign Language for sixth graders. In addition, I did a seventh grade English class. My qualification for the English class was my English minor in undergraduate work. Unfortunately, those students were very unruly, and I did not enjoy that year at all.

In February of that school year, I noted in my journal: "Tired at work. Kids not obedient. A few that don't care ruin class for others. Wish I could enjoy my job. *I guess I was idealistic about teaching.* Parts of it I enjoy; but don't enjoy always keeping kids under control. Wish they would just behave." Where was that opening day motivational speaker from Teacher Institute now?

My view of teaching had changed from joy to drudgery. But God in His faithfulness sent some encouragement my way. The following day after that journal entry, I noted that Alison and I attended a women's ministry meeting at First Assembly of God. The speaker was Carmella Coleman from First Wesleyan. She spoke about seasons of our lives and used a country music song to drive home her point that we should "stay in the game (or dance)" every season of life. The song was "I Hope You'll Dance." One line spoke of some mountains in the distance that could intimidate and tempt any traveler to "throw in the towel" or "sell out" any interest in the venture. That's what I wanted to do, just get out of teaching altogether and write off my years in college as a loss. And those mountains in the distance? For me, they represented those four more years of teaching that I would have to do before becoming age sixty so that I could retire!!!! I resolved that evening at the ladies meeting, "I'll just stay in the dance *today*," one day at a time, like the song was telling me.

In May I opened a birthday card from my friend, Lolly, from church and read words that leaped off the card toward my discouraged heart: "Have a day bursting with all the hopes and dreams that you have dared to dream! Take hold and shine—today's your day." That card really helped me turn fifty-six in 2003. What a God of encouragement! He would take care of those *four mountains* in His own way and time.

It was a mixed blessing and disappointment when eight of us non-tenured teachers were presented with "pink slips" at the close of that school year because of budget cuts. It was a "proration year." We were all told that if the state legislature came up with more money, our jobs would be posted and we could reapply for them.

That was actually what happened. Of course, some of those eight teachers took other jobs. I reapplied. But that spring we had been briefed on a new federal law that was going to change my destiny. It was called "No Child Left Behind." We were warned that teachers could no longer be assigned to classes outside their fields of expertise. I had been teaching English "out of field." The principal and Site Based Council had recommended me for the following year. Alas, when my job was posted, a local woman applied who had a Master's in English and could become "highly qualified" in Spanish with a few courses from a college or university. The school system was trying to come into compliance with the law; therefore, she got the job, and I was looking at a jobless fall ahead of me. We now had a higher house and car payment.

Allan and I prayed and watched for job openings. Since he was now retired, we even considered moving within or out of the state if something turned up elsewhere. I considered a position at a school twenty-five miles away but thought, "No, that's too far away." The summer continued, jobless.

There had been another need in my life, besides a job. I needed to feel used of God. Graduate school and teaching had pushed any active ministry aside. Helping Allan with his Sunday school classes was all I had time for.

When I attended a ladies Aglow meeting, I surprised myself during an invitation for prayer when I burst into tears and told the guest speaker, "I just want to be used."

The speaker was the positive, vivacious Susanne Cox who wore the label of "First Lady" at the wonderful Kingwood Assembly of

God in Alabaster, AL, where Joel had done his Master's Commission work. Her pastor husband, Ron Cox, was admired by all for this loyalty to his disabled first wife for many years until her death. Then God gave him pretty Susanne. She had been a single missionary to India, helping restore victims of sex trafficking.

Susanne prayed for me; then she did the coach hand-slap that said, "You go, girl." I dried my tears and waited for God to answer that prayer.

Allan found a way to keep me busy that summer. He had volunteered to become the church librarian and bring some order to the chaos stored in boxes in a spare room. He assembled Wal-Mart bookcases, installed check-out card pockets, and labeled book spines with his improvised Dewey decimal system, *a la Gravely*. During our tenure there, starting with a few boxes of books on one side of the room, the collection grew to almost 4,000 items, including books, videos, and CDs. Some of these were fairly rare and had been stored away for years. A widow of two pastor-husbands donated her two late husbands' libraries. Church members shared their resources or picked up items at garage sales to contribute. Librarian Allan recruited family members to help out any time he caught us idle. Thus I was familiar with all the wonderful Christian books and tapes that were donated.

One old cassette tape series in particular caught my attention. Rick Olsen, one of the early workers with the Assemblies of God Youth Alive high school ministry, shared the joy of seeing interdenominational campus fellowship groups developing in local high schools. Young people in one town in Texas decided that God must surely love them as much as the kids in Sherman, Texas, where a revival broke out. Uh huh, He sure did. Revival spread to another and another location through the high school groups. These testimonies emboldened me to pray, "Lord, wherever I am hired, I'd like to be the faculty sponsor of the Christian group there." I had observed Debra Downs faithfully serving in that capacity during my internship.

One day during that summer, I remember pouring out my heart with tears to God. I reminded Him that I had worked *so hard* to finish college, that I had given teaching my best shot, and that I was willing to work for our family. It had not been easy since my hearing loss seemed to be growing worse and I often had trouble hearing students, even with my hearing aids. God has ever been my ally through this life, an even greater—far greater—ally than my wonderful earthly dad or super-husband had been. The Lord had something very special for me just ahead.

POINTS TO PONDER

1. Positive Christians often encourage fellow Christians without even knowing it. Praise be to...the God of all comfort, who comforts us in all our troubles...". II Corinthians 1:3-4
2. Current events in our culture have far reaching effects on us, often quite memorable. "Trust in him at all times, O people; pour out your hearts to him, for God is our refuge." *Selah* Psalm 62:8 NIV
3. Career changes don't diminish God's work in us. "...being confident of this, that he who began a good work in you will carry it on to completion until the day of Christ Jesus." Philippians 1:6 NIV

CHAPTER 19

WEST BLOCTON?
BIBB COUNTY?

SHORTLY BEFORE THE 2003-2004 SCHOOL year was to begin, I got a call one Sunday morning from a dear friend from my past, Peggy Rowe. Peggy had once been a pen pal of mine when she was a youth and I was in my twenties. She had also once worked with Allan at Vocational Rehabilitation. She got right to the point. Her familiar voice was telling me that she was now employed as guidance counselor for a small rural high school in adjoining Bibb County. The school, West Blocton High School (WBHS), was desperate for a Spanish teacher. It seemed that no one was available to work in that remote location. *Did I know of anyone who might be interested?*

Peggy had no clue when she picked up her phone that day that she was being part of a miracle in my life, an answer to prayer. When I told her that I was definitely interested, she gave me contact information and directions to the school, which was located *forty miles* from my driveway!!! That was the only down side of the whole situation.

My interview with the principal, Mrs. Suzanne Jones, went well even though I forgot to wear my hearing aids. She offered me the job, and I accepted. I was as desperate for a job as her school was for a Spanish teacher, the perfect match. The teacher I was replacing had left with her family to be missionaries in Mexico. She had been the faculty sponsor of the Christian group, called First Priority (www.firstpriority.org). I was delighted to take on that responsibility too, along with Peggy's help.

Within a week I was wearing old clothes, preparing my future classroom, and painting the old podium when a gentleman peeked in to see what all the noise was about. (I was pounding a paint bucket lid shut.) He was a Bibb County Board of Education member who assured me that the board would vote in favor of hiring me, especially at such a late date before school opening. Hiring a coach might require some deliberation, but a willing, qualified Spanish teacher would certainly be approved without objection. That sounded so good to my ears.

When I got home that day, Allan greeted me and told me to sit down. The new Tuscaloosa County High School (TCHS) had been built only *three* miles from my driveway. Someone from that school had called to interview me for a Spanish job; its administration was also desperate in a last-minute situation. I turned my options over in my head. What should I do?

I thought of Peggy, how she had recommended me. But her school was forty miles from my home. I thought of the WBHS Christian group I would be leading and the friendly country people, my kind of folks. But TCHS was only three miles from home. I thought of the desperate principal at WBHS with no talent pool to draw from while TCHS was near the University of Alabama with all its resources. I remembered Psalm 15:4b, about the upright person "who keeps his oath even when it hurts." (NIV) Didn't I tell the principal that I was accepting her job offer? It would be so hard to call her and decline. Besides, would I fit into the energetic TCHS Spanish department at my age with my hearing impairment? At WBHS *I alone would be the Spanish department*, actually the entire foreign language department. The WBHS Spanish textbook was better than the one used at TCHS in my view!!!

I thought, "Maybe the forty miles would not be so bad with all those library tapes to listen to."

I chose West Blocton and have never regretted it.

THOSE FOUR MOUNTAINS – FOUR YEARS

The country song had admonished me not to fear mountains in the distance. As mentioned, in my mind those mountains represented hard climbing ahead, the four arduous years I would have to "endure" teaching teenagers before qualifying for retirement from the Alabama teaching system. I did not expect to "enjoy" them. Well, God thought differently. His long-ago words to Joshua came thumping their way into my soul as I listened to an old chorus tape from the First Assembly library. The rousing melody and lyrics from Joshua 1 proclaimed,

> *Every place on which your foot shall tread, I have given to you, I have given to you. No man shall be able to stand before you. I will be with you. I will be with you. Be strong and courageous. Do not tremble or be afraid, for the Lord thy God is with you <u>wherever you go</u>.*

Why, I even felt a stirring of anticipation at what lay ahead. God can level a mountain.

The second week of August launched my new career in the little "Mayberry" community of West Blocton, AL, in Bibb County. The faculty and students welcomed me warmly. One of the First Priority students left a note of welcome and encouragement, taped to my classroom door! The assistant principal visited my class the first day and told the students in no uncertain terms that misbehavior would not be tolerated. Administrators with muscle are wonderful!!

My predecessor, Mrs. Collins, had done a great job leading the Christian club, First Priority (FP). The students had heard that I would be their new sponsor. I heard the intercom during morning announcements state that FP leaders would be meeting in my room during the morning break. They did so and planned their first meeting. Wow! This organization was truly student-led. During their first weekly meeting, I met a local youth pastor who brought several students in his car to the 7:00 A.M. session held in my room. I also met a local adult worker and county FP leader for the middle and high school; she presented me with a FP T-shirt. Students conducted the meeting. Commitment was in place here.

Spanish classes went smoothly. I found out that I would also be teaching eleventh grade English, including research papers. Rural schools had longer to comply with "No Child Left Behind." (Eventually, I became "high qualified" in English under that law through experience and Praxis test scores.) Some of my journal entries read: "Still enjoying classes." "A good week at school. Kids are learning." "God is giving me grace to be a teacher at W. Blocton. (Ephesians 4:7) The ride to/from school is spiritually refreshing to me."

Of course, there were some students who were challenging. But in this rural area, parents still wanted their children to behave at school. Corporal punishment by administrators was permitted in Bibb County, with witnesses. Some students requested the paddle in lieu of suspension so that their parents would not discover their crimes at school and mete out further punishment.

There was another check to mischief in place at WBHS. Another teacher, told me about a little discipline system she and a co-worker had developed. After two warnings, if a student continued to disrupt instruction, he or she was sent to another teacher in order to give the first teacher some respite and to place the culprit in an unfamiliar environment with different peers.

This swift handling of disruptions is exactly what is needed in teaching. If school districts require phone calls to parents, referrals to counselors, write-ups, and pages of documentation, then punishment for misbehavior is so slow in coming that it appears to the class that nothing is being done. I began to think that Bibb County was Alabama's best kept secret!!

The First Priority students planned their meetings using a four-week rotating format of strategies. One week was more "in-house," for members. The next week a particular student testimony would be planned so that similar students could be invited. Then, the third week youth pastors or students shared from their experience with God. The fourth week was reserved for more aggressive outreach, a "hook" endeavor to catch some fish for the Lord. I suggested a speaker for their September "hook" event, John Causey.

John attended my church in Tuscaloosa. One of the team captains, he had been on the offensive line for Alabama's Coach Gene Stallings's national championship team. Since he worked a pharmaceutical route in Bibb County, he was familiar with the area and delighted to come speak for us. On September 9, I posted flyers around the school with a photo of John in his Crimson Tide jersey. Everyone was invited to attend the 7:00 A.M. meeting on September 11, 2003; we started praying and expected several football players to be there.

This "9/11" date was so different from the tragic one our country experienced two years earlier. I felt God's presence in the old school library as John spoke to thirty-five students. He told them that the football game is over in four short quarters, but what Jesus gives us lasts forever, with no end. He got a ring (and a limp) from his football days, but Jesus gave him something everlasting. John admitted that he felt a little nervous as a speaker.

He said, "Put me in front of 80,000 football fans and tell me to block someone, and I'm not nervous. But speaking makes me nervous."

He did a great job. The students connected with him and his sincere humility.

Six days later I participated in my first "See You at the Pole" event at 7:00 A.M. in front of the school around our flagpole.

(www.syatp.org) About twenty-five students gathered and prayed in groups, just as they themselves had planned. The area First Priority director, Joel Frederick, was present. Joel was a graduate of WBHS and very popular with the students.

In October, I had the pleasure of recording in my journal: "Good day at work. Got to witness to... [a student who confided he was tired of life]." "Good day at school. This year is so much better than last two. It's worth driving for." "A good week at school, getting more rest." My daily drive to school became a seminar on wheels as I listened to Focus on the Family radio broadcasts and tapes from Allan's library project at First Assembly.

That fall I got to know the community of West Blocton better and found that it was a Small Town, USA, that enjoyed fun. It was more alive than Andy Griffith's Mayberry. People were very supportive of the families, schools, and churches. For example, (according to one story) during one losing football season, the team finally won an away game. About 1:00 A. M. the old team bus came rolling back into town carrying some excited teenagers and bus driver. She could not resist blowing the bus horn coming through town. People came to their doors in pajamas and cheered and waved to the heroes, whose heads and arms were hanging out the bus windows. WBHS had won that night; there was joy in "Mudville"!!!

Mt. Carmel Baptist Church was just up the road from WBHS. Its pastor for years and years was Brother Simpson. He probably baptized, married, and buried more people in the area than any other minister. His church loved the school. Each fall the teachers were treated to a back-to-school breakfast in the church fellowship hall.

That was only the beginning. On the eve of the annual homecoming game, Mt. Carmel hosted a community bonfire, pep rally, and free "Turnip Green Supper" in the local ball park, named appropriately Simpson Park. Usually about 1500 folks attended.

Most people in the crowd were probably alumni of the school. The church members spent the previous day washing gobs of turnip green leaves and soaking lots—lots—of large lima butterbeans to cook for the event. Of course, cornbread was on the menu. And a side table of hot dog "fixin's" was prepared for anyone who did not eat *country*. As friends and neighbors enjoyed the food and fun, the WBHS cheerleaders of yesteryear stirred up some school spirit with their old-fashioned routines before the current cheerleaders took over at the pep rally. The coach and team members were on hand to receive encouragement from a community that loved them. Allan drove up from Tuscaloosa to experience this event with me.

Another good part of that October was marching in the Homecoming Parade with the First Priority float to identify with God's people and let everyone know whose side I was on. I had been doing some extra walking to get in shape for that march.

The parade was held in early afternoon, and students were dismissed from class if they chose to attend. Again I was impressed with the community support. The streets of the old downtown were lined with adults, children, and teens. Marchers tossed candy to the bystanders. Some locals sat in lawn chairs or their porch chairs. Everything paused for the parade. After all, the pretty girls waving from the convertibles were probably cousins, daughters, granddaughters, or friends. The marching band did its best.

That homecoming week I also did my first WBHS Spanish Club field trip to a Mexican restaurant in Tuscaloosa. Students were excited to get out of their locality and have some fun together.

I found that the students were affectionate and easy going. There was usually harmony among them, with few fights. Their good behavior afforded them the increasingly rare privilege of having a mid-morning break for about ten minutes. They loved getting themselves some snacks, nachos with cheese, or drinks and just hanging out along the lockers around the hallways. Teachers sometimes gave naughty students "break detention" in the class-room to deprive them of that wonderful ten-minute interval of juvenile bliss. This proved to be an effective behavioral upgrade.

The majority of the students rode the school buses to school and could not attend club meetings before or after school. To accommodate them and encourage extra-curricular participation, the school devised a clever scheduling maneuver. Once a month club sponsors could hold a thirty-minute club meeting during their planning periods, and all members of a particular club were dismissed from class to attend. One of the faculty members arranged a master schedule for the participating clubs. That is how I held my monthly Spanish Club meetings.

One week the First Priority students wanted to know why *their* club could not hold a meeting during school hours on club day like other clubs. I checked with the administration and got a green light. So, we set November 13, 2003, as our first school-day meeting. We had a *date.* We had a *place* because my planning period "happened" to be the same period that the gymnasium was not in use; we expected a crowd. We needed a speaker or format.

No problem. God loved the kids at West Blocton as much as the kids in Sherman, Texas. He already had a speaker in mind for us. Our date was near the date of a community-wide, weekend revival series led in part by evangelist Darrin English from Muscle Shoals, Alabama. My school counselor friend, Peggy, arranged for Darrin to come and be our November speaker.

The club period was only the last thirty minutes of the ninety-minute class block, my free period. Darrin arrived early to pray in the empty gym. I joined him and felt the presence of God there. The school janitor stepped in for a moment and later told me that she felt God in that place too.

We had no idea how many students would attend because First Priority had no club dues or official roster of members. Anyone could attend our pre-school meetings, and anyone could attend this school-day meeting. And who would not want to "get out of class" to go sit in the gym and listen to a speaker?

Crowd control was a concern of the administration. The ratio of one faculty sponsor to a gym full of students was worrisome. But Peggy and some of the other Christian faculty members also came. The bleachers were about two-thirds filled. The students sat in rapt attention, hanging on every word Darrin spoke. He seemed totally given over to the control of the Holy Spirit, explaining to his audience that Jesus could relate to all of earth's sorrows and bad deals. He gave a specific invitation only for those seriously interested in making a commitment to Christ to come and stand at center court and confess the Lord as their Savior. At first there was total silence, and no one moved. Finally, one student came forward, one for whom I had felt a particular burden. Then a few others joined him. As their peers watched respectfully, Darrin led the whole group at center court in a sinner's prayer and then asked for a show of hands of those who prayed and meant it. About eight hands went up.

The assembly ended. Our First Priority students and Darrin spoke individually with those who had come forward, collecting contact information. Some of those new baby Christians remarked that they felt "something" pulling at them to respond. I had to go teach Spanish and English, somewhat anticlimactic. Later I remembered Susanne Cox's prayer for me, that I would be used of God. He was giving me my heart's desire. Yes, indeed, God did love the kids in West Blocton.

The next weekly morning meeting of FP was encouraging. A senior football player gave his testimony, and the students planned a bowling event in Tuscaloosa (no bowling alley in West Blocton).

December was a busy month with final exams to prepare and two clubs to sponsor. Allan did our Christmas gift buying. The FP students suggested area director, Joel Frederick, for the December gym meeting. He spoke to the majority of the student body at his old Alma Mater. For his closing invitation, he set up two clipboards and asked students to sign the sheets on the clipboards if they wanted to connect with God. Two lines formed as sixty-three students waited to leave their contact information for follow-up.

In early January, 2004, I had the privilege of completing the first of four special photo albums for our children. Charles was approaching his thirtieth birthday. I did not know if that would be painful for him or not. So, just in case it was, I did an album of memories of his first thirty years on earth. I could hardly believe that thirty years had passed since that first night in Decatur General hospital when I kissed his newborn cheeks and told him, "Someday you'll be a man, but for right now, you're my little baby."

The new spring semester at school was good; there were new students and a fresh start. There was one problem in my classroom that was difficult to deal with. The students discovered that I could not localize sounds because of my hearing impairment. A few of them made sounds in their throats to disrupt instruction, and I could not tell who it was since I could not determine the origin. I felt successful as a club sponsor and teacher but sometimes felt a total failure as a disciplinarian. John Maxwell's book *Failing Forward* was a tremendous encouragement to me. I took pages of notes from it. I simply did not have the personality of a police woman, and the students knew it. Teaching probably toughened me, but I did not want to be hard hearted.

But I had to keep on going, failure or success. Each morning I punched the trip gauge on my car's panel and said, "Lord, I'm obeying you again today, driving eighty miles to teach where I believe you sent me." He was honoring that obedience by touching lives. One of the many taped sermons I listened to en route to school was one by John Kilpatrick of the Brownsville, FL, revival. He explained that Joshua pointed his spear toward the city he was fighting to capture for the Lord because the Lord was giving it to him. (Joshua 8:18) He continued to hold up that spear till the job was done (v. 26). I would continue to stand in my place until my assignment there at WBHS was finished.

Joel Gravely's two-year involvement with the Master's Commission ministry proved helpful to WBHS that spring semester. Being somewhat familiar with that ministry and its leaders gave me confidence to request their help. By simply asking for someone to come to WBHS, one of MC's Hispanic leaders, Abraham Ortega, came to speak at a Spanish Club meeting; the students loved him. His topic was "Growing up Hispanic in California."

Abraham and his MC team came with a "bang" on February 19 for our monthly gym meeting. They really got our attention with their opening percussion number done on metal garbage can lids!!! Very impressive!!! That explosive opening was followed by testimonies and "human videos" set to music. Crowd control was no problem when the audience was so focused on what they were seeing and hearing. MC had perfect freedom to share the gospel with these public school students since our meeting was a Christian club gathering and attendance was voluntary.

MC was so popular that it was easy for the administration to consider having them do their school-wide, anti-drug Conquest assembly program. Conquest satisfies the school's annual requirement to inform students of substance abuse dangers. The presentation on March 12 was secular, but the MC teammates could legally witness to students after the assembly ended. All the above arrangements just took emails, phone calls, and talking to the principal. While I did not preach or sing, I could do phone calls, emails, flyers, and chats with a friendly principal.

Sadly, that principal's husband passed away suddenly with a heart attack the week before our February gym meeting. A somber seriousness hung over the entire school as we grieved with our beloved Mrs. Jones. Thursday of that same week a student of nearby Brookwood High School was killed in a one-vehicle accident on her way to her First Priority meeting before school. She was a leader in that club and a strong Christian. Several of our students knew her personally because they had played on community softball teams together. They were shocked and numb. Their mortality bells had been run. I believe many hearts were tender for Master's Commission's message. Later on, one of our students admitted that the Brookwood girl's death had made her assess her walk with God and press in closer.

Since Abraham Ortega and MC now seemed like special friends to our school, it was no surprise when some of our students came to school excited to tell me that they had attended a drama workshop at a local church and saw Abraham and MC there. In fact, MC was doing the instruction!! The Second Baptist Church of Shady Grove got inspired and started a drama team in their church with a large group of excited kids ready to do something for God.

In May, 2004, an issue of *Christ for the Nations* magazine had an article by Robert Shone admonishing Christians to get a passport and pray about doing ten-day mission trips. He said that first we should have our passports in hand; then we should begin praying for God to use us.

That advice really resonated with me. I made a mental note to follow up on it as soon as possible.

One tradition for closing out the WBHS school year was the annual faculty/senior softball game. I signed up to play; then the doubts set in, especially when I saw the black eye of one of our softball girls. A softball had hit her in the eye. Ouch! Also, I did not want to make a total fool of myself. So, I started praying, "Lord, don't let me get hurt, and don't let me strike out."

God answered those requests. I actually hit the ball once past the third baseman, but I forgot to run. When it occurred to me to take off, the humor of the moment made the senior female shortstop start laughing instead of getting the ball and sending it to first base. Thus, I got on base. I hit the ball the second time up to bat, but it flew directly into the glove of the pitcher, Big Sammy.

Sammy was the batter I feared most as I stood trying to be an out-fielder. Sure enough, he knocked a high flying ball that was doing a perfect arch coming down in my direction in the outfield. "Oh, dear," I thought. "Here goes." But much to my relief, the ball kept going over my head and out of the park. I was glad to forfeit that homerun. The faculty won after all. My leg muscles were sore for days from running the bases.

The WBHS school year was winding down. The classes and clubs were thriving. Of course, there were some struggles among the victories. I was sometimes tired from all the teacher duties and getting up at 5:30 A. M. most days and 5:00 on First Priority days. Sometimes the FP students had personal issues that had to be addressed. But by the end of the year, I was able to sum it up by saying, "More highs than lows this year!!!"

One final low that school year occurred just after I gave the last final exam and got all my grades in the computer. I carried a dressy outfit to wear to that evening's graduation ceremony, man-datory for faculty members. But I got a phone call from Alison telling me that she had taken my precious husband to the emer-gency room for chest pains. Allan had been scheduled to go see a heart doctor the following day for an arteriogram, but his pain was so strong that he decided to go get checked. Since his doc-tor had a cancellation in his schedule, he took Allan in for the arteriogram a day early and decided to insert a stent because of a blockage.

My principal told me to skip the graduation and go be with my husband. The entire heart procedure was over by the time I arrived at the hospital. I really did not like the sign above the wing Allan was on. It read "Acute Cardiac Care Unit." I entered his room and saw his wonderful smiling face. He was doing swimmingly and was very thankful it was all over. Sharon and Luis came from Arkansas to check on him. He has been fine since; I cannot keep up with him on his daily walks. His recovery went so well that in June he accepted the position of president of Lakewood Property Owners Association that year!

Reflecting back over that year made me realize that it had been one of those four mountains I once saw in the distance, mountains I had dreaded climbing, the four years left before retirement. I was glad I had decided to "dance" and not sit out that year and write off teaching as all bad. The first mountain had not been so bad, thanks to the Lord. One down, three to go. The year reminded me of Zechariah 4:6-7 with its question, "What are you, O mighty mountain?...you will become level ground." (NIV) The mountain leveling was all done not by might nor by power, but by His Spirit. But I was ready for a break. After all, as someone said, the three main reasons for being a teacher are June, July, and August!

IN THE GOOD OLE SUMMERTIME

During the summer of 2004, an unexpected financial and ministry opportunity came my way. My friend from college, Diane Fowler, conducted a four-week English academy for nine children visiting Tuscaloosa from Korea with their guardian. Diane offered me a position as tutor, with pay. Besides English, I also shared some Christian children's songs with the students. I earned $80, just enough to get a U. S. passport. That magazine article about ten-day mission trips was still on my mind. Allan decided to get his passport as well; he did not want to miss any action ahead. Now, according to the article, I needed to pray and see what God would do.

Near the end of July, Alison moved out to begin her career as an English-as-a-Second-Language (ESL) teacher in adjoining Shelby County. We assisted by pulling a U-Haul trailer behind the old Jeep. She was excited, and we were proud of her for all her hard work in graduate school. That trip was a milestone for us because it marked the first time in thirty years that our home was without one of our children. We missed them and were very thankful for phone calls and emails.

At the same time, we wanted each one of our children to have a life of his/her own, a life that would glorify their Savior. We had done what we could to prepare them for independence. Two supporter certificates hanging on our walls reminded us that Charles and Sharon were nationally appointed missionaries. Joel was helping to lead worship with his church youth group. Alison joined a weekly group that was reaching out to some eighty Hispanic kids in their neighborhood. That group was an extension of the fast growing Church of the Highlands in Birmingham, which she joined. The old apostle John was right when he said, "I have no greater joy than to hear that my children walk in truth." (III John 1:4 NKJV)

As both a school secretary and a teacher, I treasured my summers off from work. But I also felt it my duty to seek God for the most profitable way to spend them. One year I felt drawn to working with international women and did some work with friends along those lines. In summer 2004, however, I thought again and again about children's outreach.

I probed for God's will by checking with our children's church director; she did not need extra help. I did a small Spanish crash course for our youth pastor's interns. But no neighborhood outreach seemed to be on the horizon.

Then, one Sunday morning as Allan and I reached the church door, there stood a friend who had a monthly ministry to the Hannah Home for battered, abused women and children. He wanted to know if we knew of anyone who could work with the children there at Hannah Home one Sunday a month. The couple who had been helping him was resigning for health reasons. Yes, we knew of someone—me. I began August 1 with a good Bible class with the flannel graph story of David and the large illustrated children's version of *Pilgrim's Progress*. Four little girls between six and nine years old prayed to receive the Lord.

This wonderful summer was winding down. I had spent time taking care of my Allan, reading great books to build my faith, and reaching out to children. As usual, we hosted our own children on water skiing adventures. Allan taught Charles and Alison how to ski. Living in Lakewood, a subdivision with access to beautiful Lake Tuscaloosa, was a dream-come-true for Allan, the ultimate water lover. Unfortunately, we had an old boat that was not exactly a dream-come-true, but it did work most of the time for summer fun.

Patient Allan taught even me, the non-swimmer, to drive the old boat. The scary part was being bounced around by wakes from other boats. Captain Allan told me to steer straight into the wake at a perpendicular angle, hold it steady, and not make any sudden moves. Sharon mused one day that those words would make good advice for life's decisions: Just hold it steady and don't make any sudden moves.

One thing was lacking to wrap up that summer. I needed to go "home" once more to the old mountain home place and spend two days with my almost ninety-five year old mother. She still spoke so lovingly of my dad and missed him. She shared a story about how she coped with her overwhelming grief when she first became a widow.

One day in her kitchen, she told me, she felt virtually overcome with grief. She prayed, "O, God, what can I do?"

"Help someone else," she heard someone say.

The voice was so real that she turned to see who had spoken those words. But she looked around and saw no one there. She believed it was from a divine source, so she began to act on the advice. When she heard that someone in the community needed help with a dental bill, she sent the money. Then she began distributing used clothing that people left at her home. Often her good cooking was passed on to others. Her mourning became manageable.

Taking a tip from my sister, Judy, I gave Mother a pedicure, an act of service that was truly an honor for me in order to repay some of her lifelong service to me and others. She could no longer reach her toes.

A bonus treat for me on my visit home was reconnecting with my high school buddy, Jane. Since I moved away from the mountain, she and her husband had discovered the Spirit-filled life and were happy Christians. That made our friendship bond stronger than ever.

I think Mother was glad that one of her children had taken up her old profession of teaching. I wondered how she would have fared as a teacher in today's world. I knew that the exciting first year at WBHS would help me to fare better there during Year Two, but each day would still have to be "fleshed out" with its challenges and met with prayer and determination.

Points to Ponder

1. How do we balance family, ministry, work responsibilities, and fun?
2. God can work wonders in any location.

CHAPTER 20

MOUNTAIN
NUMBER TWO

WITH THAT CLOSURE TO SUMMER, I was now ready to tackle that Mountain #Two in the distance, another year of teaching. It started August 5, 2004; at least that was the first day of my classes, each one with thirty-plus students. All went well. The freshness of a new semester, a new year, invigorated me.

Faculty members were required to work the ticket sales table for at least two home football games. That duty gave me another opportunity to see the fun-loving side of the West Blocton community. People came and enjoyed the band, the food, the friendships, and the game, whether the team won or lost. The scene was a social event for Friday nights.

Near the end of the August, Allan and I got renewed strength for spiritual "mountain climbing" by attending the All-Church Summit gathering at Garywood Assembly of God in Hueytown. Various workshops were designed to enhance ministry giftings. The general session featured the Georgia state superintendent, a Brother Brumbalow. He pointed out that often Christians are just waiting for an opportunity, a chance, to serve God. His Indian chief story was very clever. The Indian chief said "chance" not "how" when greeted. He said, "I know how; I just need a chance." (How often I had felt like that Indian chief.) Danny Duvall gave a strong prophecy before the sermon that had said virtually the same thing. Danny had been the speaker at camp the night Joel surrendered his life to the Lord. We will always be grateful for his obedient service to the Lord.

At the Summit, Superintendent Brumbalow called for the audience to respond to the challenge for service by coming forward to offer ourselves as vessels in God's hands. Allan and I made our way to the front. As people responded, the praise team began singing a chorus affirming that God an use anyone. I believed that for us and Bibb County students!!!

The WBHS First Priority students wanted to reach out to their peers by hosting a Fifth Quarter event after the next home game. A local youth pastor helped to lead the charge. It happened in the middle school gymnasium across the road from WBHS on Oct. 1, after the exciting Friday night football game. The game narrator was happy to announce the event for us. Of course, flyers had been on the school hallways that week. Two other local youth pastors provided the music. Mt. Carmel Baptist and Peggy's church, New Life Assembly, took care of the pizzas and drinks. Students worked hard setting up chairs and serving the food. After Joel Frederick spoke, several students responded to his invitation. One of them was a student of mine. I was one of the first waiting to hug her after her prayer. The students had wanted me to attend; I was so glad I did. My heart was singing as I drove home through those now familiar twists and turns through the countryside. My pillow welcomed me about 1:00 A. M. A country preacher once remarked, "Don't pray for God to use you. Make yourself available, and He'll wear you out!"

In mid-October we chatted with Charles in Louisiana, where he was making himself available to God on staff with the ULALA Chi Alpha chapter. While WBHS was gathering for football on Friday nights, Charles was helping to lead the weekly international student meetings. Those students decided to show the popular new Mel Gibson movie, *The Passion of the Christ.* A Christian student from India requested posters from Mel Gibson's association and did a good job promoting the event. Charles was struck with Bible illiteracy in our country when an American student there asked afterwards, "You mean this was all true? This really happened?" Someone gave that inquirer a New Testament.

He asked, "Who was Matthew?"

An international student wanted to know, "Did Mel Gibson add the whipping part?"

They were asking good questions to people with answers. It was great to know the Chi Alpha ministry was "on duty during their watch" and did not fail those seekers but had answers to their questions.

In late October at my school, Master's Commission team members did their second annual Conquest Assembly for the whole school and chatted with students afterwards. They agreed to return in a few days for our First Priority club day meeting in the gym.

There was one change in the attendance policy for club day this year. Since our club had no official roster, the administration decided that students could only be dismissed for our school-day meetings if the students came by my room and signed up in advance. That list of names had to be circulated to the faculty prior to the meetings in order to dismiss students. So, I notified students via the morning announcements to follow that procedure; I stayed after work to type up those names. Then I sent an email and gave a hard copy of the list to the faculty and staff. It was a little more work, but no sacrifice is too great for Jesus, and it was so, so worth it. Around fifteen students responded to the gospel invitation at the close of the meeting. It was great to partner with Master's Commission.

I wish I could say that all these decisions swelled the ranks of First Priority and all the converts became glowing examples of a work done in their hearts. Sometimes it was discouraging not to see apparent fruit for our efforts. We had to leave the results to God. Our FP students attempted follow up and invited others to their youth groups. Local youth groups did grow. One undeniable statistic was encouraging. The number of teen pregnancies at WBHS was down.

For the November FP club-day meeting, I had to do another long list of names for the faculty because about 200 of our students signed up to get out of class and come hear a very special speaker. He was Jeremiah Castille, a former football star at the University of Alabama under our renowned Coach Paul "Bear" Bryant. Jeremiah's life was a shining example of what the Lord Jesus Christ can do for a man to make him a new creature. His relatives who rejected the Lord had not fared as well as he had.

One of our WBHS coaches had known Jeremiah at Briarwood Christian School in Birmingham when they were co-workers. When I invited him to come speak, he was willing and told me to call his wife to arrange the date. When the date arrived, alas—he called from highway I-459 to say that traffic was backed up three lanes. Since I was on my planning period, some of our First Priority network friends and I went to prayer in my room. If the traffic jam lasted too long, the club period would be over. We prayed for God to work a miracle to get him there on time. He arrived just before 8:00, and we started at 8:10 A. M.

Jeremiah Castille really "connected" with the students. He charged them not to let peer pressure keep them from God's call. After all, those peers will also be in line on the Judgment Day. Although Jeremiah did not call for a public commitment, he did lead the student body in prayer and felt that many there responded to the call of the Lord that day.

Thanksgiving, 2004, was a milestone for our family. Mother celebrated her ninety-fifth birthday; she still lived alone in a newer house that her sons and grandsons had physically built for her.

At the annual Thanksgiving meal, she was surrounded by a host of children, grandchildren, and great-grandchildren at her son Ronald's home just down the road. All our children were there except Sharon and Luis. There were enough male cousins to have two flag football teams square off in the field that Ronald had cleared off and marked for the occasion. Older uncles now served as officials for the game. In previous years they had been in the action themselves. As I mentioned, Thanksgiving was always really an annual Childers family reunion event. After all, it fell near Mother's birthday and anniversary. We enjoyed honoring her each year. Ironically, her youngest grandson, Judy's son, was also born on her birthday, so he had a cake as well.

Holidays are wonderful. They refresh us for that return to duty. Something else refreshed me as I returned to teaching in December. It was the coming of a special guest for one of our morning First Priority meetings. She was none other than our younger daughter, Alison. She led worship with her guitar, testified, and taught. There was God's handiwork right before my eyes. She brought some chips for snacks and told the students that they were "all that and a bag of chips." Teenagers can eat any time.

Another refreshing, food-related event happened on Saturday, December 11, 2004—a pizza party. Allan and I had been assisting Mr. Fields and his wife in the monthly Hannah Home outreach to battered women and children. He asked me to be in charge of the entertainment for the moms, youth, and children for their Christmas party. He would take care of bringing the pizzas. I turned to an ally for help. She was a devoted Christian lady who picked up FP students who did not have transportation for our morning gatherings. We will call her "Jane." I asked her if her church's newly formed drama team could come perform at the party. She agreed, by faith.

Jane attended Second Baptist Church of Shady Grove. After agreeing to bring the drama team, one night in bed all the details of a "human video" filled her head. Now I just needed a head count of her group for pizza orders.

"Thirty," she said.

Mr. Fields did not seem to mind the expense at all. As he picked up the Cici's pizzas that Saturday evening, Allan and I met the team at the one-and-only traffic light in Brookwood, AL, and led the way to the home in order to enter the security number at the front gate.

Those teenagers were well received by the mothers and children temporarily staying at the home. During the program, two female drama team members who were WBHS First Priority and Spanish class members, shared their testimonies about coming to the Lord. One of them had once had to flee to Hannah Home herself, along with her mom, to avoid someone abusive in her mom's life. When the team did their choreographed "human video," they passed out unlit candles to everyone and dimmed the lights. They chose the beautiful song, "Go Light Your World" by Chris Rice, to play as they moved throughout the audience and began lighting all the candles held by guests at various tables.[1] One verse of the moving lyrics mentions an abused woman with an unlit flame in her life and exhorts Christians to take her their light. The room became brighter and brighter, just as the song was teaching. It was very impressive.

When the Shady Grove pastor spoke of God's love and forgiveness, one teenage girl responded to his invitation to make a public commitment to Christ. She fell into the arms of my two Spanish students who had shared their testimonies. They wept together. It was worth every college course, every ornery pupil, every test I had had to grade—all of it—just to see that beautiful sight that cold December night.

That was the same cold December that Charles came home from Louisiana for the holidays and did not let the temperatures stop him and some friends from a camping trip to the Sipsey

Wilderness in the Bankhead National Forest, near Mother's old one-room school sites. The forecast called for a night time low of twenty degrees. Apparently our long-ago camping trip to Cheaha Mountain did not turn our kids against camping. Luis and Sharon have even helped plan multi-family campouts. Alison's camping zeal even contributed to a career change later on.

Joel once took a buddy to my old mountain home to show him the waterfall on the big bluff and camp out under a cave-like over-hang. My brother Ronald had purchased that land and shared it with family. But when the adventurers heard that coyotes had invaded those benign woods and recently there had been a mountain lion sighting in that same cave, they decided to camp out in Uncle Ronald's cozy house. Professionals later removed the mountain lion.

After Christmas, Charles, Sharon, and Luis headed to the annual Chi Alpha SALT meetings where some "vision casting" usually occurs. The Arkansas Chi Alpha caught a vision to partner with Bolivian college students to plant Chi Alpha chapters in Bolivia; the U-Ark chapter had some planning and work to do to turn those dreams into reality. Allan and I didn't know at the time that we could help out with those dreams.

BACK TO WORK (FUN) AT SCHOOL

Back at school in early January, 2005, our Spanish Club sponsored a special low-admission event for the school. A live Mariachi band came to perform. Their opening number was "Sweet Home Alabama," and the band captured the hearts of those students from the first delightful opening chord, even though the words were sung with Hispanic accents. I enjoyed hearing the old Marty Robbins song, "El Paso," done in Spanish. Students wanted to be photographed with the band. The event was lots of fun, though a "flop" as a fundraiser for the club.

When Allan and I made our January trip to Hannah Home, we took a young man from our church and his fiancé came along to work with the teenagers. The drama team leader and three youth from Shady Grove also came to help. Allan and I conducted the children's class. I chose a new Child Evangelism book that Allan had ordered for the church library. It was an illustrated biography of George Washington Carver, the father of synthetics. He was a humble Christian man known more for his discoveries using peanuts than his walk with God, but he left a tremendous godly, as well as scientific, legacy behind at his beloved Tuskegee Institute in Alabama.

Thus, my theme that day was peanuts. After a Bible lesson and the Carver story, I hid peanuts for the kids to find. We tossed peanuts into a large can. Then I said that if anyone there had not received the Lord into his/her heart, to come over to the side to talk to me afterwards. Then I placed the bowl of peanuts before them to eat and watched little hands try to crack the shells open. I got absorbed in watching their childish delight, but one little girl ignored the peanuts and walked directly to me. She wanted to pray.

I asked, "You have never asked Jesus to live in your heart?"

Her answer was just shaking her head to say "no."

I prodded, "But you want to?"

The head nodded up and down, up and down, and that face told me that she meant it and really wanted to. Within moments, thank God, another little sister had entered the kingdom.

The January club day First Priority event was extra special. One of the girls who had told her story at the Hannah Home pizza party told it again before her peers at school. She was only in the ninth grade but very bold in her faith. Joel Frederick spoke and did a Q & A session with the students. He responded well to their questions. The inquirers and the audience seemed to enjoy that format. My ninth grade student was allowed (by her Spanish teacher, Señora Gravely) to come to class late since she was needed to counsel students who lingered for prayer. When she finally arrived outside my door, her face was glowing. She had led another girl to Jesus.

In the spring Allan and I watched Jerry Falwell speak on TV. His topic gripped me. He spoke on *maximizing a short life time.* He advised being focused and concentrating on fewer talents, not being a Jack-of-All-Trades. He urged viewers not to give up but saturate our lives with *much* prayer. He went so far as to say that all our failures are prayer failures. Ouch. Of course, he was currently diligently working on one of his legacies, Liberty University. I can listen to advice from someone like that.

One thing I had begun to pray about was my fatigue from work. Even Alison noticed it when she came home for her spring break. (My school was in session that week.) Some of that fatigue was alleviated by that free pitcher of sweet tea on the teachers' cafeteria table. It must have been the best sweet tea in the South; it really got me through those long afternoons.

Another prayer item was that short-term mission trip. I had my passport. The *Christ for the Nations* magazine article said that was step one. Step two was prayer. The answer was just around the corner. Sharon called one day to recruit us for a mission trip team to Bolivia scheduled for early June. She could use another Spanish speaker. She needed me; I needed my faithful bodyguard; therefore, Allan was recruited.

During my spring break in late March, Allan and I worked on a support letter to notify friends of our proposed mission trip. Several responded with financial gifts. We would use our savings for airfare. Our flight was scheduled for the day following the end of my 2004-2005 teaching contract. All the semester exam review of Spanish verbs with the students was going to prove very helpful in more ways than one. What an exciting way to conclude Year #Two at WBHS—holding in our hands two airline tickets to Bolivia!

POINTS TO PONDER

1. We need to feel needed and useful. Are opportunities to serve closer than we think?

2. Comment on Jerry Falwell's advice to narrow our focus for more effectiveness. Any supporting scriptures?

3. Have you ever considered children's ministry? ...your Father in heaven is not willing that any of these little ones should be lost. Matthew 18:14b

CHAPTER 21

BOLIVIA AND BACK

ALLAN AND I ARRIVED IN Sucre, Bolivia, some twenty-four hours after leaving home. Sharon, Luis, and some of the Arkansas team members greeted us. They had arrived a few days earlier. Although we had had stops in three U. S. and three Bolivian airports, we felt refreshed because we had napped in two of the locations. We were able to attend a Sunday evening church service and go out to eat afterwards at a Bolivian restaurant.

It was during our departure from that restaurant that we had our first encounter with the ugly face of Bolivian poverty. Small children approached us (at approximately 10 PM) to try to sell us their small hand crafts. Allan noted some fear on the little faces. Our missionary host, Howard Nutt, explained that often the children are beaten at home if all their goods are not sold. But... here's where Jesus got involved that night by the restaurant!

As we were piling into Howard Nutt's van, he noticed that an older vehicle came along. A kind woman he recognized picked up the little street children. Later we learned the whole story behind this amazing woman on wheels, the one I later called the "Mother Teresa of Sucre." She was Ana Colque. She was often out after dark searching for desperate street children. She usually took them to the Shalom orphanage that she founded. At Shalom she could keep the children until she could legally offer them a home inside its walls.

Mr. Nutt took us from the restaurant to the campus of Universidad Unidad (Unity University) and showed us the dormitory apartment which would be our lodging while there in this lovely old colonial city with its Spanish red-tile rooftops. Meals were served in the school cafeteria downstairs, but our team let us sleep in for breakfast the next morning and sent up our food later. We drank only bottled water.

Almost immediately we got involved with doing what we had come to do, reach out to college students and assist with the establishment of a campus ministry among the hundreds of college students in Sucre. Our U. S. campuses are blessed to have such well known ministries as Campus Crusade (or Cru), Intervarsity, and Chi Alpha. The Arkansas Chi Alpha chapter was committed to birthing its counterpart in Bolivia.

The secular university there in Sucre pre-dates Yale or Harvard. It is called the University of San Francisco Xavier and is divided up by its various disciplines, called "*facultades*" throughout Sucre. One such *facultad* was situated directly across from one of the thirty-plus churches established by Howard Nutt in his tenure in Bolivia. The church had a thriving college-aged ministry in place. Some of those church members joined our team to witness in the atrium of the *facultad*. Sharon and Luis were both artists who could do pencil drawing portraits. As their subjects sat still, posing for their free portrait, I was able to share the gospel in Spanish with them, using the Evangelism Explosion (EE) format.

One young man was ready to pray to receive the Lord. I decided it would be better to have Allan involved at this point, so I summoned him over to lead the prayer. He led in English, and I translated into Spanish. That young man accompanied us all the way back to the Bible school campus. We got him in touch with local Christians for follow-up.

One student from the local church convinced his professor to let our team speak in her class. Luis shared our purpose for being in Bolivia. Serving Jesus is fun and adventuresome!!

Back at the Bible school campus, we got more acquainted with our hosts, Howard Nutt and his wife, Jerri. They were truly veteran missionaries who had labored long years for the Lord. As a result, there were over thirty churches alive and growing, a radio station, a Bible school, rehab center, and orphanage.

The Bible school was housed in a defunct hotel with a lovely courtyard. The Nutts had added more floors to the original structure. It had sufficient space to rent some lower level rooms to a private school, to house resident students, to hold classes, and to provide guests rooms for mission teams. The whole venture was initially funded through gifts from the Jimmy Swaggart ministry the year before his career was marred by scandal. When that source dried up, allies of Mr. Nutt in the home office of the Assemblies of God were able to divert some funds his way to continue his dream.

We were honored to be a part of the continuing vision of Mr. Nutt. He was the only Bolivia missionary who responded to Luis and Sharon's letter offering to bring a team to found Chi Alpha Campus Ministries on Bolivian soil. The University of Arkansas (UArk) became determined to make a ten-year commitment to seeing a Latin American Chi Alpha raised up. This year was the launch year.

UArk chose Bolivia because their own Chi Alpha chapter had several Bolivian alumni now back in their homeland. UArk had a special arrangement with the Bolivian government that allowed Bolivians studying at UArk to waive the out-of-state tuition rate. Thus, Bolivians made up a sizable portion of international students in Fayetteville, Arkansas. UArk Chi Alpha chose Sucre because Howard Nutt was the only one to welcome the offer extended to several on the field.

Mr. Nutt seemed like a modern day apostle to us. In his office he shared about trials and victories over the years, of spiritual warfare, of friends and adversaries. It was a record of faithfulness.

Even during his wife's illnesses and homesickness, they stuck it out. Now God was sending along some additional help.

The Bible school had an unheated chapel. No one seemed to use heaters there, not even the wealthy. When chapel was over, everyone stood outside a while in the sunlight, like lizards absorbing heat. We were over 9,000 feet above sea level in the Andes Mountains in the month of June, Bolivia's wintertime and one of its dry months. We did not suffer altitude sickness except once when Allan forgot to wear a hat outside.

Our dorm had a basketball goal on the edge of the courtyard. One day I played a game of HORSE with Luis and a teenager from the private school. The teenager, I found out, was from the Shalom orphanage. A Bible school student, Alex, sitting across the table from me in one of our morning classes was one of the original abandoned children taken in by Ana Colque years before. Yes, God is the Father of the fatherless. (Psalm 68:5) There sat one of His sons, a life made over again from sorrow to happiness. Alex wore a beautiful smile. I wanted to see this Shalom home. On Wednesday I got my wish.

Ana gave up her off day to give our team a tour of the Shalom (peace) orphanage which she directs. Ana was a graduate of the Unidad Universidad Bible school, a middle-aged single lady devoted to the Lord's work. She served as director of the orphanage and administrator for other areas of ministry at the school. She took us from room to room, building to building, as she told the history of the miracle around us.

ANA'S STORY

In her early teen years Ana's dad died, and her mother had to be hospitalized. With no social services to assist, life was tough, but one day she found herself in a Christian gathering. There someone showed her the love of God and explained His wonderful plan to receive eternal life through faith in the sacrifice of His Son. That day she gave her life to Jesus. He took it and made something beautiful with it. He led her to attend Bible school and later start the Shalom home for abandoned, unwanted, or orphaned children.

Ana is "Mother" to many now. In her office she pulled several photo albums from a bookcase showing pictures of "her children." The pages showed the children, first as she found them, sleeping on cardboard boxes on the cold streets of Sucre, then current shots of their happy faces. Their biological mothers did not do albums of baby pictures because all their resources were spent on survival. Prostitution is legal in Sucre; there are many unwanted little ones. Some are actually abandoned to fend for themselves. They learn to make things to sell to tourists, to steal, or to compete with hungry dogs for garbage on the streets. Ana says that the children she rescues always ask the same questions: "You mean I can stay here? You mean I don't have to leave?"

The miracles that brought Shalom into existence began when Ana befriended a few boys. She requested from Howard Nutt a simple spare room without windows for night lodging for them. He gladly provided the room for Ana. (See http://www.hnutt.net) Then a friend treated Ana to a vacation in Oakland, Maryland. There she shared her vision of establishing a home for Sucre's desperate children. One woman took Ana's dream to local churches, and soon a confederation of churches of various denominations pooled their resources, faith, and enthusiasm. They decided to back Ana's "peace" home with $50,000 per year, as well as make annual trips to Bolivia to do hands-on construction work on group homes, to make curtains and shelves, and simply to love the children—the easy part. The city government granted the land with the stipulation that buildings be erected within two years. Ana has to look to God for daily provision of food and water. Water is delivered in Sucre by trucks and deposited into underground reservoirs. She has to recruit house-parents and staff workers who are willing to lay down their lives and ambitions for the sake of the children and the Lord.

Now several buildings are a reality on two sites. Former street kids are graduating from high school; some are going to Bible school and becoming pastors. (Today, Alex is married and serving the Lord in India.) Ana is very proud of the children. One young boy there, she said, feels called to India as a missionary. I heard her address him with the affectionate "mi amor" (my love). I wondered, "Did he ever hear that before Shalom was his home?"

One building Ana showed us was not quite complete. An apartment at one end could be a home for grandparents. She offered it to Allan and me. The children had not experienced the luxury of having grandparents. I wanted to fill that role, but after prayer, Allan and I felt that it was not God's role for us. I would return to the states and tell others about her work. (See www.shalomesmicasa.com. Facebook: www.facebook.com/shalomandseeds.)

MISSION TRIP WINDS DOWN

As our team traveled in Bolivia from churches to campuses to the Bible school, the UArk Chi Alpha campus pastor, Ronnie Hoover, began to "pick my brain" about Spanish grammar. Luckily, just days before, I had done thorough reviews with my high school students to prepare them for their final exams. Without any notes or charts, I could explain all the regular and irregular verbs in all the tenses, something I cannot do at any given moment without some review. Ronnie studied his notes and verb charts well and was not afraid to attempt some communication in Spanish. Today he can even preach in Spanish. It was a joy to give him that little push, like a parent with a hand on the bicycle seat. I guess that is one of my callings, to be a "pusher." It does not bother me at all that my students far exceed the early skills I give them or my own current skills. Giving that push to a missionary-pastor who loves Bolivia was especially fulfilling to me since I did not get to go be a missionary to Hispanics myself.

The grand finale of our week in Bolivia was a fun party at the Bible school. We invited all our contacts of the week to let them see Christians having fun. Allan and I served at the greeting table. I did not mind the pretty *señoritas* giving Allan a kiss on the cheek. That was the customary greeting.

Ronnie Hoover assured our hosts, the Nutts, that his Chi Alpha in Arkansas was serious about a ten-year commitment to return to guide and extend the ministry of Chi Alpha in Latin American. The UArk chapter has kept that promise since 2005. What an honor it was to be a part of the first team. Today that ministry has expanded to Santa Cruz, Cochabamba, and other cities.

The UArk team left for the U. S., but Sharon, Luis, Allan and I traveled on to Cochabamba to visit Luis's paternal, Bolivian grand-parents, aunts, uncles, and cousins. He had not been there since he was a teenager, but their affection for him was evident from the first day. Everyone was very gracious and welcoming toward us. Only one aunt spoke English, so my brain got a work out serving as interpreter much of the time.

Those two memorable weeks ended so soon. The *Christ for the Nations* magazine article had been correct. Every Christian should do short-term mission trips. They are life changing. I had to send a follow-up "thank you" letter to those who had helped make our Bolivia trip possible. We took more than suitcases home with us. We carried home a fresh determination in our lives to get involved in God's work. Ronnie Hoover remarked that at our age we were supposed to be thinking about sitting down and relaxing. But the opposite was what we were feeling. Allan and I were wanting to get back home and make our final years count even more for Jesus as they were counting down.

BACK TO THE USA

When Allan and I arrived back on U. S. soil at the Miami airport, I went directly to a water fountain and drank all the water I wanted. We had used water sparingly in Bolivia, consuming only bottled water. No one wastes water when bathing either. Bolivian showers consist of getting wet, turning water off, lathering body with soap, and then turning water on for rinsing. Water is heated by the sun on rooftops, and showers work best at mid-day.

At first the usual USA routine resumed. Our July 4th weekend was special in 2005 because we got to host Joel and Alison for a time of water skiing and picnicking on Tuscaloosa's Black Warrior River, followed by grilled steaks and watching *National Treasure* with Nicholas Cage. Wow, our son-in-law, Luis, really does resemble Nicholas Cage. Then our patriotic church, First Assembly of God, did a July 4th BBQ. It was fun to be home again with kids and our church family but would never forget our new family in Bolivia.

Then the summer of 2005 took a different turn in July. I got involved as never before in my 95-year-old mother's caregiving. She had not seemed to need care before. She was Miss Independence on two feet. But on a recent visit, she agreed to have an eye exam done. The report was not good. She had advanced glaucoma and macular degeneration in both eyes. She was losing her eyesight. Her children had noticed that she had *not* noticed the bread crumbs and ants on her kitchen floor or the fruit flies on decaying food. She sometimes complained of it being so dark inside, even with sunlight coming through the windows.

It was a poem (not a song as usual) that inspired me to action. I saw the following poem in a book I was reading that reinforced to me that God had assigned to me a certain amount of Mother's caregiving:

There is some place for you to fill,
Some work for you to do,

That no one can or ever will
Do quite as well as you;
It may lie close along your way,
Some homely little duty
That only needs your touch, your sway,
To blossom into beauty.[1]

After fasting and prayer, I felt that I should go stay with Mother as long as it took to get her some help with housecleaning and some type of meals-on-wheels. With my siblings' help, we got both goals accomplished. I had to be away from Allan for a week; I missed him. But I recalled that Mother and Dad had lived apart for over five years in order for Dad to work in Chicago to provide for the family. What was my week away from Allan compared to their sacrifice for years for us, their children?

Not only did *their sacrifice* inspire me, but also another poem that I found in one of Mother's favorite books of poetry "nailed" the posture I should take. The poem's title was "My Mother," written by Ann Taylor. It speaks of a mother's tender care for the child during its formative years. Then, in the final two stanzas, it shifts to role reversal:

When thou art feeble, old and gray,
My healthy arm shall be thy stay,
And I will soothe thy pains away,
My mother.

And when I see thee hang thy head,
'Twill be my turn to watch thy bed
And tears of sweet affection shed—
My mother.[2]

I did shed those tears as I watched the aging process take its toll on Mother's mind and body. What an honor it was to do what little I could for that special woman! She even began to look forward to the van pulling into her yard, bringing her weekday lunches. I knew she would have one nourishing meal and one human contact per day. It was difficult to help out while living two hours away. My brothers checked on her often, and my out-of-state sister provided a call-line device which Mother wore in case of emergencies. I returned to my home feeling that my mission was accomplished for the time.

One Saturday in 2005, Allan, Alison, and I attended a very special wedding in Bibb County, near West Blocton. That day marked the end of an era for my friend, Peggy Rowe, the WBHS counselor who had called me about my job there. She became the wife of John McKay.

The day marked the end of an era for me as well. No longer would I be spending Wednesday nights at Peggy's home. Allan had suggested that I ask Peggy if I could sleep at her home on Wednesdays so that I would not have to get up so early on Thursday mornings to drive from Northport for the First Priority meetings. She readily agreed. Walking her two lovable dogs, Fender and Precious, was relaxing after a day of teaching. I didn't know following two wagging tails was so therapeutic. Dainty little Precious left love offerings of baby carrots on my bed; she would tolerate no sharing of anyone's affection with dear old chubby Fender.

I had also enjoyed attending Peggy's church on Wednesday evenings. But now, I knew the newlyweds needed their privacy, and I needed some respite from the grueling schedule I had followed for two years. Sponsoring two clubs and trying to teach with excellence was just too heavy a load. I had a hard decision to make when the fall school bells began ringing in my third year at WBHS.

POINTS TO PONDER

1. God may prepare us today for a task in the future. (Example: Tip in a magazine article.)

2. What do the Ten Commandments and Jesus say about honoring parents? Honor your father and your mother... Exodus 20:12 NIV ...do not despise your mother when she is old. Proverbs 23:22b NIV

CHAPTER 22

MOUNTAIN NUMBER THREE SCHOOL YEAR

IN AUGUST, 2005, I RELUCTANTLY gave up leadership of First Priority. One of the Christian coaches took my place as sponsor. I would have preferred stepping down from Spanish Club sponsorship, but no one else could fill that role.

That same August, a famous hurricane changed the Gulf landscape, hundreds of lives, and our nation. Hurricane Katrina struck with a vengeance and changed many agendas. The youth group Joel assisted cancelled a white-water rafting trip because fuel prices soared; his church sent a team to help with Mississippi clean-up efforts instead. Our local church fed breakfast to 500 storm refugees in one of the University of Alabama's sports complexes.

An interesting twist in our Bolivia story came because of Hurricane Katrina. Our rooftop lost a few shingles even though we lived four hours inland. We reported our loss to our insurance company but did not expect an inspector until more serious complaints were dealt with. To our surprise, during our Sunday lunch, a young insurance adjuster knocked at our door. We invited him to join us for lunch. He accepted and explained that his company decided to address claims farther away from the hardest-hit areas since transportation and communication around the Gulf were difficult.

The insurance adjuster agreed to submit our claim but expected little help. He was wrong. A check for about $2100 arrived soon, about what we had used from our personal savings account for the Bolivian trip. Serving God is so much fun. He sprinkles surprises and rewards all along the way.

YOU'RE IN THE ARMY NOW!

Speaking of surprises, in early September, our son-in-law, Luis, surprised us with an announcement. He felt it was time for him to transition out of college campus ministry. After earnest prayer, he decided to join the U. S. Army and fulfill a long dormant dream to serve in the military. He would report for two months basic training at Ft. Benning, GA, in January, 2006. Adventure lay ahead for him as he served Uncle Sam. They had contributed well during their tenure in Arkansas. There Sharon was even able to use her decorating skills by assisting Dana Hoover with beautifying the new Chi Alpha House.

About this time I began to have a growing concern that I still had three unmarried adult children; the oldest was thirty-one. I intensified my prayers for them. But a dear saint of God gave me some instruction about my concerns.

At the fall state women's conference at the Springville Assemblies of God camp north of Birmingham, I had the rare privilege of joining some older ladies in a dorm room for afternoon prayer. I voiced the need for mates for my unwed children. That is when I got the instruction from a special lady, Dean.

Dean had served as greeter years before at Garywood Assembly of God near Birmingham, AL. One day she greeted and befriended a worldly church visitor who would go on to become a missionary and pastor's wife, v. g., Susanne Cox, the "First Lady" of Kingwood Assembly of God. Susanne was one of the conference speakers that weekend and was the one who had once encouraged and prayed for me when I felt so unused by God. Now I was in the lodge room with the woman who had extended friendship to and mentored Susanne.

I will never forget Dean's words to me that day. She actually placed a hand on my sternum and told me to rest about my unmarried children.

"It's better to die single than marry the wrong one," she said.

She went on to describe the agony of a young boy from a broken home who had asked, "Why can't we have a normal family like other people?"

So, I would wait for God's timing and God's choice for my dear ones. The wait did prove lengthy but –oh!! – so worth it.

Back at school, not only did I have some respite by relinquishing my role in First Priority that fall, 2005, but some relief from driving came via two young Tuscaloosa teachers who also had to make the long drive. We split the driving duties up three ways as we carpooled. The arrangement helped with the gas expense as well. It was a joy to get to know them better and hopefully sow into their young lives. One of them rejoiced during that year that her husband became born again and was a new man! I shared with her that Alison and I had prayed an "agreement" prayer for her husband one day as we drove somewhere. (Matthew 18:19) It is nice to have a daughter for a prayer partner.

This particular school year was sadder than any other in my lifetime. Shortly after it ended, the community had said "goodbye" prematurely to two teachers, two students, and four parents of West Blocton middle and high school students. One of our high school female athletes was seriously injured in a car accident that left her partially confined to a wheelchair with some brain damage. The following year she was crowned the homecoming queen; this community knew how to wrap arms of love around its own. As each death occurred, SGA students came by the classrooms to collect donations for families. Students willingly forfeited their snack money for the cause and grieved along with families of the fallen.

With a *little more time and energy*, I noticed that I was able visit Mother, to be more involved at church, and help with Allan's church library project. Some of us church ladies did a lasagna Sunday meal for college students; I sold the idea to the ladies. It just took a few phone calls to make it happen. Everyone contacted was very willing to help. Allan and I also had more time for hosting our children, water skiing, or touring with Joel and Alison the Montevallo American Village replica on his birthday.

Charles came home more often that fall, sometimes to itinerate and build his support base. He came late September to escape the pounding of Hurricane Rita, then for Veteran's Day, Thanksgiving, and Christmas. Looking back, I see these visits as a gift to us because (unbeknownst to us) he was soon to depart for missionary service to Belgium.

NEW CHURCH HOME

In December, Allan and I decided to transfer our church membership to the new Assembly of God church plant closer to our home. Thus, after several years with a loving church family, we were given a formal farewell with prayer from our friends at Tuscaloosa First Assembly of God, but Allan retained his position as librarian there.

During that prayer time, a close friend advised me to pursue mentoring younger women when I got involved with the new church. While at First Assembly, my friend, Lolly, and I had formed the tongue-twister team of "Lolly and Dottie" and with help of others had led a women's group for a time. We met in various homes one Saturday morning each month. We chose Saturdays so that husbands could babysit; we chose homes with a room in the house to accommodate any children who did not have a babysitter at home. The church paid for the babysitter at our meetings. Each month we tackled a spiritual topic and a practical topic. Our topics for the first meeting were these: (1) How to stay in love with your husband. (2) How to make him trust you with money. Those home meetings were a way for women to bond together and to have basic mentoring by more experienced women. As a result, their husbands did more networking as well. (Titus 2:4)

BRING ON 2006

Allan and I did not attend a lot of movies, but in January, 2006, we had to check out the newly released *Chronicles of Narnia,* since the series by C. S. Lewis was a childhood favorite at our house. Even the none-reader, Joel, relished the series. Lewis portrays the reason for Christ's sacrifice so skillfully in the "Deep Magic" episode in which Aslan (Jesus) sacrifices himself to rescue the erring child of Adam. Of course, Aslan did live again and royally outsmarted the evil ones.

Time with Allan was always a precious commodity. He gave me a priceless compliment one day. I mentioned a quote in the January 1, 2006, *Evangel* magazine. A pastor from Iceland, a former fisherman, said a wife could be to her husband either a sail or an anchor. Allan immediately said that I was a sail to him!

One day Allan showed me Proverbs 31:25b from the "Noble Wife" passage in the New International Version: "...she can laugh at the days to come." The days to come? That meant I did not have to dread being older or teaching juveniles another year and a half. Being at mid-year of the school year meant that I was midway finished with climbing that mountain Number Three of those dreaded "mountains in the distance" before retirement. It was going to be all right.

Allan and I were privileged again to host Charles in January, 2006, so that he could do more extensive itinerating to boost his budget for overseas service in Belgium. We caught him still long enough to treat him to an early birthday gift, a meal at Tuscaloosa's original, famed Dreamland BBQ and a basketball movie, *Glory Road*. Our firstborn was now thirty-two. It's a noble calling to simply "keep the home fires burning" and provide that haven of rest and stability, especially in our ever-transitioning society. Maybe we were now in Parenting Part III, parenting adult children.

In February, Mother moved into my nearest brother's home, just down the road from her. Independence has its limits when the body becomes frail and week. The next month her household items were entrusted to her various children because the house would have to be sold to finance her stay in a nursing home.

Those words, "*nursing home,*" had always been dirty words in our family; all the siblings felt that we would NEVER put *our* mother in one of those places. But she had lived so long that her would-be caregivers were no longer able-bodied enough to lift and care for her themselves. It seemed there was no other alternative. At least we personally knew some of the staff at the local nursing home, and Mother probably had more visitors and kisses on her forehead than any other patient.

In April, we journeyed to Ft. Benning to see Luis graduate from basic training. He said he had had more opportunities to witness for the Lord in one month there than in an entire year on the college campus. The younger troops called him "Preacher." They requested prayer before one qualifying drill in marksmanship and went on to set a record at Ft. Benning; that accomplishment was mentioned at the graduation ceremony.

Another opportunity came for Luis to walk out his faith when a commander ordered Luis and his group of soldiers to do some community service work. Luis called a local church and asked for suggestions. In no time, his group of soldiers delivered sacks of shelf goods for the church's food pantry. He learned later that the church had recently had more requests than usual for help with food. These extra supplies from the U. S. Army men were especially appreciated at that time. Luis's future assignments would take him to Ft. Gordon in Augusta, GA, and to Ft. Bragg in Fayetteville, North Carolina. The latter assignment would greatly affect our lives just ahead.

In early May, Joel had his college graduation, and the family clustered around him for his special day. He donned a cap and gown at the University of South Alabama in Mobile. He now carried a diploma that definitely unlocked some doors ahead in his life.

Soon another school year was history. First Priority had continued on with its new faculty leader. The Spanish Club and classes had been a pleasure. We did field trips to a Mexican restaurant in Tuscaloosa and to the annual state Spanish Club convention at the Ferguson Center on the campus of the University of Alabama. The campus was such familiar turf for our family, but to the WBHS students, the University seemed "so big!" It was a joy to expand their worlds and give them the opportunity to compete with their peers. Some of them were winners in their respective competitions, and they all enjoyed themselves. Their club sponsor, Señora Gravely, enjoyed the event as much as they did.

SUMMER, 2006, OPPORTUNITIES

One Sunday night in June, 2006, our new church had a special evening of praise, prayer, and waiting on the Lord. I requested prayer for direction for any summer ministry I could render the Lord. Then there was a message in tongues with an interpretation. These words were followed by some weeping and just sitting or kneeling before the Lord. The time was so special that nobody wanted it to end; no one wanted to leave.

The next day I received a call from the pastor's wife asking me to go ahead and launch the "Young Women's Core" group we had discussed. She was excited, and I was as well. I got started on some phone calls. Two other ladies in the church, Vicki and Shelley, helped me lead and make our Wednesday night sessions fun and interesting. Mentoring younger women was enriching for the leaders as well as the younger ladies, and it was biblical since we were following the Titus 2:4 model. The leaders decided to use Carolyn Mahaney's book, *Feminine Appeal*, to steer our discussions each week.

Allan served as mentor to a group of young golfers in the church. Sometimes we wives joined them afterwards for a meal. Allan also led a study on Dietrich Bonhoeffer.

In late June, 2006, we helped Alison move to her new home in a suburb of Birmingham. A friend of hers purchased a home large enough to have several Christian housemates there. These young women became life-long friends for Alison, real "soul sisters." They all attended Church of the Highlands near Birmingham. Alison thrived with her friends and the church's interest and outreach groups. Her camping group later did some camping in Puerto Rico, and that planted a little idea in her head that played out later on and even involved us! She was no camping wimp, even if her parents were.

Another window of opportunity for me began to open. (I've never waited around for my church to assign me a job but kept an open mind to anything the Lord might prompt me to do, anywhere.) I felt a growing concern for the children in our own neighborhood. Little did I know that 2006 would be the last full summer I would live in our dear Lakewood "resort" home.

I took a yellow legal pad one day and went around to the homes and did a survey, asking if the children would be interested in a Bible club. One girl about twelve lit up and said, "I'd love to have a Bible club."

That settled it. She had two younger siblings also interested. They were unchurched at the time. So, a weekly club began in our home. Friends from church and the neighborhood helped me.

On July 27, I had the privilege of praying with that twelve-year-old to receive Jesus as her Savior; she lingered after club to request that prayer. Soon afterwards, her family got back into church. Incidentally, July 27 just happened to be day I had prayed that prayer myself back in 1962.

In July we enjoyed some wonderful family times at the beach on the Florida Gulf coast with Sharon, Luis, Alison, and Charles. Joel couldn't make it. Charles really needed to "veg" since he had been working twelve-hour days to raise his support to be a missionary to Belgium. He had at last reached his financial goal and was waiting on his VISA. He was building up his French proficiency by listening to tapes during his long road trips.

Charles told us that listening to a different type of CD on a road trip had been a deciding factor in his decision to go abroad. Joel had burned a CD from a free download of John Piper's account of the life of the brave Adoniram Judson, who served in Burma in an earlier century. Piper admonished young ministers to be willing to serve on foreign soil if God so directed.[1] Heaven's tug gripped Charles's heart that day, and he knew it was time to start working on that French and proceed ahead toward Belgium.

Charles was able to stay longer with us than the others at the beach. He treated us to ice cream at an outdoor tourist area in Seaside, FL. Since I got my fingers sticky with the ice cream, I left Allan and Charles to find a public bathroom to rinse my hands. A Hispanic maid was waiting to service the one-person bathroom. I explained to her in English that I only wanted to wash my fingers and would not be long. Her blank look told me she had not understood my English, so I explained again in Spanish. She smiled and nodded. When I finished using the sink, she still could not do her task because another and another patron kept going into the bathroom.

I sensed a witnessing opportunity with this person who was stationed there with nothing else to do but listen to me. I struck up a conversation in Spanish and eventually led her in prayer for salvation. She confided that she had recently been having sadness daily with tears but now she felt free and happy (*libre y alegre*). I called her a few days later and found that she was still joyful and had told her children about the experience. She had been reading the book of John as I had suggested.

By the end of July, Charles was all set to leave for Belgium as soon as his VISA arrived. So he left Louisiana behind and came to live with us until the VISA came. A new chapter in his life was about to begin. Our home was always open for our children in transition. Over time, it seemed that just "keeping the home fires burning" was one of the roles assigned to Allan and me. It is not a difficult role.

POINTS TO PONDER

1. Consider the expanded possibilities for communicating if we master a second or third language.
2. Embracing the role of mentor can be rewarding. Do it with prayer.

CHAPTER 23

TRYING TO FINISH WELL

WITH A WONDERFUL SUMMER BEHIND me, it was time to embrace my final year of teaching in the Alabama public schools back at West Blocton High School. This year my two younger teacher friends took jobs elsewhere, so I was alone again in my car for those eighty miles a day. Thanks to Allan's library work at church, I had a bountiful supply of free cassette tapes and CDs to listen to as I rolled along the interstate and country lanes.

One such tape really impressed me. I had to go home and make notes when my hands were free from the steering wheel. Since the topic was finding God's will for our lives, I knew I would get to practice this sermon soon when I reached retirement and faced the looming question, "What now?"

The teaching was done by Andy Stanley, son of the famed Baptist pastor, Charles Stanley. Andy taught on knowing God's will, which he divided and defined in three categories:

1. Sovereign Will - will occur regardless of what people do. (Example: Jesus will return again.)
2. Moral Will - what He has taught us to do or not do in His word.
3. Personal Will – individual will for our lives.

His strategy for success in obedience to these three areas looked something like this:

We should be familiar with #1 and #2 so that we can narrow our options in decision making when it is time for #3.

Andy explained that his concept of staying in God's will is more like walking through a canyon rather than walking a tight rope. We stay in the broad canyon as we keep our hearts surrendered. When we have difficulty with decisions, we should check with other Christians and saturate ourselves with Bible truth to know God's perfect will (Romans 12).

In the third area (personal will of God), I felt that the neighborhood Bible club should close since my "platter was full" with involvement with the Women's Core group at church and the responsibilities of teaching since school was in session.

Instead of a Mexican restaurant field trip the fall semester, I decided to take the Spanish Club students to a live Mexican folk ballet performance in the state capital of Montgomery, followed by lunch and some free time at a large mall. Some sixty-four students piled into two buses and away we went. They thoroughly enjoyed the trip. I enjoyed seeing them enjoy it and making good memories. Those guys kept me young!

But curricular and extra-curricular activities can take a toll on the body and mind. My physical and spiritual resiliency ran low. In late October, I was attacked with a flu-like sinus infection with chills, fever, and a painful throat. A doctor gave me a steroid shot and a prescription for antibiotics. I missed five school days and a church service on Sunday.

That Sunday morning I turned on my TV set and heard an older Baptist preacher named Ed Young, Sr. Right away he said something like this: "God's got you in a time-out. You've been so focused on the small pictures. You need to see the long picture."

He had my attention. It was true. I had been so focused on job responsibilities, Spanish Club meetings, events, and lesson plans that I had forgotten to think of the students and co-workers as eternal people with eternal destinies. How could I have forgotten after the premature goodbyes of the previous year?

As I sat on the sofa and listened to Ed Young, I felt convicted and really repented deeply to the Lord. I suddenly realized that the pain in the back of my throat was *gone*! Before it was painful to swallow even my saliva, and I certainly could not bear to clear my throat. The pain totally left even though I still had a scratchy voice.

Since I was now more focused on the Lord, I quickly altered lesson plans when I called a dear Pentecostal lady to be my substitute teacher the following day. She mentioned that she was sitting there watching the movie *End of the Spear*, a dramatization of Nate Saint's martyrdom in Ecuador. I scrapped my lesson plans and told her to show that movie (with Spanish subtitles, of course, to make it educational). She did just that and even paid for another day's rental so that the students could finish it the following day.

The next Spanish Club meeting was also on a more spiritual note. One of my students shared slides of her mission trip to a Latin American country, where she served impoverished children. The club voted to donate $500 to that mission program for children. God is so good to re-orient us when we have wandered off course. And Jesus loves, really loves, the little children!

Meanwhile, the Luis and Sharon Saavedra military family was ordered to report to Ft. Bragg in Fayetteville, NC, by November 15. Their furniture followed later, days and days later, but they still offered to host us for Thanksgiving. Allan thought nothing could be finer than to be in Carolina Thanksgiving morning, 2006. That year Allan, Joel, Alison and I spent some time with Allan's brother and his wife (Ben and Martha Gravely) rather than the Alabama clan as usual. We all enjoyed spending family time together, touring NC State, and visiting a potential future church. That trip to NC proved to be a scouting trip.

A LITTLE TALK WITH ALLAN

The call of his home state seemed to be resonating in Allan's brain (and heart). He had been with me in Alabama since 1972. He had recently been doing some thinking, extra thinking. One day we had a talk.

Allan pointed out that I would be retiring from teaching at the end of the school year. I would be able to draw my teacher retirement pension in any location on the globe. Outside Alabama, I could work full-time if I wanted to do so and still qualify for that pension check. He had always wanted to get back to his home soil. Furthermore, none of our children lived in Tuscaloosa any longer. Of the four of them, Sharon now needed us worst of all. Her soldier husband was soon to be deployed to Afghanistan with his unit; she would be alone in North Carolina. Why not move there?

Why not, indeed? It seemed exciting to me. Mother was situated well in a local nursing home with family constantly checking on her. We just needed to sell our home and find one in North Carolina.

On the long Thanksgiving Carolina trip I had some luxurious time to read a good book that Allan had borrowed for me through interlibrary loan. It was *The Lives of the Three Mrs. Judson's* by Arabella Stuart. That free loan service is a gold mine and budget saver!

Having a daily quiet time with the Bible and reading worthwhile biographies has always been my way of obeying the advice (command) of Jesus in Mark 4:24-25b, "...Be careful what you are hearing. The measure [of thought and study] you give [to the truth you hear] will be the measure [of virtue and knowledge] that comes back to you, and more [besides] will be given to you *who hear*. For to him who has will more be given...." (*Amplified Bible*)

This particular biographical book teaches a valuable lesson for any Christian. It is this: suspend judgment about your life's success until the Judgment Day. (I Cor. 4:1-5)

SUFFERING FOR THE GOSPEL

The book I carried along for the Thanksgiving trip was three biographies in one since it portrayed the lives of the three wives of Adoniram Judson. Probably the first one, Ann, impressed me the most. She and her young husband were just beginning to see some success in their missionary efforts in Burma when war broke out with the British. She could have escaped to safety but chose to stay there because her husband had been put in prison. She made almost daily visits to that prison and negotiated with prison guards to get food to him. She sent correspondence back to the West about their ordeal; these accounts were followed with intense interest and made the Judsons well known.

After two suspenseful years, Adoniram was finally released. Ann wrote of her regret that "two years of precious time have been lost to the mission, *unless some future advantage may be gained, in consequence of the severe discipline to which we ourselves have been subject.*"[1] (emphasis mine)

The editor, Arabella Stuart, could not restrain herself from commenting on Ann's words by quoting a Dr. Dowling.[2] I would add my comments to Dr. Dowling's to say to dear Ann, "Your labors were not in vain and, indeed, there was future benefit through your sufferings."

As mentioned before, our own Charles was challenged to report to a foreign duty station after hearing the account of the Judsons' sacrifices. A college in Alabama bears the name Judson in honor of these heroes, Adoniram and his three wives. The Burmese Christians still love them. The Judsons could say with Paul, "Now I rejoice in what was suffered for you, and I fill up in my flesh what is still lacking in regard to Christ's afflictions, for the sake of his body, which is the church." (Colossians 1:24, KJV)

Seeing suffering for the gospel fleshed out in our earthly bodies speaks a message to everyone: the cause of the Lord Jesus is worth suffering for.

Ann went to an early grave, but God's promise is sure. "For God is not unrighteous to forget your work and labour of love, which ye have shewed toward his name, in that ye have ministered to the saints, and do minister." Hebrews 6:10, KJV

North Carolina was fun at Thanksgiving, and in December, back in Alabama, our family enjoyed a wonderful Christmas together. We were able to Skype Charles in Belgium at no cost. Parents of missionary children do not sacrifice as much as those of long ago who had to wait months for letters from their sons and daughters in distant lands. It was so good to see him on a computer screen and hear his voice. My sacrifice did not seem as great as Hannah's in the Bible, but I determined to have a "Hannah mindset," one that says, "No sacrifice for the gospel is too great." In light of the sacrifice of Jesus, how can we withhold anything from the Lord?

Spring semester, 2007, was all about *closure*. I was winding down my time at WBHS as a Spanish and English teacher, but I still wanted to give the state its "money's worth" and not be a "lame duck" teacher, just marking time till retirement.

We let our church know that we would be leaving. Allan and I made sure the Alabama retirement pension would be in place when needed and that we would be able to access the savings fund I had with the retirement system. It would come in handy with moving expenses. Just $10-$20 per month in investments over the years had paid off with compounded interest growth. It was a special account accessible only after resigning, retiring, or dying!

Spring break in March found Allan and me headed to North Carolina again for house hunting. The beautiful Bradford pear trees were blooming everywhere. They looked like big fluffy balls of white. Sharon's apartment in Fayetteville, NC, was our operating base; Luis had now deployed from Ft. Bragg to Afghanistan.

We prayed and did some house researching online. It is always good to be specific when we pray. We definitely wanted (1) a house with vinyl or brick to avoid that dreaded paint brush, (2) a house with no stairs to climb in our latter years, (3) a house with a garage or carport to avoid rainfall when getting into or out of the car, and (4) a house located between Fayetteville and Raleigh. Allan's brother was in Raleigh; a church we were considering was near Raleigh. Also, we wanted to give Sharon and Luis in Fayetteville some space from their Gravely in-laws.

Location was a big factor since desirable homes in our price range were mostly found between the urban areas. After eliminating some older brick homes with all their aging problems, one day—there it was!! THE HOUSE. It was a newer home, vinyl, and one-level in the Angier community just off Hwy. 210, a connector to Fayetteville and Raleigh. The back deck and screened-in porch reminded us of a beach home. We peeked through the windows and front door panels to see a spacious open area of kitchen, living room, and dining room. We could imagine our children, future grandchildren, friends and home groups filling up that space! We imagined many happy faces and scenes there. A military family had already moved out and really wanted to sell.

My researcher husband saved our realtor, Mr. Walton, all the effort in locating our home. But we had not seen the interior yet. Mr. Walton came in pouring rain to show us the inside of our dream home. He attended the Apex, NC, church we visited during our Thanksgiving trip, the church that our son, Joel, had recommended.

Well, we needed some more closure that spring, namely, closure on two houses, one in Alabama and one in North Carolina. Real estate details lay ahead!! I was thankful Allan had once done real estate.

The Alabama home that had seemed like a lake retreat for our children had to be painted and cleaned up for sale. That living room Crimson Tide red carpet had to go. Imitation wood flooring replaced it, and a contract came soon.

Allan's desire to live near Lake Tuscaloosa had paid off big time. Our house appreciated a great deal because the city of Northport was moving our way. As mentioned, the new Tuscaloosa County High School was built only three miles away. With TCHS came more stores, banks, restaurants, and fast foods. Our elementary school zone was more and more desirable for young families. Allan took care of the housing transactions while I returned my focus to teaching.

WBHS did not participate in the annual Spanish Club convention my last spring there. The date was on a day that school was not in session, and I accompanied my husband to his fiftieth high school reunion in Charlotte, NC. He enjoyed the event, especially seeing a former English teacher who had recommended him for honor's English and, consequently, set a new course for his future scholastic efforts. Teachers really do touch other lives.

I was very happy to learn that the *predecessor* of my WBHS job would also be my *successor*. Mrs. Collins had left to be a missionary to Mexico four years earlier; her family was returning to West Blocton. Mexico was becoming dangerous. She would resume her former duties in her classroom just as she left them. I had held her place for her. My students would be in good hands. My prayer for a successor had been answered very well. (Numbers 27:15-16)

At last, May 25, 2007, arrived. Back in 1965, it had been my high school graduation day, the day I walked away from my high school feeling free from schoolwork. This year, it was my official retirement day. I also walked away from this dear old high school with a wonderful free feeling. My duties there were finished. WBHS had given me a gift, self-esteem. There I had felt fulfilled as a teacher. I no longer considered myself a failure in that line of work and was so grateful for four wonderful years in a niche where I fit at last after my arduous investment into higher education and discouragement in the early years of teaching.

That final year at WBHS was the finale of my twenty-four and one half years of service in the State of Alabama educational system. I was sixty years old; that age qualified me to draw the Alabama retirement at a rate based on my three highest paying years. Initially I had only hoped to survive a minimum of three years as a teacher wage earner; that was the plan that I had worked, according to Coach Bryant's advice. Thanks to WBHS, I was able to serve my students six years in Alabama.

I could only wonder what would lie ahead in Allan's home state, North Carolina. Was I willing to go with this man, just as Rebecca was asked in Genesis 24? Oh, yes. ABSOLUTELY!

POINTS TO PONDER

1. Faithfulness at a duty station should not diminish till completion of the assignment.
2. We marvel when God does things that we never would have thought about. (Isaiah 55:8-9) Our job is to trust Him as our lives unfold.
3. Should we be specific when we pray? So I say to you: Ask and it will be given to you; seek and you will find; knock and the door will be opened to you. Luke 11:9

CHAPTER 24

LOOKING EAST TO NORTH CAROLINA

THE FIRST TWO WEEKS OF June were spent at Sharon's apartment in Fayetteville, NC. From that launch pad, I scouted for a teaching job, but schools there were still in session, and principals were still trying to close out their school year and were not focused on hiring for the fall.

Although there was no success in job hunting, we did enjoy a great time with Sharon. We celebrated her birthday early at a Vietnamese restaurant; I made her a key lime pie. She experienced the soldier-wife loneliness from the absence of her husband away at war. Until recently I had been clueless about the tremendous sacrifices of our military families.

Allan, Sharon, and I also celebrated Father's Day together. We went to church together and ate out. I even got in on the gift giving and presented Allan with a Carolina blue shirt and a UNC baseball cap. He was pleased, pleased!! That Tar-heel glowed with delight. He proved that "you can take the boy out of Carolina, but you can't take Carolina out of the boy."

Back in Alabama we saw Alison and found out that she and Charles would help take *this* girl out of Alabama. Alison had just returned from a trip to Belgium where Charles had hosted her and taken her to Paris for some touring. She also paid a visit to my

German friend from Northington and Belmont Apartments days, Godula, now a widow in Germany. Alison also had summers off as a teacher.

Charles was sacrificially planning his vacation time for our up-coming moving dates. We would close on our Alabama home July 13 and on the NC house July 16. How thankful we were to know that Sharon's home would be available to us during that transition weekend. And how thankful we were that Alison and Charles would assist in loading the large U-Haul truck and the U-Haul trailer to be attached to the Jeep and help us with the driving. Families are wonderful, God's idea!! We were also thankful for long-time friend, Ronnie Fowler, and one of Charles's Chi Alpha friends, Craig Woodham, for their help in loading the household goods. We felt as if we were the aging Abraham and Sarah starting over in a new place.

Our transition promise came from Psalm 107:7. "He led them by a straight way to a city where they could settle." NIV

The *city* was Angier, NC. The *straight-way* was along comfortable interstates and, near the end, along a state highway. Alison and I drove the Jeep. It was stressful to accelerate up an entrance ramp of the Interstate and not know if it would be clear to merge into traffic. Having to stop on the ramp with a heavily loaded trailer's weight behind our vehicle was not that easy. But time and again it seemed an unseen hand had cleared the way before us. The little caravan arrived safely in NC. Allan was home again.

I had prayed that the real estate dealings would transpire without a "hitch." That prayer was answered, and we moved into our new home in peaceful little Angier, pronounced "ANN-jer" by the locals.

OUR NEW LIFE IN NC

When God begins to nudge us to change our circumstances, He is so gentle yet persistent. I felt His nudges at times months before leaving Alabama as I made my journey home at the end of the school day. There was that insurance company billboard that said, "Let's talk about your future." It seemed I should respond to God (not the billboard) and say, "Yes, Lord. Let's talk." Then, there was that beautiful sunset just over the horizon with the accompanying desire for other horizons ahead, different horizons. Anticipation had begun to grow.

Finally, when retirement was a "done deal," I began to wonder what mindset I should assume in my new surroundings. Should I act as the old horse turned out to pasture? Should I be ambitious and seek part-time employment, some mini-career? Was God putting me on the shelf?

The answer to all these ponderings was "NO." But I had to wait a while to get that answer.

Meanwhile, God had a special treat for us, especially for Allan. All of his life, this NC native had wanted to see the famous Outer Banks (OBX) off the coast of NC but had never had the opportunity. He got his wish almost free of charge! That wish came true through military contacts.

Since Luis was currently deployed to Afghanistan, Sharon leaned heavily on the military wives support group known as Protestant Women of the Chapel (PWOC). She got to know one of the leaders well (we will call her Mrs. M) and agreed to do some art for the upcoming conference speakers. The art would be included in "illustrated sermons" and later presented to the speaker as a gift. Sharon was treated to a visit to Mrs. M's home in beautiful Manteo in the Outer Banks. There they made plans for the conference, and Sharon began preparing her art. Mrs. M truly enjoyed being a hostess. Since her husband was also deployed, she even invited Allan and me to come and visit and stay in her home near downtown Manteo. Did we accept? Oh, yes.

Mrs. M's mom was also in town and led our tour of Manteo and fed us fresh caught shrimp. We also saw the famous Wright

Brothers Museum at Kitty Hawk, Nags Head beach, and the large sand dunes on Kill Devil Hills. From the top of the dunes, we saw the vast Atlantic Ocean on one side and the Roanoke Sound on the other side. Allan had learned to swim as a young boy in the Sound near Wrightsville Beach at Wilmington, NC. He was in his element at OBX. God was so good to His "boy" to give him this little vacation.

In late July, my waiting for an answer about employment was finally over. I was hired for a full-time teaching job within twenty-four hours of the interview! It seemed miraculous. Here's how that incredible feat happened.

I always searched the online job listings in education very carefully. I really wanted a position at that high school situated only three miles from my home, but—alas—there were never any Spanish or English positions open. Reluctantly, I did apply for a middle school Spanish job about fourteen miles away. Then in late July, I finished an interview for an English position at a junior high next to the nearby high school.

At the conclusion of the interview, I thought, "Why not just drop off a resume at that high school, even though no opening is posted?"

After all, I had all my paperwork with me, and I was dressed up in a power suit.

By this time it was about 5:00 PM, but the school's front door was unlocked, and a few students were on the parking lot. The school office was unlit, but I saw a light in a back room. No one responded to my loud knocking, so I started back out to my car. But just before reaching the school's front door, a gentleman in business casual clothes came out a side door.

"Hello, is the principal here?" I ventured.

He replied, "That depends. Are you an angry parent?"

I assured him I was only a teacher looking for a job. He said, "Please tell me you teach Latin."

I said, "No, Spanish. And I know there are no openings, but I just wanted to leave a resume."

He surprised me when he said, "There might be."

He was the principal. He invited me to sit down for an impromptu interview. Just the day before, the newly hired Latin teacher had decided to work elsewhere. Since Latin teachers were scarce and the new school year was at hand, the principal and counselor were considering reworking the master schedule to add other units of Spanish and an online unit of Latin II to accommodate the demand for foreign language courses. The principal checked my references, cleared my employment with his superiors, and the next day offered me a job teaching Spanish I and II. Yippee!! I accepted.

The principal's wife attended our first faculty session and met me. She said her husband came home that night of our interview and told her that my stopping by his office "was like a gift; she just walked in." I agreed. The job was a gift from my heavenly Father. My duty station was only three miles away from home!

By working full-time and drawing my Alabama retirement, Allan and I were able to get out of debt. That had been a goal for some time. Since he had to take an early retirement, we were not as financially sound as we had wanted to be when we left Alabama. But since Allan was retired, a major benefit of his having more time was his watchful management of our finances. He was able to move our debts to low interest rates, save us hundreds of dollars, and expedite closure of outstanding accounts. He is my resident accountant!

Soon school began, and I began getting acquainted with another rural community as distinct as West Blocton. This one also enjoyed Friday night football (with a *very* winning team) and several other sports and clubs. Most of the students were well behaved and were earning their Spanish credits for advanced diplomas.

One club was missing at my new school, Harnett Central High School (HCHS). There was not a Christian fellowship group for all the students; there was only one for athletes.

In September, I found out that no one was organizing the national "See You at the Pole" event. By this time I had discovered the strong Christians among my students. They were eager to participate in such an event, so a few of us Christian teachers encouraged them to go for it.

About thirty-five students, parents, and teachers circled around the pole and prayed in late September. A small nucleus of teenage friends stayed afterwards and held their own devotional time before school began. They wished this could happen monthly.

This hunger in the students made me pray about starting a First Priority chapter here. First Priority was unknown in this area, and I was unsure about where to begin. I cleared the idea with the administration and ordered a CD-ROM from the national FP office. The excitement about the club among the Christian students grew. This venture needed to be saturated with prayer.

I set aside the morning of Saturday, October 13, to fast about that unruly fourth period class and also the establishment of First Priority at HCHS. But school was going to take a back seat to my interests for a while. Mother died that night.

My younger brother, Ruel, had called earlier that day to tell me Mother was having trouble breathing. She told him, "I'm going; I'm going."

Nurses gave her oxygen and a shot of morphine. A nurse found her sleeping soon, but fifteen minutes later on the next check for vital signs, the nurse noticed that Mother had left this life.

MOTHER'S STORY

My mother's life would make a colorful movie or TV series. In fact, a life with some parallel chapters was portrayed in Catherine Marshall's *Cristy*, a novel and TV series about her own mother's days as a one-room school teacher. Though I do not possess the writing skills of Catherine Marshall or Laura Ingalls Wilder, some space here is due to the recounting of my mother's singular life.

That life began in humble circumstances, in the home of poor sharecroppers, Virgil Grover Harris and his young bride, Annie Greenfield Hampton Harris, both of Lawrence County, Alabama. Annie had a full-blooded Indian grandfather. Little Mae (Mother) was the second child and first daughter. By age four she was already babysitting younger siblings so that her mother could work in the fields. Eventually she had six brothers and three sisters; all but the short-lived youngest worked in the cotton fields of the landlords. In her later years, she was still able to list in order the various landlords they served.

Each fall the children's schooling had to be delayed until "the crops were in." School was a delight for Mae. Unlike her siblings, she loved to learn and read. She studied her lessons until Papa made her turn off the lamp. Because she always had to work in the fields in the fall, she always had to catch up with her classmates and classes, which had already been going for two months.

Her senior year finally arrived in the fall of 1927. Sometimes she had to ride her horse to Mt. Hope High School near Moulton, AL. One day it reared up when she tried to mount. She removed the saddle to find a small burr below the saddle blanket. She graduated in the spring of 1928, right on time with her class.

A dream developed in Mother's heart to become a school teacher. But how? Her Papa knew a way. In 1928 he asked a lawyer that he knew for a loan for his Mae to go to college one year. The lawyer agreed. One year was all that was required then for a teaching certificate. Since the Great Depression began the following year, it is doubtful that loan would have been made in 1929. I am so thankful that Mother studied hard and kept up with her age group.

Promotional leaflets from Livingston State Teachers College (now the University of West Alabama) in Livingston, Alabama, lured her to that campus in southwest Alabama. An aunt and uncle rode the train with her to this exciting destination. She truly lived the college dream that year, enjoying her classes and bonding with her roommate, Christina.

Sadly, during that year she came home after hearing the news that her little five-month-old baby brother, Curtis, had succumbed to pneumonia. But over all, it was a rewarding year of good grades, new friends, and "that college experience."

With college behind her, she was ready in the fall of 1929 to begin her ten-year teaching career. She relished those days of being the one-room teacher in Lawrence County. Tall boys towering over her five-foot-two frame had to obey her or leave the school. Down through the years many of her students looked her up and came by for a visit. Two notable (and providentially placed) students in her class were sisters, Vivian and Viola.

Miss Mae was boarding with a local family that sometimes discussed Mae's marital status. She told the lady of the home her usual line, "I'm not getting married until I find someone who doesn't smoke, drink or 'cuss.'"

Her own mother had told her she would die single for such a standard in Lawrence County. But Miss Mae's hostess instantly commented, "I know just the man for you, Bob Childers."

It turned out that Bob sometimes made extra money carrying local folks to town in his car. It also turned out that Mae's students, Vivian and Viola, were his sisters. She sent a message home with them. They approached Bob with a question, "Are you busy Saturday?"

"Yes. Why?" he asked.

"The teacher wants to hire you to take her to town."

He quickly decided, "No, I'm not busy."

That Saturday Mae (Mother) saw Bob (Dad) for the first time and instantly fell in love, she said. I really believe God enjoys His match-making. There is much behind-the-scenes activity in heaven in the implementation of Psalm 68:6a: "God setteth the solitary in families...." (KJV) Dad's dark black hair, car, and musical skills helped the implementation along, no doubt!

Their courtship was the talk of the community. Both were about twenty-seven years old. His shy proposal came something like this:

"Do you suppose we'll ever marry?"

Her response: "Not if we don't set a date."

His response: "All right. You pick a date."

It was settled within moments. Mother chose her birthday, November 24, 1937, near Thanksgiving. They were married in Mother's classroom and moved into their modest first home with its limited furnishings. Their two solitary lives became one.

During the winter months when Dad could not work outdoors with logging or farming, he was willing to let his teacher-wife raise his education level up from fourth to eighth grade. But at that point, he decided that was enough. Mother no doubt knew that life with a poorly educated man would be difficult, but she made that decision and stood by it throughout the years of hard farm work. Once she left that school, she never taught again in the classroom except briefly in a private school in Chicago or in public schools as a substitute teacher in later years. She reminds me of characters in Willa Cather stories who leave a measure of culture behind to embrace a more difficult pioneer life.

Mother did continue teaching until December of the following school year. That is when she and Dad welcomed their first child, Bobby Ray. Her teaching career ended as motherhood began.

During some of her years of teaching during the Great Depression era, the school board could not afford to pay her full salary amount. Instead, she was given promissory notes called "conscripts." While she was still single, the total amount of the conscripts was finally paid, and Mother had a small "nest egg" to become a property owner. A relative had told her about some cheap land in nearby Morgan County. She purchased several hundred acres of woods and farmland as she continued to teach in Lawrence County.

One section of the land became a gift to Mother's parents, the sharecroppers who never owned their own place. Family members cut timber from the land to build them a home. A son-in-law did the electric wiring. My grandparents lived just down the road from the old "L" shaped house that became our home after Mother's teaching career ended. There the young parents welcomed the rest of their children.

Those two love-birds were excellent role models for us in the art of staying in love. (None of their eight children experienced the agony of divorce.) It was common to see Mother and Dad holding hands throughout their marriage. They enjoyed forty-five years together. Although Mother relished her college and teaching days and Dad thrived in his church in the role of song leader and deacon, probably both of them considered their greatest accomplishments to be their eight children, twenty-one grandchildren, twenty-nine-and-counting great-grandchildren, and the twenty foster children they hosted in their humble home during their retirement years. Everyone knew that Mother's heart was big enough to love them all. Many of them have made their way to her door to spend some time with "Mother" or "Grandmother." Some of the foster children still attend our family reunions.

When we left her in Alabama in July, 2007, I really did not expect to see Mother alive again. A friend who worked at the nursing home had told us that Mother was becoming less responsive. I took comfort in an account of one of my heroes who left his aging father and mother behind to go to a distant land. That hero was John Paton, missionary during the 1800s to cannibals in the

New Hebrides Islands in the South Pacific (now Vanautu). After John's elderly dad prayed with him before his departure for the islands, John said he "knew to a certainty that when we rose from our knees and said farewell, our eyes would never meet again till they were flooded with the light of the Resurrection Day."[1]

I felt the same certainty in my farewell to Mother. We wait with the Patons for that resurrection light to flood our new eyes that will not have glaucoma, cataracts, or macular degeneration. Come, Lord Jesus.

Mother's funeral was conducted at a local funeral home to accommodate the number of people we expected. My siblings asked Allan to lead a prayer at the service. He wrote such a touching prayer tribute that one relative called later and asked for a copy. Below is the prayer in its entirety:

A Prayer of Commemoration and Thanksgiving for the Life of Mrs. Mae Harris Childers

OCTOBER 17, 2007

Let us pray.

Our Father, we are thankful for the life of Mrs. Childers. We who are gathered here are sad because she is no longer with us, but we are grateful and joyful that she finally has entered fully into eternal life with her Redeemer.

We are thankful, Lord, that by your sovereign mercy and grace you called her to yourself when she was a young woman, and showed the outworking of your grace in her life in more than seventy years of a faithful life.

We are thankful, Lord, that we have known and benefited each one of us, in some way or other, from the life and labors of Mrs. Childers.

As a Christian wife and mother, she diligently taught the precepts of your Word at home to her children and at church as a teacher.

As wife, mother, foster mother, grandmother, counselor, and friend–she was a patient, kind person, able to endure hardship with calmness and fortitude, and, by her example, to inspire others to live in the same way.

Lord, help us to take from her legacy some semblance of these qualities for our own lives because we know that their source was her faith in You, her Savior.

We thank You that her labors on earth are now ended and that she is safely home with You. Our prayer is that the memory of her life will always remain fresh in the minds of those who knew and loved her. In Jesus name, we pray. Amen

On the back of the printed funeral service program, our family was able to include the gospel by using the beautiful words from Ronnie Freeman's song, "Home Forever," and also to have it playing along with other songs as people were being seated.[2] (I had asked him well in advance for his permission to use it when I saw him at Alison's Birmingham church.) Its words both soothe and direct inquirers toward Jesus by inviting them to follow the believer home to a place with no more blinded eyes; they warn of delaying in making that lifetime decision to say an eternal "yes" to the Lord.

The minister, a former pastor of my parents, honored both the Lord and Mother in his remarks in the chapel and also at the graveside service several miles away. That October day in Alabama was sunny and pleasant. Mother's children sat in a row of chairs alongside the open grave. It was front-row seating for a close-up viewing of death. That unwelcoming hole looked like an enemy. But the minister said, "Even here we are victors."

Yes, we do not have to be intimidated by death. This last enemy will be defeated one day. (I Cor. 15; II Cor. 5:1) But the same chapter that promises the demise of death closes with a charge to Christians still on earth to be "abounding in the work of the Lord." (I Cor. 15:58 KJV) There was some unfinished work of the Lord waiting for me in North Carolina. I returned to pursue it.

POINTS TO PONDER

1. God can be our "constant" in times of change.
2. In Jesus, death has lost its sting although separation is painful.
3. God provides in His time and in His way. Meanwhile, we develop patience.

CHAPTER 25

FIRST PRIORITY IN NORTH CAROLINA!

THE DAY THAT MOTHER DIED, I had been praying about that difficult fourth block class at school and about the opening of a new First Priority chapter at Harnett Central High School (HCHS). Those prayers were swiftly being answered. When I returned to NC and my classes, even the students in that fourth block class seemed to have sympathy for me because of my recent loss. One ornery football player even walked to the front of the room and gave me a hug. Teenagers really do have a capacity to love and reach out if given the opportunity. There were still challenges in the class but some improvement.

And plans were taking shape for our first meeting of First Priority. Three other Christian teachers joined me to help lead the group. The principal gave us approval. The day to begin arrived on October 31, 2007. I reminded the students that Martin Luther had started something for God on October 31, the Protestant Reformation. I also told them that in all future meetings they would be in charge and I would be seated in the back of the room. We chose 7:00 A. M. Wednesday mornings for our meeting time, in my classroom.

The students wrote a "thank you" note to the principal. One student personally thanked me for starting the club. Her mother told me later that her tenth-grade daughter had been discouraged and sensed that her school was becoming so "secular." These young people were hungry for God. They met together before school on their own initiative to pray and have devotions. I knew that God loved them as much as He loved the kids in Sherman, Texas, or West Blocton, Alabama. I felt expectant of good things ahead. I was not disappointed.

The weekly meetings were running between fifteen and twenty students. They planned their own music and speakers or activities. I sat in the back of the room. Then they decided to join other clubs on the monthly Club Day during school-day hours and host a meeting in my room. On the first Club Day, some forty-three students crowded into my classroom.

On another occasion, some of the FP girls set up a table in the indoor atrium between the cafeteria and the gymnasium with a First Priority poster they had made. There they solicited students to sign bandanas to be sent to our soldiers at war. All this was their idea.

Just as the national office recommends, our group had a supporting network of pastors and parents who gave of their time and resources. One grandfather gave a donation of money shortly before his death. I gave a tithe of the meager inheritance money from my mother to buy biscuits and juice for one of our breakfast outreaches.

Christmas Blessings, 2007

Our first Christmas in North Carolina was especially wonderful. All of our children were here, but not Luis. He was still in Afghanistan. We also got to see Allan's NC Gravely relatives. We ate together, played "Mafia," saw the *Amazing Grace* movie on William Wilberforce's life, attended church, and even did a family portrait.

The family decided to give each other a personalized prayer, scripture promise, or blessing to be read aloud on Christmas morning. I still treasure all of the personal words my family gave me: a poem from Alison that she wrote herself, an exhortation from Allan to keep on sowing gospel seeds, a Proverbs 31:31 prayer from Sharon that God would give me everything I deserve. But one encouragement from Charles was soon to happen. He wrote: "Mama, for this year, I'm praying for the revival that's to come in your school."

A revival? I knew enough about revivals to know that they begin with prayer and "prayer burdens." The FP students and I already had a weighty concern for the students at HCHS. One afternoon after school, one of our FP students dropped by my room for a chat about a "burden" he had. It had become a dream in his heart. We will call him Jay.

Jay, a senior, was one of our leaders. I learned that Jay had mostly attended Christian schools or been home-schooled his first eleven educational years, but before his senior year, he had felt God leading him to attend public school. He came to HCHS and got involved with First Priority. Now he sat in a desk and shared that he could envision a student-led youth rally in the school gymnasium. I was cautious.

Such an endeavor, I knew, would take lots of work, coordination, and prayer. I was already seemingly "maxed out" with my teaching responsibilities. On the other hand, I did not want to dampen Jay's enthusiasm. I counseled him to first run this idea by his godly, pastor father and also his youth pastor. If they agreed, he should come back and talk to me further about it.

He came back with a "green light" from both! He assured me that he would do all the work; all he needed from me was to get clearance from the school.

On January 21, 2008, I was off work for Martin L. King Day. I was in Fayetteville with Allan and Sharon, but they did not need me to line up contractors for the house they were "flipping," so I had some time to pray. (Sharon, the ultimate Proverbs 31 lady, bought a house. With her dad's help, she was renovating it to sell, even while her husband was deployed!)

As I sought the Lord, I seemed to be getting some green lights of my own, some "yes" and "amen" promises about the youth rally idea. These positive words lifted right off the page to me:

Proverbs 16:3 – "Commit to the Lord whatever you do, and your plans will succeed." (NIV)

Mark 9:23b – "Everything is possible for him who believes." (NIV)

Matthew 7:7 – "Ask and it will be given to you; seek and you will find; knock and the door will be opened to you." (NIV)

Psalm 108:13 – "Through God we shall do valiantly; for he it is that shall tread down our enemies." (KJV)

In late February, Allan and I attended a youth rally organizational meeting in Jay's home with his parents and youth pastor. I shared with them that it had been easy to lead the charge for the See You at the Pole event and setting up First Priority, but I did not feel the strength to take on the youth rally. They all assured me that local churches were going to work together to make this new challenge happen. I had already secured permission from the principal; my part was almost over.

True to their words, Jay's family and the other Christians whom they recruited took care of all the financial and decision-making efforts for the rally. There was a rental fee for the school facilities. Jay set up intercessory prayer cells to cover the event, before and during the rally. We chose Saturday, April 12, 2008, for the date. Meanwhile, we continued our weekly meetings.

During one of our February morning FP meetings, one of our female athletes shared an amazing healing story with the club. Her coach and other athletes attended since she was the speaker. She wanted to tell the story of her Aunt E.

I remembered the day that the athlete stopped one morning by my door where I was required to stand sentinel before class. She stopped to request prayer for her aunt who had just suffered a stroke. I asked her how old her aunt was. She said Aunt E was in her late seventies. She did not want to discuss age; she insisted, "Would you just pray for her?"

I said that I would. After she left to get to class, I lifted up a brief prayer: "Lord, if you are not finished with this lady, would you raise her up?" Others were praying as well.

By that afternoon, Aunt E was off life support and out of the hospital. When I asked the niece the next day or two how Aunt E was doing, she said, "Oh, she's out at Wal-Mart."

That recovery was really an encouragement to this young believer.

For our early April Club Day, FP asked a favorite teacher to speak. He was a math teacher from Romania. He shared very clearly to the fifty students packed into my room that salvation is by faith in what Jesus did to take our punishment, not in our puny good deeds. He explained that he used to go to his Catholic priest to confess his sins in order to be ready to die. Unfortunately, he usually sinned again on his way home! What could he do, move in with the priest? The students listened to every word. American missionaries had shown the teacher God's simple plan of salvation, and the Holy Spirit made him a new person as he transferred his trust to that plan (Christ's work on the cross) instead of his own efforts.

Our April 12 rally date was fast approaching. Everything was ready. A consensus of the steering committee made Jay himself the main speaker. A youth band from a local church would lead the music. The prayer team would be next door in the school auditorium throughout the rally; they would come to the gym at the end to be altar workers. Several folks were fasting and praying.

Finally, that Saturday came. The Crossroads Church youth group band did a wonderful job leading worship on the gymnasium floor. Jay poured out his heart as he spoke so earnestly to his peers at the first annual HCHS youth rally. When he gave the invitation for commitment, about fourteen young people responded. Our FP members made mental notes of those people for follow up. One young lady buried her head against a counselor's shoulder and made her surrender to the Lord.

Christians also made deeper commitments. I noticed one of our FP students leave the youth band, kneel at our "gym altar," and pray for a while. Later, he wiped his eyes and returned to his band position. Only he and the Lord know what commitment was made there, but I know that he volunteered to speak at a future Club Day meeting, before members of the student body who came.

That April day is now history. It spoke volumes to me of what young people can do for God with a little help from the older crowd. I think the spiritual climate that all the prayer produced that spring enabled our students to endure the painful, tragic death of a student who was a dear friend to many. She was killed in a one vehicle accident. Our FP students were able to console and challenge many others who were also grieving.

A PRAYER STORY

Speaking of the "older crowd," about a week after the youth rally, I had a lesson in another use for older people: PRAYER. It happened at 3:44 A. M. EST on a Monday morning. I woke up suddenly because it seemed that I heard the voice of Charles from our living room calling me, "Mama."

Since I knew that Charles was in Belgium, I took this semi-dream or whatever it was as a cue that I was needed to offer up prayer for Charles. I wanted to be sure that I would not drift back to sleep, so I got up and went to another room in the house so that I would not disturb Allan. First, I prayed for Charles's safety, then for his ministry efforts.

After work that day, Allan picked me up, and we rode through beautiful NC countryside to a plant nursery on the edge of little Coats, NC. As he selected some small fruit trees for our yard, I could stand the suspense concerning Charles no longer.

There in remote Harnett County I reached for my cell phone and dialed Charles's number. He happened to be sitting at his computer where the free call was going through. His mellow voice said, "Hello."

When I told him about my prayer, he explained that he was fine, safe and sound. He was grateful for the prayer for ministry efforts. Usually his evangelistic team went out on Thursdays, but that week they decided to go witnessing on Monday. Charles said that the people they contacted "didn't want to stop talking" that day. I had heard of these "over-the-ocean" prayer stories from others but had not been involved in one till then.

Prayers of older—or younger—people must be big on God's agenda. Near the time of this experience I had noticed that the old and gray prophet Samuel told Israel it would be a sin for him to *stop* praying for them. (I Samuel 12:23)

Our prayers for Luis in Afghanistan were heard. He came home safely in time to help Allan and Sharon complete the flip house, sell it, and make a good profit.

BACK AT HCHS

At Harnett Central we continued to pray for direction for FP and our lives. The students chose speakers from among themselves or youth pastors. They planned the once-a-month "hook" activity to reach others. One Saturday, one of my co-sponsor teachers, her sister, and five students went to a local nursing home to sing to patients in the Alzheimer's unit and to plant flowers. The patients sang along on most verses of familiar hymns.

One FP student wanted to have her eighth grade teacher, Mrs. B, come speak. Mrs. B was a local pastor's wife. At the time, she was a retiree who had "done what she could" during her tenure at the Harnett Central Middle School (HCMS) by hosting a Bible study for students there. (Mark 14:8) She agreed to come speak in May at one of our Wednesday morning club meetings. Her testimonies were so refreshing. She told of her comeback from cancer and her son's comeback from a car accident. He suffered a broken back in a car wreck and was told he would never walk or drive again. But he was currently serving a short-term missions assignment in Greece, driving a shift-stick car, and officiating basketball games! In addition, Mrs. B's middle school Bible study group had now grown to 80-100 students under the leadership of a husband/wife teacher team who built upon her foundation. I saw that we FP teacher sponsors were standing on the shoulders of some faithful workers over at the middle school, as well as parents and pastors.

As the school year drew near its closing, our FP students planned their last Club Day meeting. They decided to have a joint meeting with the Fellowship of Christian Athletes in the school cafeteria. They wanted the format to be a mini-concert and testimony time.

That day, May 23, 2008, the cafeteria was filled with students. I stationed myself near the open door of the cafeteria kitchen. Workers were busy within preparing the daily meals, making the usual kitchen noises. Three FP girls sang with a back-up tape. The student who left the youth band to pray briefly at the youth rally shared his testimony. Then Jay, a member of the school choral group, began a solo *a capella.* He chose a simple chorus. His voice swelled out over the microphone and seemed to fill the atmosphere, "Jesus, Jesus, Jesus...." Suddenly, the clanging of pots and pans ceased. I looked to my side and saw that three lunchroom workers had come to join me in the doorway. Then Jay spoke about the Lord. At one point he said he tends to get tearful at the mention of the name of Jesus. One lunchroom staff worker encouraged him, "That's OK, baby."

Jay was leading everyone in a prayer of commitment as the bell rang to end club period. These FP kids were not ashamed to own the name of Jesus before others. How they encouraged me to lay it all down for Him! It seemed to me that Charles's Christmas prayer for revival was being answered. I enjoyed telling him about it. But he currently had some other things on his mind.

POINTS TO PONDER

1. William Carey exhorts us to "expect great things from God and attempt great things for God."[1] God honored the attempt to launch a youth rally. What do you feel inspired to attempt for Him?

CHAPTER 26

TRAVELS AND
ANOTHER ROMANCE

AS USUAL ON MY FIRST day of summer vacation, I took some time to fast and pray and to offer up to God my current concerns: Allan's health and some type of challenge for him in his retirement, Alison's possible transition to Puerto Rico, ministry opportunities for all our family, and Joel's full-time campus ministry work at the University of Maryland where he mentored young men. One interesting item on my prayer list was a developing relationship between Charles and a former staff worker back in Lafayette, LA, Amanda Meadows.

Charles went to Louisiana, his missions base, in June to itinerate in order to fatten his missionary budget and to have time to pursue Amanda. Allan and I wanted to see him, so we decided to fly to Tuscaloosa the same weekend that Charles was going to speak at our former church, Tuscaloosa First Assembly. Amanda had agreed to accompany Charles there. Our friends, Ronnie and Diane Fowler, agreed to host us that weekend; other friends provided lodging for Charles and Amanda.

Alison picked us up Friday at the Birmingham airport. Allan, Alison, and I arrived at Steamer's Restaurant (our rendezvous location) on the Black Warrior River a few minutes before Charles and Amanda did. Soon I saw the pair crossing the parking lot, or should I say, floating across the parking lot? Each one seemed to be enjoying the other's company a great deal! My boy looked so happy, happier than I had seen him in a long time.

Of course, Amanda was treated to a tour of Tuscaloosa, which included the beautiful University of Alabama quad, the new football stadium promenade with statues of championship coaches, and finally some ice cream at Jack's Hamburgers.

Saturday afternoon Diane hosted a fun back yard get-together with several friends. Then there was Sunday church. It was a great weekend, except Allan got a migraine and could not attend the church service. Amanda seemed to feel fine with the Gravely clan and wanted to proceed with the courtship. She was a super girl, the daughter of an Assembly of God pastor and his wife in Colorado. She also felt a call to missions and had been serving for some time with Eric Treuil at the Lafayette Chi Alpha where Charles had served for five years.

PUERTO RICO

Another summer trip opportunity came in July that would require airplane tickets for sure. We were going to an island in the Caribbean. We got involved in this adventure because Alison decided to leave her ESL teaching career behind in Alabama and move to Puerto Rico to improve her Spanish. She had taken a nine-month course at Samford University in Birmingham to be a medical interpreter, but the tremendous responsibility that accompanies being accurate in that field drove her to hone her fluency in Spanish.

Why Puerto Rico? Since Puerto Rico is a U. S. territory, Alison could relocate and work there without the red tape other Latin American locations would entail. She had already made that scouting trip to the island with a group of her church camping friends. She even had a job and a temporary free place to stay for a few days. I honestly cannot remember if she invited us or if we invited ourselves to go along as she got established!

The trip to Puerto Rico was very interesting. We toured two old sixteenth century Spanish forts, hiked in the famous El Yunque national rain forest, and got to hear the little green tree frogs, the *coquíes*. I even imitated the evening sound one of them was making in the patio bush. It answered back to me several times, although I was clueless about the direction of that conversation.

Our hosts those few days were gracious missionaries who were just beginning to learn Spanish. I was able to share some Spanish tips with them. The wife missed her grown daughters. I understood. Moms and grown daughters have a special relationship of mutual respect. (It reminds me of the lemur cats in Madagascar. I read that the mothers and daughters remain close throughout their lives.)

I mentioned to my new friend in Puerto Rico that, in her absence, God would provide her daughters with other "mothers," according to the promise in Mark 10:28-30. At the same time, she could be a "mother" to daughters of other women, even Alison. She did keep a motherly eye on Alison during her time there. Alison's Spanish improved tremendously, and (as usual) she made some first-class, lifelong friends, more "soul sisters" who love God.

YEAR TWO AT HCHS & EUROPE!

The 2008-2009 school year seemed a rerun of the previous one as far as classes and activities went, except perhaps with less intense prayer. First Priority Students were really stepping in and planning and conducting their own meetings.

EUROPE? ME IN EUROPE????

The highlight of that fall was the expectation of a trip to Europe for Allan and me. We could go visit Charles during my days off for Thanksgiving if I took off Monday and Tuesday of that week. If we did not go see him then, we would not get to see him for a long time. The entirety of his Christmas vacation would be spent visiting Amanda at her parents' home in Colorado. We were very pleased with that.

So, we got some extra warm clothes for the trip and got our lost passports replaced. I worked on my French by reading more in my French Bible. Years before I had decided to read it just five minutes a day to build my vocabulary. I do not know pronunciation but can read it somewhat.

That memorable trip was almost surreal to us. We saw Belgium, France, and England in whirlwind fashion. Charles was a gracious host and good cook. He knew how to maneuver through train stations and markets. We left his town of Liege to travel by train *below* the English Channel—about twenty miles—to England.

The homes in Belgium are very vertical since land is scarce. Visitors usually don't knock on the front doors since the family can be found on one of two or three floors. Instead, a handy doorbell rings on all levels of the home, and an equally handy microphone allows the person on the street to identify himself. If he is a welcomed guest, someone within will press an unlock switch to admit the visitor. That made a lasting impression on me, and God used it months later in a corrective dream to identify an area in my life that needed attention.

For Allan, he had a dream come true. Charles arranged for us to stay with a British friend in London who drove us (on the left side of the road) to Gravely, England, where perhaps Allan's ancestor, Joseph Gravely, had lived before coming to farm in Virginia in the 1700s. We were too late to attend the Sunday service in the ancient Gravely church; a church bulletin board flyer advertised the Alpha Course for newcomers or inquirers in Christianity. The old church cemetery's tombstones had dates from multiple centuries. The thirteenth century knight, Robert d'Gravely, was buried inside the church.

A waitress at a local restaurant/pub told us that there in that village the "a" is pronounced *long*, not short as the Virginia and North Carolina Gravelys prefer. Charles said that he suddenly experienced an identity crisis!

The next day our host in London had to go to work. We were on our own. We had just enough time to visit the British Museum (with its special Babylon display) before heading back to Charles's apartment for the night. France was waiting tomorrow!

In Paris, we found a cheap hotel near the Louvre art museum, but it was closed on Tuesdays. A young Alabama Chi Alpha missionary to Paris joined us for some daytime touring at another art museum housed in an old train station. Nearby I saw an old, street-beggar woman trembling in the November cold, holding a cup with a bare hand that needed gloves. I gave her one of mine, knowing I could replace it back home for a dollar. We had been briefed not to give money to beggars to avoid being swamped by them.

That cold, cold evening we saw the Eiffel tower from a distance. It suddenly began to twinkle all over with blue lights. Charles said he had arranged that display just for us! Aggressive street vendors were selling key chains of miniature Eiffel towers to tourists. Charles coached me on pronouncing "Jesus loves you" in French so that I could purchase key chain souvenirs for our other children and witness to the foreign vendor from the West Indies at the same time. What a cold way for a tropical man to make a living!

Before that night, Charles had been thinking of bringing Amanda to the Eiffel Tower to propose. But the cold and the aggressive vendors made Charles decide that he needed to choose another location. She had agreed to come to Belgium just after Christmas. He wanted to give her a ring and make their engagement official then. He would just have to come up with another unique, romantic place.

The following morning we went outside Paris a bit to see Versailles palace and grounds, where French royalty once resided. I saw the tiny bed and bedroom once used by Queen Marie Antoinette. Another room had been used by Napoleon for billiards. He had borrowed the Mona Lisa painting to hang on his wall while he resided there. The gardens and all the gilded extravagance were impressive to us, but it seemed the French had grown disdainful of their ancient royalty. They had allowed the American metal sculptor, Jeff Koons, to display pieces of his modern work right in the middle of the elaborate rooms. That evening we went back to Liege to rest in Charles's apartment.

Finally, we went to Brussels for Thanksgiving Day. We got to eat American Thanksgiving food after all. We went as Charles's guests to a meal for all the American missionaries in their fellowship. It was held in a building used for Belgium Chi Alpha meetings (actually Chi Alpha is called Students for Christ there). All three of us Gravelys got to stay in that building that night so that we could get to the airport early the next day. Our trip was winding down.

At the Brussels airport, the Christmas decorations were beginning to be displayed. The Christmas carols were not yet playing. People everywhere were busy. They seemed to prefer dark grays and browns in clothing for easy cleaning. Charles stood out not just because he is 6'5" but because he wore a bright green hoodie. It was time to tell him farewell.

BACK TO THE USA

When Allan and I arrived at JFK airport in New York, my ears recognized a beautiful instrumental version of "Joy to the World" on the airport speakers. It was good to be back in our USA!

Christmas was fun with the whole family except Charles here in North Carolina. He enjoyed a white Christmas in Colorado, meeting his future in-laws. After the holidays, he and Amanda flew to Belgium. She got a glimpse of Belgium in cold December but still said "yes" to his marriage proposal in a snowy, historical setting near his home, after a fancy meal at a special restaurant. (Her future home lay as far north of the equator as Quebec, Canada.)

Now Amanda and her family had some wedding planning to do. The groom's family had plenty to keep them busy. What a packed year lay ahead!!

POINTS TO PONDER

1. Should successive generations evaluate their heritages and traditions, rejecting some or keeping some?
2. Families and fellow Christians can do global networking. It facilitates maneuvering between cultures.

CHAPTER 27

ONE PACKED YEAR–2009

THE COMING YEAR OF 2009 was historical for our family and nation in many ways. We were anticipating a July wedding. I worked on the last of four "Turning 30" scrapbooks, this time for Joel, our youngest. Sharon and Luis received orders from the Army to relocate to Ft. Lewis, Washington, near Seattle. (When Luis completed his officer training, the Army thought it best to place him away from the men he had once served with while he was enlisted status.) America watched the swearing in of our first African-American president, Barak Obama. Alison was living her dream of teaching post-secondary students because she was hired to teach for the University of Puerto Rico. Allan was happy to have a troublesome bone spur removed from his spine; the spur had been causing him extreme pain. He would also turn seventy in 2009 and be totally surprised at his surprise birthday party. Allan and I began attending a church closer to our home than the Apex church forty-five minutes away. Soon Allan was leading a home group in our living room, just as we had dreamed. Joel would change jobs. Allan and I would again get involved in an Evangelism Explosion program. And I would retire, again! Whew!

Our new church was very supportive of First Priority. The pastor arranged a Fifth Quarter event there for FP after the last varsity basketball game. His friends from the large Fayetteville Manna Church came to help out. It was a good outreach event but not as well attended as we had hoped. One of those friends from Fayetteville was a youth pastor and quarterback for a professional indoor football league there. Later that year, he was a guest speaker for a school-day club meeting. The athletes loved him, and he represented the Lord well.

During my April spring break, Allan and I had the distinct privilege of touring Washington, D. C. with our other hosting son, Joel, who now lived in that area. We saw famous sites such as the White House, the Capitol Building, the Library of Congress, and Arlington Cemetery. Equally or more fulfilling to me was getting to see Joel lead worship at his twenty-something fellowship group and attending his church, Covenant Life in Gaithersburg, MD. He had a tremendous network of friendly friends.

It was during this final semester of teaching that the "Belgium Doorbell Dream" came one night. It was definitely some of that chastening promised in Hebrews 12, the kind that someone has described this way: It "hurts so good."

I dreamed that I was in a second-level room in a Belgium home. Charles told us that Amanda would be arriving soon, so we were expecting to hear the doorbell, followed by her voice on the speaker outside. The bell sounded, and we answered the buzz from the speaker. But the voice below was that of an older woman. She got right to the point as she addressed me: "You are pretty and have a good personality, but you've got to do something about the mean streak in you."

The dream ended abruptly. When I woke up, I had very clear recollection of the mystery woman's words. As I searched my heart, I realized that I had allowed some hardness of heart to creep in, perhaps through toughening myself for the classroom or majoring on disappointments. I resolved to heed this warning and meditated on an old Petra song, "Don't Let Your Heart Be Hardened." Petra's advice for a mean, hardened heart is to keep a meek, pure, thankful heart before the Lord.[1] A Christian mother, wife, and faculty sponsor can't afford a reputation as a "meanie." And God's reputation is at risk too. Thank God for the Belgium Doorbell Dream.

In May, First Priority hosted its second annual youth rally in the school gymnasium. Again it was student planned and directed. A Campus Crusade college student spoke. He and others had attended one of our FP meetings recently when we hosted a college ministry panel. On that panel, we also had an Intervarsity representative, and one teacher shared about a Christian sorority she had joined at UNC. Our students needed to think ahead to their college days and plan to get "plugged in" with Christian support groups there as they had done in high school.

My days of sponsoring First Priority were coming to a close as I approached the end of the school year. I had hoped that other chapters would open here in NC as they had in Alabama, but that did not materialize, so that desire had to die.

I sent an email to our entire faculty to request a replacement for me as club sponsor. A dedicated Christian history teacher who worked two doors down the hall agreed to lead the following year, and three others offered to help her. I had prayed fervently for this to happen one day when I saw in Numbers that Moses prayed for a replacement. - Moses said to the LORD, "May the LORD, the God of the spirits of all mankind, appoint a man over this community to go out and come in before them, one who will lead them out and bring them in, so the LORD's people will not be like sheep without a shepherd." (Numbers 27:16-17 NIV) God was faithful again as He was at WBHS.

With public school teaching in my "rearview mirror," I could begin to focus on an upcoming wedding, one for which I had prayed especially fervent prayers. Charles and Amanda set Friday, July 17, 2009, as their wedding date. The big event was planned on Friday since their Louisiana church had Saturday services.

All of our family, except Luis, traveled to Lafayette, LA, to witness the coming together of two lives dedicated to the Lord. Luis could not get a pass from his military officer training in Augusta, GA, to attend. He sacrificed again and again for our country.

It was a pleasure to meet Amanda's happy parents, the Meadows. Her mom, Billie, shared that a year earlier at Christmas as she was flipping pancakes on her griddle, she suddenly noticed Amanda, her single daughter. Her mother's heart sent up a special prayer that Amanda would have a mate. Billie had felt that Charles was definitely "a keeper" after first meeting him in the past. I certainly agreed.

The wedding ceremony was outstanding. The officiating pastor was the Chi Alpha campus pastor, Eric Treuil. His touching personal comments about the two young people standing before him, in whom he had invested so much, simply made the ceremony perfect. Eric was at times humorous and at times a little tearful. He reminded Charles that Amanda loved her dad; he reminded Amanda that Charles loved his mother. He vouchsafed Charles's character when he affirmed that he was confident that Charles would still be by Amanda's side fifty or sixty years later, God permitting.

The happy couple planned a fun reception in the Chi Alpha Café building with plenty of food. Charles requested that I dance with him as Amanda danced with her dad. I did my best since he asked, but I am not a good dancer. A disc jockey provided non-obnoxious music. The able bodied tried their skills at line dancing. No one seemed in a hurry to leave. The bride and groom were thoroughly enjoying themselves with their loyal friends. Some had come great distances. Finally, the really-really newly-weds made their exit between two rows of well-wishers with sparklers in their hands. A new family had just been launched. God's blessing seemed all over the event.

That day proved to me that Miss Dean was right, back in that ladies prayer meeting at the state convention. Years before she had rebuked me for worrying about my unwed adult children. She warned me that it was better to be single than marry the wrong one. There had been some dead-end relationships along the way in my children's lives, but since I agreed with Dean, I never felt a need to push any of our offspring to hurry to the altar. When uncertain about God's will in various relationships, our family simply prayed, "Lord, bless it or block it."

Nothing blocked Amanda's entrance into the family; contrariwise, there has been only blessing. And the Lord did such a good job finding Charles a mate that I decided I would let Him take care of the last two single Gravelys.

After a honeymoon in Shenandoah Valley, Virginia, Charles and Amanda set their faces toward the both grueling and rewarding task of budget-raising, otherwise known as itinerating. They systematically contacted Louisiana churches to request a window of time in the church services to present their call and need to the congregation, just as Sharon and Luis had done in their early marriage to be home missionaries. Foreign missionary couples are required to have a higher budget figure than single missionaries or home missionaries. The Assemblies of God does not have a pool of funds with which to pay their missionaries. Support comes from churches and individuals. The down side of this method is the lapse of time; the up side is that the sponsors or supporters know their missionaries personally and can pray for them and visit them on the field.

About a month after the wedding, Allan and I looked into becoming "home missionaries" in an Evangelism Explosion (EE) program. Allan had fond memories of his involvement in EE over twenty years earlier. He sensed a growing desire to get involved again. After some Internet research, he found that one church in our area had such a program; it was Colonial Baptist Church in Cary, NC.

That summer Colonial was hosting a "Come and See" version of EE to offer the opportunity to anyone who wanted to "come and see" how EE works. Guests were allowed to go out witnessing with regular members of the EE teams. Allan and I, especially Allan, felt like "Br'er Rabbit in the briar patch," back on familiar ground.

That summer marked the beginning of over nine semesters with Colonial's teams. We and those faithful evangelists block off Monday evenings as a time set aside for sharing our faith. Sometimes we repay a visit to someone who visited church; other times we knock on apartment doors or chat with college students strolling across campus at NC State. Often we do a religious questionnaire in order to engage someone in a discussion about his or her soul's eternal destiny. Sadly, we had not been able to persuade a church closer to home to engage in a deliberate witnessing attempt such as EE. Colonial has graciously permitted us to join them although we do not attend that church.

When I began to dread the twenty-three mile trip from Angier to Cary to do EE after a day at work, I reminded myself of a testimony in Bertha Smith's book, *Go Home and Tell*, describing the 1927 revival in Shantung province of China. A pastor there admitted that before the revival came, he was too lazy to go to the next village to preach. After the revival, he traveled by foot a twenty-five mile circuit to preach in village after village. If he could *walk* that far, surely I can travel in a leather-padded car to go share the gospel; I just make sure to get a good nap before heading to Cary.

We all knew that Sharon and Luis would be leaving us in October, Army's orders, to go to Ft. Lewis, Washington. They had finished their time in Augusta and returned briefly to Fayetteville. They stayed with us a few days as Luis "cleared base" from Ft. Bragg to prepare to report to his new duty station at Ft. Lewis, Washington, near Seattle and Tacoma.

Sharon really wanted to help give her dad a surprise "Turning 70" birthday party, but we had to plan it a little early before they departed. Since we were both now retired and both *at home* all the time, it was very, very difficult to be sneaky. Most of my phone calls and emails to arrange the party had to be done when he was gone or in the shower. He was expecting Joel, Sharon, and Luis (our stateside kids) to be together for cake and gifts, but he had no idea that the living room would be full of our friends. They parked in the neighbors' driveways. We did it. He was totally surprised.

A few days after the party, Sharon & Luis had to depart for Washington, but Sharon prayed that her dad would be able to lead someone to the Lord on his actual seventieth birthday, October 19, 2009, during the weekly Monday night outreach visits with EE at Colonial Baptist. That did not happen Monday night, but the following day, it did!!

Allan & I were returning home from a trip to Raleigh, when he remarked that he would like to tour the campus of Meredith College.

"Yeah," I agreed, "let's see the fall leaves on the trees there." It was a beautiful "Indian summer" day.

We turned off the highway to see the school he had often heard about but never seen. We strolled around the quiet campus for a while, taking in the pretty fall scenery. Then we came to a non-functioning water fountain surrounded by a small shallow, now-empty pool. It had an inscription impressed into the white cement. As I recall, it read, "And whosoever will, let him take the water of life freely." (Rev. 22:17c KJV) There was no water, no life, no movement in the fountain; apparently all the water had been turned off for repairs or budget cuts. The school had once been owned by Baptists but had become privately owned. The fountain seemed symbolic of something that once had offered "living water" to hungry people but now did not.

As we were checking out the old, unused fountain, a coed approached us. She welcomed us to her campus and answered some of our questions. She was very friendly and helpful and did not seem in any hurry to move along. Somehow our conversation turned to God. She listened thoughtfully, and eventually Allan led her in a prayer of surrender of herself to the Lord. She told us enthusiastically about a favorite chaplain on campus and recommended that we check out the chapel. We did just that before heading on down the highway toward home. Later I was able to make Facebook contact with the student. It was a privilege and pleasure to meet her.

Allan and I had moved to North Carolina to support a soldier's wife, Sharon, during her warrior's deployment. Now they were safely relocated in Washington State on the opposite coast. Americans are very transient folks. Soon another family shuffle was going to alter the proximity of our clan members.

POINTS TO PONDER

1. Psalm 71 is for older saints who still want to be useful for God.
2. Proverbs 18:22 "He who finds a wife finds what is good and receives favor from the LORD." (NIV) A friend said if a man found a wife, he was probably looking for one. People can cooperate with God in this process.

CHAPTER 28

An Unforgetable Year

If 2009 was historical, well…it cannot compare with 2010! It started with a bang when Alison decided to move back home from Puerto Rico. Like Elijah's brook, her job at the University of Puerto Rico was drying up. (I Kings 17:1-7) The school did not offer her sufficient classes for her financial needs. It was great having our younger daughter home again. She and I began some part-time work for the Central Carolina Community College system, working with ESL and GED students.

Allan worked a while for the 2010 census. Charles was ordained for ministry. He and Amanda picked up a little money by being "extras" in the *Secretariat* movie, filmed in their city of Lafayette, LA.

Then there was that phone call on Easter morning and another one on Mother's Day morning. First, Sharon and Luis called early April (Easter Day) to announce that Sharon was pregnant, after over ten years of marriage! Then, Charles and Amanda called on Mother's Day to tell us their news; Amanda was pregnant. We felt as if we had just won two lotteries! We would have to wait till the following November and January to meet our first grandchildren; Allan would be seventy-one years old.

Allan's Unknown Family Discovered
The summer of 2010 marked a wonderful milestone for Allan. He discovered some lost family members. He had left his North

Carolina heritage behind him since his twenties and rarely got back "home." He had settled into Alabama with me since 1973 and participated in my family connections with few from his own lineage. No wonder he was thrilled to connect at last with some Carolina cousins he had never met!!

Through a new family at church, the Shelors from Virginia, we learned that they were just a few of many cousins from the Shelors of Floyd County, Virginia, all Allan's relatives. In the early 1800s two young Jefferson sisters, first cousins of Thomas Jefferson, had married two Shelor brothers and settled in that lovely mountainous area. One of the sisters, Nannie Luvenia Jefferson Shelor, was "Grandmother" to Allan's dad and "Mother" to Allan's staunch old matriarch, Grandmama Nan (Nannie Luvenia Shelor Gravely of Monroe, NC).

The Shelors multiplied abundantly in Floyd County and even held a bi-annual family reunion on their own Shelor campground, originally the property of patriarch Captain Daniel Shelor. Captain Daniel's old iron furnace (or its replacement) still stands there today. He fought in the Revolutionary War and was awarded land for his service. In his sixties, he took off to fight in the War of 1812 but arrived too late. The war was over. His patriotism was passed down through his descendants; many Shelors donned military uniforms to stand behind their country.

Allan seemed to have found a family he never knew existed although he knew some family history. To me it seemed that this was God's reward to him. The Shelors welcomed us with open arms; we were allowed to stay in the Shelor lodge on the camp property, simply because we were "family." (See http://shelorfamily. org/lochist.htm.)

While staying in Floyd County, we went an hour's drive east and took a short tour of Henry County, home place of the Gravelys. There we gleaned more Gravely history from a distant cousin, Desmond Kendrick, who happened to be the county archivist. He provided photos of Allan's grandfathers through successive generations back-wards to the son of Joseph Gravely himself, the Leatherwood, Virginia, patriot from England who fought in the battle of Guilford Courthouse in North Carolina and helped stop Cornwallis. We saw a split-log tobacco curing shed Joseph had built and the land he once worked as a farmer in the late eighteenth century.

We learned that Patrick Henry had once defended one of the Primitive Baptist preachers in the Leatherwood area when it was illegal to be a Baptist preacher in Virginia. Patrick Henry had retreated to the mountains near Leatherwood to escape malaria near the coast; a historical marker points toward where his home once stood, and two counties bear his name, Patrick and Henry.

Our guide, Desmond, showed us some of the old Baptist meet-ing houses and took us to a nearby grassy cow pasture. The pasture included a neglected family burial plot of six of Allan's grandpar-ents. Some graves had been marked off with a small fence and preserved. Other tombstones had been knocked over by grazing cows and lay hidden among the tall grass. One lost grave there was that of Grandfather John King, the one-legged preacher.

But John King's testimony has not been lost. This early pioneer left a tremendous legacy in his day. Allan was thrilled, actually super-excited, in later research to find in a book of early Baptists in Virginia the actual account of John King's conversion and in-fluence. It seemed amazing to me for him to stumble upon the record of his ancestor's journey of faith.[1]

It was interesting that within a few miles radius of Joseph Gravely's habitats, we could stand in front of gravestones of these King and Gravely men who ultimately gave me my husband; their time on earth was not in vain, at least not from my perspective!! Allan was the great-grandson of the great-grandson of Joseph Gravely. He was experiencing a certain reunion with his fathers. I noticed that Acts 13:36 in the French Bible says that David [at death] was reunited with his fathers, "...a été *réuni* à ses pères...."

(emphasis mine) Allan thoroughly enjoyed this small token of a reunion here on earth; I enjoyed seeing his happiness.

Allan also attended the 200-year-old Thanksgiving family reunion of his mother's relatives near Greenville, NC, the Tyson-May reunion. I found out that in North Carolina, the old saying holds true: "It matters who your pappy is."

A LOCKET FOR ALISON

During all the happy family times, like Amanda's mother, I noticed my unwed daughter Alison, alone. My mother-heart, like Amanda's mom's, was also longing for my daughter to see a mate walk into her life.

One day in a local store, I noticed a pretty locket-necklace on sale. It opened up to provide space for two small photos. I had a locket with my photo across from the love of my life, my Allan. Alison had no one to photograph for that space. I bought that locket that day and hid it in my dresser drawer, not telling anyone except the Lord. I prayed that He would bring the right man to fill that spot in Alison's life and his photo to fill its spot. I looked forward to the day that I could pull out that locket from the drawer and present it to Alison when she would become betrothed. It was something of a "faith image," a reminder until the answer became a reality.

My other daughter held a special place in my heart and prayers too. She was experiencing pregnancy. Everyone was thrilled for her and Luis and couldn't wait to meet little John-John.

POINTS TO PONDER

1. Has your life ever changed course when an opportunity vanished or "dried up" like Elijah's brook? (I Kings 17:1ff)

2. God knows all generations from beginning to end. (Isaiah 41:4) Find other scriptures to verify this statement.

3. Standing on the shoulders of previous believers encourages our generation. Try interviewing an older Christian.

4. Just as the locket example illustrates waiting "until" a promise materializes, there are examples in the Bible of others who did just that. (Ezra 8:29; Luke 22:16; Exodus 3:12) Can you find others or cite examples in church history?

CHAPTER 29

LITTLE LUIS–OR JOHN'S–APPEARING

LUIS AND SHARON'S EARLY MARRIED years were very busy, too busy to include babies. They traveled extensively to intenerate as home missionaries. Then they both had a serious bout of illness from toxic mold beneath their house in Arkansas. At last, when they wanted to begin a family, no baby came. A friend in Fayetteville, NC, hand wrote a lengthy word of encouragement to Sharon and told her that God put life in Sarah's dead womb.

Later when Luis and Sharon were living in Augusta, GA, they requested prayer at their home group meeting about the possibility of adopting a child. The hostess that night spoke up and felt she had to say, "God put life in Sarah's womb."

Still no baby came.

But one night during their tenure in Augusta where Luis had his officer military training, Sharon dreamed of having a fair baby boy. Someone in the dream commented that the child's name was "John Moore."

When Sharon woke up, she thought, "John Moore? Who would name a baby 'John Moore'?"

But afterwards they attended a founder's day service at their home church, First Assembly of God in Augusta, GA. There they learned that the founder was a champion in God's kingdom, named John Moore. His tenure at Augusta First stretched over several decades. (Rev. Moore won many to the Lord during his last days of battling cancer, even his Jewish pharmacist. He was a pastor to many in Augusta outside his church.) Sharon just had to elbow Luis and mouth the words, "John Moore." She had told him about the dream.

Still no baby came.

Out in Washington, the military pair found another healthy church to attend and serve. Sharon assisted a friend in children's ministry, something she thought she would never do. That friend had adopted three precious children. Luis and Sharon followed the friend's example and signed up for parenting classes to be foster parents, leading perhaps to adoption ahead.

Luis wanted to be sure about a military career or other options, so they set aside one Saturday in early February to fast and seek God about their future. They got an answer in an unusual way! Sharon got pregnant. Their little baby boy was born to them nine months and five days later. They never attended those parenting classes but were thrown into a lively, first-hand parenting practicum. Being a dad was a factor in a later career decision for Luis.

During those nine months of pregnancy, Sharon discovered the preciousness of feeling a child develop within her. She found out on her birthday that "it" was a boy. God does put life in a barren womb. (Psalm 113:9) And she and Luis decided they would give their little one the name Sharon heard in her dream, John.

Sharon told me throughout her pregnancy that she would really like for me to be present for John's birth. That did not seem possible since she was now on the west coast, but I assured her I would come as soon as she knew she was in serious labor and called me. The call came November 10, 2010, just at the end of my school day. I happened to be on the phone with Charles and Amanda when she called, so they were alerted to pray.

I rushed home and began checking flights to Seattle-Tacoma. It seemed that the best plan would be to leave early the next day so that I would not arrive during the night and inconvenience everyone. Thus, I arrived around 4:00 PM the following day, Veterans Day. The baby still had not arrived. A military couple picked me up at the airport and carried me straight to the hospital. Sharon got her wish after all; I was there as that tired heroine (after some forty-one hours of labor) pushed little John into his daddy's hands. John's healthy cry was welcomed by all, especially the exhausted, brand-new mama. Luis cut the umbilical cord; pregnancy just ended and parenthood began.

The new parents decided to name their firstborn "John Moore." The Rev. John Moore did not have a living son, but he now had someone carrying his name. Sharon wanted to add "Luis" since he looked so much like Luis, even from birth.

At last Allan and I were grandparents. I had not expected the instant bond I felt with my grandson. It was amazing how I loved that little guy. I think I was the second person to kiss him. Sharon was the first, of course. Allan joined me a day or two later to help out at the Saavedra household.

SOME THOUGHTS ON FASTING

It is interesting that I noticed only recently that old journal entry about Luis and Sharon's day of fasting, ironically nine months before seeing their biological son. It reads: "Sat., Feb. 6, 2010 – Sharon & Luis fasting today about Luis' future voc." That same day I recorded a scripture that caught my eye, Prov. 10:24b "…what the righteous desire will be granted."

While fasting is not a "silver bullet" to get what we want from God, sometimes food loses all appeal as our souls want only something from God, or more of God Himself, and that is all that matters really.

Unfortunately, in my early days after receiving the baptism of the Holy Spirit, I sometimes thought of fasting as *the* way to propel myself into a higher plane of spirituality. After all, I read so many biographical accounts of the great Christians who told of drawing closer to God through prayer and fasting. Surely, I thought, fasting must be the key. I lost far too much body weight during those days and fasted many times when the Holy Spirit had not led me to do so. My thin body was a concern and offense to my family. Finally, I read that the highly successful healing evangelist, Smith Wigglesworth, rarely fasted unless he felt specifically led of God to do so. I saw that perhaps I was offering God my lunch sandwich for more of Him; something akin to Simon the sorcerer's offering money to buy spiritual power in Acts 8. However, it is true that God is a *rewarder* of those who diligently seek him. (Hebrews 11:6)

Little John Moore certainly was a tangible reward nestled in his parents' arms. Could I possibly love the next grandson as much as this one? I would find out in about two months.

POINTS TO PONDER

1. There's nothing like a baby to spice up life!
2. Even spiritual disciplines should be done in moderation.

CHAPTER 30

OFF TO COLORADO

CHARLES AND AMANDA'S NINE MONTHS of waiting for little Aidan Isaiah Gravely came to an end when he arrived January 24, 2011, all nine pounds and nine ounces of him, in Lafayette, LA. His arrival coincided with Sanctity of Life Sunday in many churches, a day set aside to pray for America to return to more respect for life for all its citizens. Amanda's parents came from Colorado to assist the new parents.

COLORADO IN FEBRUARY SNOW

The preciousness of Aidan's life was a wonder to all of us. Surely no two people ever relished their roles as parents more than Charles and Amanda. They wanted to publicly dedicate Aidan to God. What better place could there be to do that than in Grandfather Meadow's church in Stoneham, Colorado? So, at one month of age, little Aidan was going to take his first of many plane rides.

Sharon suggested that all the Gravely clan join the Meadows for the happy event. She and Luis could come from Washington State; the rest of us could come from the East. Lodging was arranged at the Meadows and a nearby Christian ranch that hosted guests in authentic bunk houses. The owners did ministry among Romanian orphans.

When we arrived at the Meadows' home, it was too late to meet Aidan officially. We just got a glimpse of him asleep. Early the next morning, I was headed to the bathroom in my pajamas with my clothes and hair rollers to groom for the day. Amanda and her mom, Billie, met me near the top of the stairs to introduce me to Aidan. He must have been having a good day because he looked right into my sleepy face framed with unkempt hair and gave me a big smile.

I instantly put aside my load and took that little guy into my arms. It took no effort on my part to love him *thoroughly* just as I did John Moore. The capacity for parents and grandparents to love another and another and another child is amazing! It's a gift from God.

The remote environs of Stoneham, Colorado, were fascinating. The town proper was dying. The train no longer came by, and the population sought work elsewhere. A home was cheaper than a car. The terrain was only slightly rolling with cattle and prairie dogs enjoying plenty of room among the brown prairie grasses. There were few trees. The town had two churches, a Catholic church and Pastor Meadow's Assembly of God church. The U. S. post office, where Amanda's mom worked part-time, had an out-house.

At Aidan's dedication service, the entire Gravely family gathered around Aidan to lay hands on him and pray for his life to count for God. Even almost four-month-old John Moore extended a hand and touched his little cousin. Indeed, "children's children are a crown to the aged, and parents are the pride of their children." (Proverbs 17:6 NIV) The family was God's idea all right.

Allan and I did not get to see Charles, Amanda, and Aidan again until June. Aidan was then about five months old. At that time, we hosted them briefly before their departure for Belgium. There their missionary (and parenting) labors lay before them. It was time to activate the "Hannah mindset" again and release them for the Lord's service. (I Samuel 1 & 2) Allan and I kept in touch with them through Skype, Facebook, and emails. Their blog helps too. (See conclusion.) Allan and I have had the privilege of being their "office staff" that gets their newsletters mailed out in the States.

But departure of one son was balanced with the good news that our other son, Joel, would be coming in the fall from Arlington, Virginia, to live in North Carolina. It seemed that every door of employment in the Washington, DC, area (FBI, police, government agencies) slammed shut in his face. He probed for God's will.

Seminary had been a default plan. But a few things had to "come together" for that plan to begin. He wanted to get free housing by being a resident assistant; he needed a part-time job and the Baptist scholarship provided for Virginia residents. All these doors did open wide for him. He was awarded full scholarship status for seminary at South Eastern Baptist Theological Seminary (SEBTS) in Wake Forest, NC. In no time, he fit right into the academic groove and began preparing himself for what God wanted for him ahead.

Joel had no idea that obeying God's leading would be very rewarding right away. A golden (I mean golden!!!) opportunity came his way. Just after Christmas, 2011, he boarded a plane to make his way to Israel with a group from the seminary, led partly by the seminary president himself, Danny Akin. Joel saw the famous sites that his eyes had only read about before on the pages of his Bible. He floated in the Dead Sea and felt the spray from a boat ride on the Sea of Galilee. And he got college credit for all those memories.

The following April, 2012, Sharon and Luis were headed our way, briefly. Luis made a decision to resign his officer commission and leave the military. The day after they arrived at our home, he was offered by phone a job at Auburn University in Alabama, teaching ROTC. He accepted. Away they went again. At least they were going to be closer than the west coast. A friend from my high school graduating class helped them find a house, and John Moore began to be raised in "Sweet Home Alabama." Uncle Joel and Uncle Charles had some concern that their little nephew might become an Auburn fan.

POINTS TO PONDER

1. There's something special about presenting our children to the Lord. Luke 2:22
2. Have you ever been to Israel?

CHAPTER 31

ANOTHER WEDDING

ALISON'S LIFE ALSO EXPERIENCED SOME transition, with even more just ahead. She let the passion of her heart direct her way to find God's will. In her heart, she felt that God had given her the gift of singing, and she had learned to play a guitar. She did not want to hide or bury her talent for leading worship, but females are not in great demand as song leaders. She checked Craigslist. There it was, an opportunity. A local church plant needed a worship leader, one who would not expect much monetary compensation. Making money was not Alison's goal; she only wanted to fulfill her calling. The church welcomed her to lead them into worship. Later she was presented with a new guitar, an anonymous gift from some donor in the church.

But there was a much greater benefit than a guitar in Alison's willingness to pursue God's call. She was soon to "bump into her tree" as she navigated through the forest of life and kept looking up at the Son.

There happened to be a sound man at Alison's new church who happened to know a friend who was interested in getting married. In fact, that friend had been praying specifically for a wife. That fact made the friend (Daniel) bold enough to follow the sound man's tip to contact Alison. He sent a friend request on Facebook. Alison noticed that this Daniel was a mutual Facebook friend of the sound man, thus not a stalker, so she accepted or "befriended" him. Daniel followed up with an invitation to a single's game night at his church. Again, she accepted.

Soon some dates were lined up, usually with Daniel appearing at our door with red roses. She really missed him when she was visiting her sister in Auburn a few weeks. I saw *that look* in her eyes and knew that Daniel was winning her heart.

The 2012 Christmas season was very special to all of us. Allan was determined to attend some of the local seasonal events we had heard about but missed in the past. For example, we participated in the *Messiah* sing-along at the historic Edenton Methodist Church in Raleigh (which Francis Asbury founded), the Christmas Sweet at Colonial Baptist, and a fuller *Messiah* performance in the Duke University chapel.

Alison and Daniel also attended the Duke University chapel performance, on a different occasion. Afterwards, they took a walk in the scenic Duke Gardens. There in that lovely setting, Daniel knelt before our lovely daughter and asked for her hand in marriage. She accepted his marriage proposal and the beautiful diamond ring he took from his pocket.

When Alison returned home from that special date, she sat down on the living room sofa to tell us all about her day and tell us her good news. She was engaged!

I said, "Alison, sit right here. Don't move. I've got a speech."

I quickly went to my bedroom dresser drawer and removed the locket I had hidden there over two years before. I shared with Allan and her how I had tucked it away by faith that the current moment would one day occur. Now it was here! That locket is still a special connection between my wonderful daughter and me. God had brought her a mate, a godly mate with a call to ministry on his own life. Now his photo is next to Alison's in that locket. God is so good!

At last, Alison would have her own home in which to exercise her tremendous gift of hospitality. But while I was thrilled for

Alison, I have to admit that there was a tender spot in my heart that let me know I would miss her when she would leave our home.

I found out shortly just how tender that spot in my heart was. A few days before Christmas, Allan and I attended one more seasonal event. The Irish hymn writers, Keith and Kristyn Getty, and Buddy Green were performing live at the Durham Performing Arts Center; it was their Christmas tour. It was a worshipful experience. One song in particular made me cry.

Kristyn's beautiful, clear voice reached my ears in the upper level of the center as she sang a song she wrote to her young daughter, Elise. The words fit my own feelings about Alison's departure from our home into her own home. I tucked those words away for future reference

But we had a wedding to prepare for. Suddenly I had to shift into a "mother of the bride" role and give attention to details ahead. All of them seemed to fall into place smoothly. (Allan held up well as the father of the bride.) I relished accompanying Alison to find that dream wedding dress at a bridal shop. Wow! She transformed into a stunning bride before those mirrors, even without makeup. The invitations, catering arrangements, wedding program, and decorations all got done.

Friends and family extended their love to the couple with a shower, a dinner, and a tea. One Puerto Rican friend sent her own wedding jewelry; she wanted to give it to Alison as her gift. Alison's former students where I worked wanted to know all the details.

Alison and Daniel chose March 23, 2013, for their wedding date. Daniel chose Joel for his best man. Charles and family arrived from Belgium for the event. We invited his in-laws, the Meadows, to come stay with us the wedding week because they would not get to see their daughter, Amanda, otherwise. That week would be the only week back in the states for Charles and Amanda. The Meadows were a godsend and took stress off us through their service to us. Luis and Sharon and John Moore came from Auburn.

Charles and Luis helped me with a special surprise for the rehearsal meal the eve of the wedding. The Getty song, "A Mother's Prayer," became the background song for a Power Point slideshow of photos of Alison's life.[1] The final verse of the song, accompanied by engagement photos, was a "tear jerker" and tugged at all our hearts. It speaks of the day when the daughter will move on to walk her own journey in this world. Alison gave me a tearful embrace. I didn't mean to make her cry. The reality of the approaching switch in her life seemed to register as she heard the words.

Allan's brother, Ben Gravely, and his wife, Martha, came for the wedding. Their daughter and granddaughter flew down from Minnesota. Alison had friends from California and Germany here for the occasion. My sister, Judy, and her husband were able to come from Tennessee. Old friends of ours arrived from Virginia. It was truly a joyful day in Dunn, NC. No one knew that Allan had had a brief migraine in the store as we picked up the wedding cake. Thankfully, in recent years he has found an over-the-counter headache pill that disables that old attacker within three hours.

Since the day after the wedding was our fortieth wedding anniversary, Daniel and Alison honored us at the reception with a surprise of their own, a pretty cake with a "40" on top; and Alison presented to us framed poems to "Mom" and "Dad." What an honor it is to raise children.

Daniel and Alison serve faithfully in their home church in Dunn through music, Sunday school, and Hispanic outreaches. They stay busy for the kingdom. And both of them still have "that look" in their eyes that reflects the love God placed in their hearts for each other. Truly He does exceeding abundantly above all we could ask or think. (Ephesians 3:20)

During their first year of marriage, the Dunn church asked Daniel to begin a Hispanic congregation. Several church members got on board and helped out. Daniel felt keenly the need to learn Spanish in order to communicate better. His mother-in-law, who can teach Spanish I at the drop of a hat, offered to do a class for his team two Saturday mornings a month for one semester. The group bonded well. I set up a website to provide them with resources. (www.spanishindunn.weebly.com) It was a privilege to empower Christians to reach the wonderful Hispanic people I have loved for decades. And it was exciting to see the love birds begin their journey and adventures together. Allan and I are glad that they are nearby and we can feel some of the "fallout" of their blessings, which always amazes us.

POINTS TO PONDER

1. Rejoice with those who rejoice, even if your own breakthrough hasn't come yet. (Romans 12:15) Your time will come. Therefore do not throw away your confidence, which has a great reward. For you have need of endurance, so that when you have done the will of God you may receive what is promised. For, "Yet a little while, and the coming one will come and will not delay...." Hebrews 10:35-37 ESV
2. What a gift from God *music* is to His people!

CHAPTER 32

CONCLUSION

GOD HAS GRANTED ALLAN AND me the privilege of seeing our four children mature in their separate walks with God. We saw their embryo "giftings" along the way during their childhoods and adolescence.

We saw Charles's ability in language arts such as reading, writing, and telling stories. Today that is useful in drafting newsletters, preparing sermons, and co-hosting a blog with Amanda. (http://www.agmd.org/u/TheGravelys)

Sharon was always decorating her room. Now she is a certified stager of homes and has her own interior decorating business. (www.saavydesigns.com)

Alison began to win poetry contests in secondary school. That skill blossomed and matured. Currently, she writes songs and has her own poetry blog. (http://alisonmacomber.blogspot.com/)

Allan always told Joel he was the best singer in the family; Joel could not believe it. His musical talents became more evident around age seventeen; that is when he picked up a guitar and within three months could play far better than I ever could! He later majored in music performance for a while, learned three instruments, and won a music scholarship for college. He has often served on church praise teams in various settings and never lets those fingertip, guitar callouses go away. He has even sung in weddings. We haven't been able to persuade him to post any music on YouTube yet.

Allan himself, my inspiration, developed his writing talent to a higher level after retirement and worked on his own book soon to be launched on Amazon. It was birthed from his passion to see the church enjoy a balance between sound biblical knowledge and experience in the Spirit's leading. His tentative title is *"Strange Fire": Can the Church Be Both Evangelical and Charismatic?*

Yes, we are all unique, and God does not overlook anyone when dispersing His gifts. Parents have to be good stewards of their children's souls and callings or giftedness. It is amazing to see what God can do with each one of them.

And Allan and I still stay busy in the kingdom as opportunities come along to serve. We want to keep bearing fruit until Jesus returns or says "time's up" for us. To do that, we know we must abide in the Vine, the Lord Himself. We look forward to each new day; our Father is waiting at every dawn to enjoy the journey with us.

I have to agree with Joel Osteen when he encourages us to line up our lives with God and see Him take us places we never dreamed of!!! I never dreamed I would get to share the gospel on three continents or get to see Washington State, Colorado, Bolivia, Mexico, Belgium, France, England, Puerto Rico, or even Washington, D. C. After all, for thirty years our money mostly bought groceries and athletic shoes for four children. Our traveling circuit was usually limited to Alabama and North Carolina. But because of those four children, our world was broadened, usually as they hosted us or needed us to come along and help out.

I marvel at God's goodness to us and all His people, first to His Jewish people and *now also to us Gentiles*. Jeremiah 32:40-41 really struck me one day: "I will . . . never stop doing good to them. . . .I will rejoice in doing them good." Our family has experienced that *goodness*.

Someone has said that God answers prayers in three ways, all valid answers: yes, no, and wait a while. It is easy to embrace the first answer, but we have learned to trust His wisdom and goodness as we embrace No. 2 and No. 3. In retrospect, we are grateful for many of the "no" answers.

We are still waiting on some of the "wait a while" answers. I compare the waiting interval to the time I have to wait for those dry tulip bulbs lying dormant in the cold winter ground to burst into life with the warmth of spring. Their beauty becomes evident in time. It is safe and reassuring to rest our faith in God's good timing. Then, other testimonies can be written. I'm looking forward to sharing them on my blog: www.legaciesthatlast.weebly.com.

Thank you, dear reader, for joining me on these pages as I have recounted the goodness and faithfulness of God to those who trust and obey Him. May He bless your journey of faith as you create a legacy that will last and last and last in His forever.

He's a good God!

The hand of our God is upon all them for good that seek him. Ezra 8:22c, KJV

WHEN JESUS BECAME REAL TO ME

by Edsel H. Steverson
(Used by permission)

AFTER HAVING GROWN UP IN a typical denominational church, attending and graduating from a church related college, and after having been a pastor for several years, I came to experience, through the grace of God, a dimension of Christian reality which I had never known before and which has resulted in the complete change of my life and ministry.

As I try to share with you something of the blessings of God in my own life, I become increasingly aware that mere words can never express the thousands of intimate experiences of wonder and joy when one's life is set on fire with the love of God. But I do pray that God may be pleased to bring praises to His wonderful name by blessing these few words to some hungry heart.

The first thing God did, before bringing me to know the complete adequacy of the Person of the living Christ in the power of the Holy Spirit, was to convince me of the sin, pride, and superficiality that filled my life. When the Holy Spirit began to reveal to me my true spiritual condition, I could not deny it for it was so obviously true. Being ever conscious that my life was not pleasing to God, I became increasingly unhappy, discouraged and frustrated.

Although I preached to others that they should pray, love and study the Word of God, forsake sin in their own lives, love their enemies, and give a real witness for Christ, I found none of these things vitally true in my own life.

For example, I believed that prayer was more or less a religious act to perform in order to work one's self up to go out and do something for the Lord. In those days, I doubt very seriously that I ever tried to pray more than five or ten minutes at a time, having never experienced the joy of true prayer in the energy of the Holy Spirit.

When I studied the Word of God, it was more or less from the standpoint of collecting facts in order to prepare sermons to preach to the people, since I had never known the joy of partaking of the precious Word of God under the leadership of the Holy Spirit.

I knew the Bible said Christians were to love their enemies and to pray for them; this I tried to do, but found it was just not so in my own heart, having never experienced the true love of God which is the fruit of the Holy Spirit.

What a soul shaking experience it was for me, although I was supposed to be an exemplary Christian, when I came to realize that my life was filled with hypocrisy; that most of what I had seen, known, and been taught in the church was superficial; that multitudes of people were lost in sin, and I was powerless and helpless to do anything about it.

But I knew enough about the Bible to know the Biblical record and presentation of the Christian faith is one of victory, power, and triumph. I knew the New Testament presents Christ as victor over every circumstance of life and even death itself. But I believed this was just for the early Christians and not for us today. I had been taught so much that victory for the Christian over the power of sin to be a future experience after death and was not to be expected until then. But I thank God with all my heart that I now know not only is Christianity a message of victory but that this victory is for all who will believe and receive today.

Along about this time a prayer-fellowship developed between a pastor friend and me. I had never known this kind of fellowship before. And as I look back, I feel definitely this was the beginning of what later proved to be a complete joyful revolution in my life. Because of this experience in prayer, I am firmly persuaded if one has a hungry heart and really and sincerely desires to know the living God in Spirit and truth, one must begin to try to pray. If one is to receive from God, one must ask, seek, and knock in prayer. Prayer is the key which unlocks the divine heart of God and through which one claims the blessings of God.

Not very long after this on Friday, March 9, 1962, the same pastor friend, mentioned above, came by to see me at the church. He brought with him a book which he had recently received from a friend. The title of this book was THE SHANTUNG REVIVAL. He had just received it and had not had time to read it. He told me that the book was supposed to be the record of the outpouring of the Spirit of God among Southern Baptist missionaries and churches in Shantung, China, in the early 1930's. This interested me very much.

I took the book and told him that I would try to read it as soon as possible, not knowing at the time God would use the testimonies in this book to open my heart to receive the answer to all the deep longings and desires of my soul.

One thing stood out more than any other to me as I read the live testimonies of these people; many of them missionaries who had gone through college and seminary and had been on the foreign mission field for many years. Many told how they were living defeated and sinful Christian lives. Many of these missionaries gave testimony to the fact, although they had been missionaries for years, that they were not even Christians. But when the Holy Spirit was poured out, they were convicted of their sad state, repented, were forgiven, and were filled with the Holy Spirit. When this happened, all gave witness of how the Holy Spirit changed their lives. Where once there had been sin, guilt, defeat, misery, unhappiness, and unbelief, there now was righteousness, victory, joy, peace, love, faith, and power in their lives.

As I read and reread this book, God revealed my need to me. I needed the Holy Spirit to come into my life. There was no doubt at all now, and it was biblical. I needed the Holy Spirit to come and do for me what I had never been able to do for myself. O how God put this truth upon my heart.

But I had been taught and believed that when a person accepted Jesus as Savior, he then and there received the Holy Spirit, and from then on it was a matter of yielding and receiving more of the Spirit. But after reading about these dear people in the Shantung Revival and about others who had received the gift of the Holy Spirit as the people had in the Bible, I knew the Holy Spirit had never really come into my heart in this manner. I knew these people had something which I did not have. I knew their lives had been changed. I knew Christ Jesus had become real to them. I knew then as I had never known before that I wanted and needed the same thing to happen to me which had happened to them.

How then was I going to claim the promise of the Holy Spirit which the Bible said so much about? I realized as never before, and as I had been preaching for many years, the only way to receive anything from God was to believe the Word of God, repent, and simply receive by faith. This was to be done without any evidence whatsoever, except the promise of God's Word. This is always the hard part. This we could never do without the help of God. But if we have hungry hearts and believe the Word of God, God will help us to have the faith to receive His promise.

God definitely was leading me all through that Friday and all the next day on Saturday. Then Saturday night around 12 o'clock midnight I knew what I had to do. In order to receive the Holy Spirit, it would be absolutely necessary to surrender my life without any reservations whatsoever in repentance and faith to Jesus Christ, and trust Him to send His Blessed Holy Spirit into my life at His own will.

So, just a little after midnight in my study at the church where I was pastor, by the grace of God, I repented of my sinful, proud, and defeated life. I asked God's forgiveness and by simple faith surrendered my all to Christ and trusted Him to fill me with the Holy Spirit. I had no idea what to expect, although I had read about the experiences of others. I just left it with the Lord and went home and went to bed.

The Sunday School hour came and passed as usual. Then it came time for the worship hour. The message I had prepared to preach that day was taken from Galatians 5:15: "This I say then, walk in the Spirit, and ye shall not fulfill the lust of the flesh." God was surely leading in the preparation of this message.

As I began to preach that memorable Sunday morning, I seemingly was not conscious at first of what had happened the night before. I was taken up with delivering the message. But, as the moments passed, I gradually became aware of the fact that I was preaching as I had never preached before. I was preaching with more fluency and power than I had ever known.

Then all at once the glorious reality of it all began to dawn upon me. The Holy Spirit had come. He had come into my life, and He was in our service.

I then began to take notice of the people in the congregation. They had never looked to me the way they did that morning. They seemingly were transfixed. There was not a sound in the entire building. And as I looked at the people, it seemed as if there was a wall of fire just above their heads. I could not see the literal fire, but that is what it appeared to be. A great pressure, a great power, a great force, had filled the building. I knew the Holy Spirit was with us.

I honestly did not know what to do. I was so happy at the wonder of it all. I had never experienced the working of the Holy Spirit before. At the close of the service I gave the invitation as usual. And several people just ran down the aisles of the church. People whom I had never seen make a move before. One elderly man, a long-time member of the church, ran down the aisle and took me by the hand and said, "Brother Steverson, I did not understand your invitation, but I just had to come down."

Another dear lady, I remember, ran down taking my hand and exclaiming, "Brother Steverson, I just love your preaching!" It wasn't my preaching she loved, it was the blessed Presence of the loving God which she had experienced in her heart that day.

It was hard for me to wait until the service was over and for all the people to leave. For my heart was burning with the holy, sweet, real Presence of the living Christ, and I wanted to be alone with Him.

After the service I went to my study and closed and locked the door. All I could do was weep and praise the dear name of the gracious Lord; for at last His Presence was vitally real and precious to me. I knew then that God had been true to His Word, and the Holy Spirit had come and made Jesus Christ real to me.

From that day, a little more than three years ago, until this very moment, the sweet Presence of the loving Christ has been in my life. In answer to prayer, repentance, and faith, the Holy Spirit came into my life and revealed Jesus Christ to my soul.

Jesus did for me in a moment what I had never been able to do for myself. Where there had been sin, He broke its power and replaced it with His deliverance. Where there had been defeat, He brought His victory. Where there had been hate, He replaced it with His precious love. Where there had been guilt, He brought

His forgiveness and cleansing. Where there had been a prayerless life, He replaced it with a joyous life of prayer energized by the Holy Spirit. Where there was weakness, He brought power. Where there was fruitlessness, He brought fruitfulness. And when He came, the Word of God literally became the living Word. Before it was a burden to study the Bible, but now it is so wonderful to have the living Word broken to your soul by the blessed Holy Spirit. Where before I had not seen the Lord work, I began to see real conviction and real salvation come into the hearts of people.

The Lord had begun to work with me in a definite way. As I began to pray more frequently and more definitely, I began to experience God's help in prayer. I shall never forget the first time I ever felt like I had really prayed. It was wonderful and truly a joyful experience. I had felt the helping hand of the Lord in prayer for the first time. But this was only the beginning of the blessings which God was going to pour out on me and many others in the near future, and which blessings have continued up until this very moment.

Of course, I did not become aware of all of these wonderful things all at once, but since that day the Lord Jesus Christ has proven the wonderful sufficiency of His love over and over again to me. And I am persuaded that He is able to save to the uttermost all that come unto God by Him.

If I were even to attempt to record briefly the blessings of God upon my life and upon the lives of others since that day, I'm sure it would require a large book to do it. For example, just recently the Lord led two dear Christian brothers, one a Southern Baptist pastor, to come and lay their hands on me and pray for me. Since that time I have been enabled by the Holy Spirit to pray in another language which has proven to be a great source of personal spiritual edification and reserve in this day of prevailing evil.

I trust, dear reader and friend, it you are living a defeated Christian life, and you have a hungry heart, that you will take these few weak words to be true, and open your heart to receive through Jesus Christ the promise of the Holy Spirit by faith.

The Bible says in Galatians 3:13-14, "Christ hath redeemed us from the curse of the law being made a curse of us: for it is written, Cursed is every one that hangeth on a tree: That the blessing of Abraham might come on the Gentiles through Jesus Christ; THAT WE MIGHT RECEIVE THE PROMISE OF THE SPIRIT THROUGH FAITH."

And in John 7:37-39, "In the last day, that great day of the feast, Jesus stood and cried, saying, if any man thirst, let him come unto me, and drink. He that believeth on me, as the scripture hath said, out of his belly shall flow rivers of living water.

(BUT THIS SPAKE HE OF THE SPIRIT, WHICH THEY THAT BELIEVE ON HIM SHOULD RECEIVE: for the Holy Ghost was not yet given; because that Jesus was not yet glorified.)"

APPENDIX II
RECEIVING THE BAPTISM OF THE HOLY SPIRIT

by Dottie Gravely

I BELIEVE THE CHRISTIAN'S FIRST step in receiving the Baptism of the Holy Spirit is to know scripturally that (1) such an experience exists and (2) that every obedient believer qualifies to receive it. Those two things need to be settled.

1. <u>Begin with the Bible</u>. Notice that this on-going ministry of Jesus is predicted by John the Baptist and mentioned six times in scriptures. See Matthew 3:11, Mark 1:8, Luke 3:16, John 1:33, Acts 1:5, Acts 11:16. Study carefully the five accounts in Acts in which regular people receive the Spirit. (Acts 2; 8:4-25; 9:17; 10:1-11:18; and 19:1-7) Read the Comforter chapters of John, chapters 14, 15 and 16. Other lateral promises include Isaiah 44:3, John 7:37-39, Luke 11:13, Luke 24:49, Acts 5:32, and Ephesians 1:13.

2. <u>Believe that you qualify</u>. John 7:37-39. Only non-Christians **<u>do not</u>** qualify (John 14:17). If you heard from a lawyer that you had inherited a sum of money, you would believe that information and show up at his office to claim your inheritance. Similarly, as one young lady shared, if a friend called

and told her that the mall was having a big sale "for women only," any woman would believe that she qualified.

3. <u>Ask for this precious gift; ask in faith</u>. It is biblical to ask for laying on of hands for it.

In addition to the Bible, there are many trustworthy testimonies in the Christian world. As mentioned in my book, chapter 21 of David Wilkerson's book, *The Cross and the Switchblade*, has clear testimony of the positive benefits of this experience. He asked many of his former drug addict converts how they knew that they would not return to drugs. Every one of them said the same thing; they knew it when they received the Baptism of the Holy Spirit.

Another good resource is *They Speak with Other Tongues* by John Sherrill. George O. Wood's book, *Living in the Spirit*, is excellent, especially chapter two.

I close with some words from the first dean of both Moody Bible Institute and BIOLA University, R. A. Torrey, in his book, *How to Work for Christ*:

The supreme condition of power in the apostolic church was the definite baptism with the Holy Ghost. The supreme condition of success in soul-winning is the same today. Many in these days are trying to prove that there is no such thing as a special baptism with the Holy Spirit, but a candid and careful study of the Acts of the Apostles will show that there is. Very many in our day also know by blessed experience that the baptism with the Holy Spirit is a present day reality. One ounce of believing experiences along this line is worth whole tons of unbelieving exegesis, no matter how subtle and learned it may be. There are thousands of men and women in this and other lands who have been brought out of a place of powerlessness into a place of power in the Lord's service, through meeting the conditions plainly laid down in the Bible for receiving the Holy Ghost. This baptism with the Holy Spirit is for every child of God, and the one who would be largely used of God in personal work must get it at any cost.[1]

ABBREVIATIONS

ESV = English Standard Version
FP=First Priority
HCHS=Harnett Central High School
KJV = King James Version
NIV = New International Version
NKJV=New King James Version
TCHS=Tuscaloosa County High School
WBHS=West Blocton High School
XA=Chi Alpha

PREFACE

1. John G. Paton, *John G. Paton, Missionary to the New Hebrides,* edited by James Paton (Edinburgh: The Banner of Truth Trust, 2002), preface.

2. George Whitefield, *George Whitefield's Journals,* edited by Iain Murray (London: Banner of Truth Trust, 1960), epigraph.

CHAPTER ONE

1. Cook, Martha, "The Lord Will Prove." See http://www.hymnary.org/text/in_some_way_or_other_the_lord_will_provi.

2. Philip Doddridge, "Oh, Happy Day." Public domain. An eighteenth century hymn that became a hit recording in the late 1960s. Rev. Doddridge's legacy (this song) has made its way into modern movies and still inspires Christians.

3. Ford Porter's tract, "God's Simple Plan of Salvation," has an interesting background story and history of being used by God to bring people into faith. One such person was a former bodyguard for Hitler who became a minister. The tract is now available in over 100 languages, with some accessible online through its website. There the Porter family shares how the tract came to be and how their ministry has grown in answer to Rev. Porter's *specific prayer for a legacy that would reach around the world and continue after his lifetime.* (www.godssimpleplan.org)

CHAPTER THREE

1. *Voice* was published by Full Gospel Business Men's Fellowship International. Demos Shakarian's book *The Happiest People on Earth* tells the amazing story behind this organization.

2. Courtney Anderson, *To the Golden Shore: The Life of Adoniram Judson* (Valley Forge, PA: Judson Press, 1987), 144-145.

CHAPTER FIVE

1. Jackie Robinson, Hall of Fame baseball star, had similar thoughts toward his brother, Frank, who died just after a motorcycle accident. He had "a burning desire to win, always win, in memory of Frank."[2]

2. Anne Schraff. *Jackie Robinson, An American Hero* (West Berlin, NJ: Townsend Press, Inc., 2008), 46.

CHAPTER NINE

1. C. Austin Miles, "Anywhere with Jesus." Public domain.

CHAPTER TWENTY

1. Chris Rice, "Go Light Your World." See https://www.youtube.com/watch?v=DtIIFJIxdUw.

CHAPTER TWENTY-ONE

1. Untitled anonymous poem quoted in R. T. Kendall, *The Anointing: Yesterday, Today, Tomorrow* (London: Hodder & Stoughton, 1998), 23.

2. Ann Taylor, "My Mother." Public domain. See http://allpoetry. com/poem/8515711-My-Mother-by-Ann-Taylor.

CHAPTER TWENTY-TWO
1. See John Piper's free downloads of biographies on his website: http://www.desiringgod.org/resource-library/biographies/ by-title.

CHAPTER TWENTY-THREE
1. Stuart, Arbella Stuart, *The Lives of the Three Mrs. Judsons,* edited by Gary W. Long (Springfield, MO: Particular Baptist Press, 1999), 104.

2. Ibid., 104ff.

"In reference to this timid and hesitating hope of some benefit which *might possibly* accrue to the cause of missions, from her terrible experience, the remarks of Dr. Dowling in a recent work, are so appropriate, that we will introduce them here."

Dr. Dowling's remarks:

Previous to the commencement of these sufferings, though a few American Baptists were partially awake to the salvation of the heathen...yet...contributions... were meager...interest it [the mission] had excited was comparatively small. Something of a thrilling, exciting character was needed to arouse the churches from their indifference and lethargy; something that should touch their hearts, by showing them somewhat of the nature and extent of the sacrifices made by those devoted missionaries whom they were called upon to sustain by their benefactions and their prayers.

Such a stimulus was afforded, when after two years of painful suspense, during which it was not known whether the missionaries were dead or alive, the touching recital of their unparalleled sufferings for Christ's sake, and of their wonderful deliverance, at length burst like an electric shock upon the American churches. ***And that shock has not yet spent its force,*** (emphasis mine) as we have recently seen in the effect produced by the simple, silent presence, in the assemblies of the saints, of the venerated man of God, who can say with an Apostle—"I bear in my body the scars of the Lord Jesus!" [Alluding to Dr. Judson's visit to America]

That worn veteran had but to arise in a Christian assembly and a thrill of sympathy was sent through the audience, and thousands upon thousands of dollars were pledged on the spot to that cause which his silent presence so powerfully advocated.

[Judson had lost most of his voice through illness in Burma. His speech was but a coarse whisper.]

CHAPTER TWENTY-FOUR
1. Paton, *John G. Paton*, 286.

2. Ronnie Freeman, "Home Forever." See www.musicservices.org.

CHAPTER TWENTY-FIVE
1. "William Carey," *Wikipedia*. See http://en.wikipedia.org/wiki/William_Carey_(missionary).

CHAPTER TWENTY-SEVEN

1. Petra, "Don't Let Your Heart Be Hardened." See https://www.youtube.com/watch?v=hiu_gpGLWy0

CHAPTER TWENTY-EIGHT

1. James B. Taylor, *The Lives of Virginia Baptist Ministers* (Public domain, 1837), 201. See https://archive.org/stream/livesof virginiab6998tayl#page/6/mode/2up/search/john++king.

2. JOHN KING. John King was a native of Brunswick County. The circumstances of his parents were extremely dependent, and his opportunities of improvement were, in consequence, scanty. His attention to religious subjects was arrested in early youth. About 1773, Elder Samuel Harriss with others, brought the glad tidings of salvation into the neighborhood where he lived, and many believed to the saving of the soul. A considerable excitement was the result. Crowds attended the ministrations of God's servants, some curious to see these New Lights, and others with sincere desire to hear and know the truth.

The ordinance of immersion also, having been rarely witnessed, excited much interest. A baptismal scene was the means of arresting Mr. King's attention to spiritual things. He attended at Harper's mill on one of these occasions, more for the purpose of amusing himself than to receive benefit; and, that he might enjoy his sport unobserved, he concealed himself beneath the mill-wheel. But the Lord's eye was upon him, and his laughter was turned into mourning. He came from his hiding place with the arrows of the Almighty sticking fast in him, and with anguish unutterable, he hastened homewards. The night was passed without rest, and he arose to behold the sun, but no hope beamed upon his benighted soul. In this state of mind he continued for many days. All society was cautiously avoided. He would wander for whole hours in the wilderness, brooding over his wretched condition, and for some time no person knew or suspected the cause of his gloom. It began to be supposed that he was suffering a temporary derangement of mind, and was called by many, the distracted boy.

After concealing his grief until he found himself more and more miserable, he determined to divulge his feelings to a Baptist minister, then in the vicinity of his father's residence. The man of God directed him to believe in the Lord Jesus Christ. He went away astonished and offended at the advice he had received. That his sin was great, he was willing to acknowledge, but he could not perceive how a holy God might accept and save him, until he should become a holy man. For this he was groaning and striving, and his heart cherished the hope, that some method of making himself better would be recommended by his spiritual adviser. In all his inquiries, he was still informed that Christ died for sinners, and that he must be saved, if saved at all, by the mere mercy of God, through Jesus Christ. At length his proud heart yielded. He saw that God could be just and yet justify the ungodly, through Christ. This humiliating truth became the joy of his heart. Now the plan of salvation was beheld in all its simplicity, freeness, and fullness. He returned to see the minister with a new song in his mouth, being willing not only to rejoice in, but to acknowledge the Saviour.

He was shortly after baptized. It has been hinted, that he was at this time quite young [age 14 or 15]. He soon cherished a desire to preach the gospel. For a long period, even after he began to exercise his talents in public addresses, he was oppressed with a fear that he was not called of God to this work. While anxious to do good to his fellow men, he was ready to exclaim, "who is sufficient for these things?" In this early stage of his Christian career, the Lord laid upon him his chastening hand. Some injury was sustained in one of his legs, which threatened the loss of life, and it became necessary to suffer amputation. During this confinement, he was brought to the conviction that it was his duty to preach. He afterwards preached for the excellency of the knowledge of Christ Jesus his Lord. As soon as the maimed limb was sufficiently healed, he began, in all the surrounding country, to declare the unsearchable riches of the grace of God. Large numbers attended to hear the youth with a wooden leg preach, and many who went from mere curiosity, returned to pray.

Thus the trial through which he was brought, redounded to the glory of God, and to the interests of immortal souls. After Mr. King's devotion to the ministry, he applied himself diligently to the cultivation of his mind. His progress in knowledge was rapid. It is said, that having married a woman of education, he received much valuable information under her tuition. She appropriated much of her time in affording such assistance as he needed. A great improvement in his manner of preaching was perceptible, and his influence was extended beyond his native county.

CHAPTER THIRTY-ONE

1. Keith and Kristin Geddy and Fionan de Barra, "A Mother's Prayer." See http://www.gettymusic.com/hymns-mothersprayer.aspx.

APPENDIX II

1. R. A. Torrey, *How to Work for Christ.* Public domain. See www. amazon.com Kindle edition.

WORKS CITED

Anderson, Courtney. *To the Golden Shore: The Life of Adoniram Judson.* Valley Forge: The Judson Press, 1987.

Cook, Martha. "The Lord Will Provide." Public domain.

Doddridge, Philip. "O Happy Day." Hymn, public domain.

Freeman, Ronnie. "Home Forever." www.musicservices.org.

Geddy, Keith and Kristin and Fionan de Barra. "A Mother's Prayer." http://www.gettymusic.com/hymns-mothersprayer.aspx.

Kendall, R. T. *The Anointing: Yesterday, Today, Tomorrow.* London: Hodder & Stoughton, 1998.

Paton, John G. *John G. Paton, Missionary to the New Hebrides.* Edited by James Paton. Edinburgh: The Banner of Truth Trust, 2002.

Petra, "Don't Let Your Heart Be Hardened." https://www.youtube.com/watch?v=hiu_gpGLWy0.

Rice, Chris. "Go Light Your World." https://www.youtube.com/watch?v=DtIIFJIxdUw.

Schraff, Anne. *Jackie Robinson, An American Hero.* West Berlin, NJ: Townsend Press, Inc., 2008.

Taylor, James B. *The Lives of Virginia Baptist Ministers.* Public domain, 1837.

Torrey, R. A. *How to Work for Christ.* Public domain, 1901.

Whitefield, George. *George Whitefield's Journals.* Edited by Iain Murray. London: Banner of Truth Trust, 1960.

"William Carey." *Wikipedia.*

THE AUTHOR HAS SOMETIMES SAID, "I have not been bored since I was nineteen years old."

This book explains why. Dottie and her family have proven through several decades that God is faithful to His own to give them a lasting legacy. She shares candidly some of the highlights along their journey of faith.

About the author:
Dottie holds a BA in Spanish and a Master's in Foreign Language Education from the University of Alabama. She has taught English and/or Spanish in Alabama and North Carolina public schools. She and Allan, her husband of over forty years, reside in Angier, NC. They have four grown children and three grandsons.

Made in the USA
Charleston, SC
06 June 2015